The Complex City

Social and Built Approaches and Methods

Editor

Caroline Donnellan

Boston University Study Abroad London, UK

Series Editor

Graham Cairns

AMPS (Architecture, Media, Politics, Society)

The Interdisciplinary Built Environment

VERNON PRESS

In the Americas:
Vernon Press
1000 N West Street, Suite 1200,
Wilmington, Delaware 19801
United States

In the rest of the world:
Vernon Press
C/Sancti Espiritu 17,
Malaga, 29006
Spain

The Interdisciplinary Built Environment

Library of Congress Control Number: 2022939761

ISBN: 978-1-64889-655-2

Also available: 978-1-64889-477-0 [Hardback]; 978-1-64889-549-4 [PDF, E-Book]

Cover image by Caroline Donnellan.

Cover design by Vernon Press.

Table of Contents

List of Illustrations

Contributors

Jie Chen is a Postdoctoral Research Fellow at the College of Architecture and Urban Planning of Tongji University in Shanghai, China. She completed her PhD on Planning and Urban Development at the University of New South Wales, Australia in 2018. Her doctoral research "The Adaptive Reuse of Industrial Heritage as Cultural Clusters in China" is highly relevant to current urban development and regeneration strategies in China. She is an architect-planner with research interests that include urban regeneration, brownfield transformation, industrial heritage reuse, and ambiguous land property rights. Her research outputs have been published in high-ranked English and Chinese journals, including International Journal of Heritage Studies, URBAN DESIGN International, American Journal of Economics and Sociology, Structural Survey, Urban Planning Forum Her article was awarded the best paper award at the 24th International Conference Information Visualisation in 2020. Selected international conferences include the 56th ISOCARP World Planning Congress; the 2017 International Conference on China Urban Development; The City and Complexity: Life; Design and Commerce in the Built Environment, the 21st Construction; Building and Real Estate Research Conference of the Royal Institute of Chartered Surveyors; the 9th International Symposium on Architectural Interchanges in Asia; and the 7th Symposium on Industrial Heritage in China. Chen's current research focuses on the development of land institution and industrial land regeneration under ambiguous property rights in Shanghai. She has research grants from the Postdoctoral International Exchange Fellowship Program in 2019 and the National Natural Science Foundation of China (Grant No. 52008300) in 2020. Chen also has professional experience in architecture, urban design, and urban planning, having worked and collaborated with well-respected design consultancies in Chongqing and Shanghai.

Morten Daugaard graduated as a Major in Social Science from the Department of Political Science at Aarhus University in 1979. He has been affiliated with the Aarhus School of Architecture since 1974, initially as a Lecturer, then as Assistant Professor, and after that as an Associate Professor. From 2019, Daugaard has been Associate Professor Emeritus at the same institution. His main fields in teaching as well as in research have been architectural history and theory, urbanism, and landscape. Selected courses include James Corner and The Agency of Mapping; Early Urban Theory, Publicity, Public Life and The Fall of Public Man; Everyday Life and the constitution of the public as acquisition of space; The Urbanity of the Network City; Introduction to Postmodern Urbanism; Poststructuralism 1980-90; and The Almost All Right Paradigm. Attached to the Centre for Strategic Urban Research is Realdania Research with the related projects: "The City without Limits, Urban Policy" and "Strategies and Qualifying Urban Landscapes." Selected publications include Qualifying Urban Landscapes in Journal of Landscape Architecture, 2010; "Qualification of the Urban Landscape – Porosity as a Social and an Aesthetic goal" in Anthology Den Grænseløse, 2011; "Network and Public Domain in After-Sprawl City" in eds. Tom Nielsen, Niels Albertsen, and Peter Hemmersam, *Urban Mutations – Periodization, Scale and Mobility*, Arkitektskolens Forlag Aarhus, 2004; and "Stirring the School" in ed. Raoul Bunschoten et al. *Stirring the City Aarhus*, 1999, Fonden Til Udgivelse Af Arkiturtidsskrif.

Khoa Do is an accomplished educator who is internationally celebrated for his exceptional people-centred and value-based leadership in the higher education arena. As Hames Sharley's Head of Design Education in Practice he leads best-practice for embedding educational leadership across the organisation with an industry practice-led mindset and approach. He is trained as an Australian architect and has had over two decades of combined experience in higher education (HE) and private sectors. His research and teaching are focused on leading interdisciplinary-integrated industry research and scholarship. Do is an internationally regarded educator, designer, speaker, and author. He is regularly invited to chair, convene, and assess awards and grants through review panels and boards. Do's contribution to HE-industry partnerships is led through new forms of thinking, creative synthesis of current and emerging discourse in industry engagement with external stakeholders in advancing simulation and multicultural design engagement approach. In addition, Do actively champions research in the areas of embedded learning in practice and develop educational pedagogical models that capitalize on the professional industry environment as a place of authentic learning through project-based learning (PBL), inquiry-based learning (IBL) and experiential-based-learning (EBL) promoting collaborative inquiry. In 2021, Do was nominated by his peers and received the GFEL (Global Forum for Education and Learning) prestigious global impact award for Excellence in Education and 2010; Do was awarded the prestigious Australian Office of Learning and Teaching Award for his sustained commitment to delivering innovation and excellence in the development of the scholarship of teaching and service to the higher education sector through the discipline of Architecture and Design. Do contributes at a national level in the HE-sector as an assessor for the Australian Grants and Awards for University Teaching, Department of Education and Training (DET).

Caroline Donnellan undertook her Bachelor of Arts (Hons) and Master of Arts in History of Art (RK Departmental Bursary) at University College London (UCL), and Doctor of Philosophy in Cities at the London School of Economics and Political Science (LSE) (AHRC Award). Donnellan taught for the History of Art Department,

UCL and is presently a Lecturer in Art and Architectural History, and Design for Boston University Study Abroad London, UK. Her interdisciplinary research in art, architecture, urbanism, cities, critical heritages, and contested histories takes a politically engaged and socially embedded approach. Selected conferences include the Association of Critical Heritage Studies (ACHS) "Futures" (2020) UCL, UK. Selected publications include *Towards Tate Modern: Public Policy, Private Vision,* 2018, Routledge. https://www.routledge.com/Towards-Tate-Modern-Public-Policy-Private-Vision/Donnellan/p/book/9780367881870 Guest Editor, Special Issue Journal, Architecture_MPS and own article "Decolonising the curriculum: US Study Abroad: London Architecture and Urbanism – Albertopolis, South Kensington." https://www.scienceopen.com/hosted-document?doi=10.14324/ 111.444.amps.2022v21i1.001 "Heritage City: Building the Historic Environment – Values and Uses – Urban Regeneration at King's Cross Central, London" in Living (World) Heritage Cities: Opportunities, challenges, and future perspectives of people-centered approaches in dynamic historic urban landscapes (eds) Maaike S. de Waal, Ilaria Rosetti, Mara de Groot & Uditha Jinadasa, 2022, Sidestone Press. https://www.sidestone.com/books/living-world-heritage-cities

Alaa El-Habashi is a Professor of Architecture and Heritage Conservation and Chairs the Department of Architecture in Menoufia University. He received a MSc in 1995 from the Historic Preservation Department at the University of Pennsylvania (PENN) and wrote a thesis about the buildings of Auguste Perret in Alexandria, Egypt. From PENN, he also received a PhD (2001) in Architecture and wrote his dissertation about the formal versus the cultural perceptions of monuments in Historic Cairo throughout the assessment of the works of the Comité de Conservation des Monuments de l'Art Arabe (1882-1954). El-Habashi's research and practices aim at founding a preservation framework that respects the specificities of local history and traditions. He has many conservation projects in Egypt such as the one of Bayt al-Razzaz and Faraj ibn Barquq water dispensary in Historic Cairo. He also has many conservation projects in other Arab countries including the Mosque of al-Ashrafiyya in Ta'iz, the Voyageur Building in Aden both in Yemen, the Idrissid Ruins in Volubilis near Meknes, the Qasbat Taourit is Ouarzazat both in Morocco as well as Sabrata archaeological site and the old oasis of Ghadames in Libya. He also consulted for the Ministry of Culture in Bahrain for the conservation and rehabilitation of the historic city of Muharraq and participated in registering the site in the World Heritage List. In such different projects, El-Habashi attempts to appropriate conservation approaches to different local values, identities, and specificities. He assisted in registering, managing, and evaluating sites listed as World Heritage, and leading capacity building programs on WH matters in the Arab World. He is a member of the editorial advisory board of the Journal of Cultural Heritage Management and Sustainable Development. El-Habashi established Turath Conservation Group

(TCG), specializing in conserving, and managing heritage sites and is founding a Centre in Historic Cairo for the Revitalization of Historic Cities.

Shuang Fei is presently undertaking her PhD at the Department of Arts and Cultural Studies in the Faculty of Humanities, University of Copenhagen, Denmark. Fei was awarded her Bachelor of Architecture and Master's in Architecture at Hunan University, China. She participated in the EPU (Eurasia Pacific Uninet) project (2014-2015) and conducted a joint renovation design on the Yifu Building at the China Three Gorges University. Fei qualified as an architect and co-founded the Sanshi design studio in 2015 which focuses on public buildings and the urban landscape. Fei also taught urban and architecture design courses at the China Three Gorges University (CTGU), Yichang. After teaching for nine years at CTGU she then worked as the leader of the Department of Architecture and Urban Planning for a further eighteen months. During this period at CTGU while working as an architect, Fei received various design awards in China. These include the 3rd Prize Supervision and Outstanding Contribution Awards in the National Green Architectural Design Contes (2014); the Finalist Awards in the 19th China Interior Design Competition (2016); and the Second Awards in the Public Architect Design Competition (2019). Fei moved to Denmark to commence her PhD research. In Copenhagen she shifted her interests from design activities to researching socio-material relationships concerning public space in cities, globalization, and the cultural economy. The focus of her research is on the dynamics and relationships of the urban environment, power, art, value, sensation, technology and public space. Based on her empirical work relating to art and networks, she is also interested in the comparative cultural complexities of difference between Denmark and China.

Angela Foster is currently a Director of the New Zealand based architectural practice, foster + melville architects (f+mA) Ltd. The aim of f+mA is to deliver projects across all of the architectural fields from commercial to residential, heritage and urban planning for a cross-section of clients. Foster initially begun working in the industry as a draftsperson at the age of seventeen. She completed her Architecture Degree at the School of Architecture and Design at Victoria University of Wellington, New Zealand in 2000 with first class honors. In 2002 Foster went on to win three New Zealand Institute of Architecture local awards in the first three years of employment before going on to set up Foster Architects in 2003. Foster Architects was very much an urban architecture firm, which focussed mainly on apartment and hotel developments. Joining forces with Melville in 2011, together they were able to continue making headway in the commercial, apartment and hotel markets around New Zealand and the South Pacific. The vision for f+mA is committed to exemplary urban design and future proofing our cities, where good architecture starts with a robust understanding of the city. As Directors Melville and Foster are involved in the local registration board as examiners for Victoria University of Wellington as course coordinators and guest critics. They also hold positions within the New Zealand Institute of Architects, as branch chair and treasurer. Foster is also undertaking a Masters of Urban Design at Victoria University of Wellington to cement her commitment to better urban design and good practice.

Viktoria K. Holmik is a PhD student at the University of Canberra, Australia in the School of Design and the Built Environment. Alongside her doctoral studies she acts as a Tutor within the School of Design and the Built Environment where she teaches the first-year Design Studio unit within the Bachelor of Built Environment. Holmik was the recipient of a Higher Degree by Research Training Scholarship in Teaching (2020). Holmik was awarded a Bachelor of Arts degree in Architecture with first class Honours from the University of Canberra. Her interest in the city, its memory and planning emerged throughout her student exchange at Leeds Beckett University in England during her undergraduate studies. Her doctoral research explores the possibility of generating a different approach to studying planned cities by testing a design method as a tool through collage theory, as developed in Colin Rowe and Fred Koetter's *Collage City*, (1978). The research proposes the development of an analytical framework that acknowledges both the objectivity and subjectivity of analysis, through drawing on the example of Canberra. Her additional research interests include studies around how the city retains its layers of history and memory, and how this can be explored in the context of planned and unplanned cities. This is coupled with investigations on capturing the complexity of the city through multi-scalar analysis that stretches the boundaries between different disciplines.

Emil E. Jonescu is a registered practicing architect with the Royal Australian Institute of Architects (RAIA) and was trained at Curtin University. Emil has attained tertiary qualifications in Architecture; PhD (Architecture Curtin), MArch (Master of Architecture) (Curtin), and BAppSc (Bachelor of Science [Architectural Science]). Upon graduating Jonescu commenced working in industry at two large municipalities: the City of Canning and City of Stirling gaining extensive and valuable design, project and construction management experience in the design, procurement, and delivery of government Infrastructure. In total his experience derives from high-impact appointments spanning two decades across three sectors: (1) officer in local and state government, (2) his own private practice as a registered practicing architect through built work & consultancy, and (3) as Course Coordinator (former) and Lecturer in the Disciplines of Construction Management and Architecture at Curtin University. Through teaching in Design, and Research Methods in Architecture, and Project Development and Appraisal and Integrated Construction Project in Construction Management, his research and discourse associated with architecture and urban behaviour has resulted in an interdisciplinary research portfolio spanning architecture, construction management, urban design, and planning. His key areas of interest include organisational behaviour; functional & political development; feasibility; architecture & diverse stakeholder engagements; surveillance theory; psychology of urban and built space; power relationships; behavioural morphology; CPTED; 'Tactical Architecture;' social sustainability; densification, inclusivity; accessibility; diverse stakeholder and community engagement. Currently, Jonescu is the Principal of Research & Development at Hames Sharley. His role creates a nexus between academic research, private sector thinking, and Hames Sharley practice in connecting academics and researchers on both a national and international scale creating opportunities for practice-led research that optimizes the organization's people and processes. His role develops opportunities for partnerships through applied practice and educational research, engagements, design innovation, and championing advancements for the community through the built environment.

Edna Langenthal is a Senior Lecturer and the Dean of the Faculty of Architecture at the University of Ariel, School of Architecture, Israel, where she teaches the first-year studio and the fifth year, final project. She received her BArch from Technion, Israel Institute of Technology, Faculty of Architecture and Town Planning. She holds an M.A. degree from Tel Aviv University, Department of Philosophy. Title of thesis: "Space, Place and the question of Home in the Philosophy of Heidegger," and a PhD from Tel Aviv University, Department of Philosophy. Title of thesis "Toward Phenomenology of Architecture: Between the Ethical and the Poetic." Langenthal is the founder and Chief Editor of Architext, the journal of the School of Architecture at Ariel University, a peer-reviewed bilingual (Hebrew/English) architectural journal. The platform discusses complex contexts regarding public, cultural, local, and global space and offers an opportunity to share thoughts and experimental research on architecture both in theory and in practice. Langenthal published "A Question of Place: Architecture between the Poetic and the Ethical" (2021), Magnes Press that revises the understanding of architectural practice while exposing it to phenomenological thought. Her areas of specialization include architecture and phenomenology, the ethical and the poetic which draw on the work of Martin Heidegger, Maurice Merleau-Ponty, and Emmanuel Levinas. Her research and teaching incorporate philosophical and ethical questions, emphasizing the link between the field of architecture and phenomenology. Langenthal is the representative of Israel in the World Association of Architects the U.I.A. and is also a practicing architect, and associate at Langenthal-Balasiano Architects.

Tom Nielsen graduated as an architect from the Aarhus School of Architecture in 1996. He has been affiliated to the Aarhus School of Architecture since 1997 and has been a Full Professor in Urban and Landscape Planning there since

2014. Nielsen has been teaching landscape architecture, urban design and urban planning since 2004. He has been teaching the MA level studio Urban Design/Landscape Architecture as well as courses on contemporary urban theory. His research focuses on the transformation of the Danish welfare city. This has included research into urban landscapes and public space, suburban transformation, urbanizing territories and the values and ethics of contemporary models of urban transformation. Nielsen has also contributed to practice as an urban design consultant in projects both in Denmark and internationally. He has worked for Gehl Architects and has collaborated with Danish architectural practices like Transform, Adept and BIG. Selected book publications include *Formløs*, 2001 [published in Danish, translated title: *Formless*]; *Gode intentioner og uregerlige byer*, 2008 [published in Danish, translated title: *Good Intentions and Unruly Cities*]; *The East Jutland Million City*, 2019 with B. B. Jensen et. al [English e-book-version *Den østjyske* million by 2017]; and *Gellerup*, 2021 with S. M. Gudmand Høyer, K. Olesen, I. Vestergaard, K. Moseng, B. G. Jensen, and R.C. Bach. Selected publications include: "New Nordic stereotypes: In search of alternative design practices for tourism in peripheral landscapes," 2021, Pasgaard, J. C., Hemmersam, P. in the Journal of Landscape Architecture (JoLA); "The Making of Democratic Urban Public Space in Denmark," *Public Space Design and Social Cohesion: An International Comparison*, Aelbrecht, P. & Stevens, Q. (eds.) (2019) Routledge; and "The polymorphic, multilayered and networked urbanised territory," 2015, in the Danish Journal of Geography.

Karen Olesen graduated as an architect from the Aarhus School of Architecture, Denmark in 1989. She has been affiliated to the Aarhus School of Architecture since 1994 and holds an Associate Professorship there since 2004. Her main areas of teaching are building design, transformation, and architecture theory. She has taught theory courses on topics such as architecture theory of the 20th century as well as the changing views of the relationship between form and programme in modern architecture. As part of her studio teaching, she has developed workshops on experimental transformation of iconic works of architecture. At present, Olesen, along with Jens Christian Pasgaard, is preparing the start-up of a new master studio focussing on the architecture of the city (running from September 2021 onwards). Her research is oriented towards two main topics: one is the unsteady relationship between programme and form thematised as open architecture and architecture on architecture. The other is the ideologies on urban design and architecture that evolved in the 1950's and 60's especially in Europe. Olesen has written and lectured about Team X and has a special interest in the works and writings of Alison and Peter Smithson. Recently, she has been part of a research group in Aarhus and co-authored *Gellerup*, 2021, Arkitektens Forlag, in which the history of one of the largest and most controversial modernist housing projects of Denmark is examined.

Jens Christian Pasgaard graduated as an architect from the Aarhus School of Architecture, Denmark in 2000. Pasgaard has been affiliated with the Aarhus School of Architecture since 2015, from where he developed his research interests which include urban design, urban architecture, strategic urban planning, and the phenomenon of tourism. From 2004 to 2014, Pasgaard was employed at the Royal Danish Academy of Fine Arts, School of Architecture, Copenhagen, where he obtained his PhD "Tourism and Strategic Planning" in 2012. Besides teaching at the bachelor's and master's levels, he also has been a supervisor at the specialised Master's program in Strategic Planning (for fully-trained professionals). At present, Pasgaard, along with Karen Olesen, is preparing the start-up of a new master studio focusing on the architecture of the city (running from September 2021 onwards). More recently, he has been involved in the cross-institutional research project "Rethinking Tourism in a Coastal City: Design for New Engagements" (2016-2019), working with analytical design proposals on different scale levels. In addition to his post as Associate Professor at the Aarhus School of Architecture, Pasgaard has been involved in several projects in practice. Recently he has been an external advisor for The Danish Association of Architects in their work on developing tools for making municipal architectural policies (2020). He has also acted as a specialist judge in the professional competition for making a development plan for the urban center of Holstebro (2019). In 2019-2020, in a part-time position for the architectural office Lytt, he has overseen two strategic-physical development plans for the coastal towns of Hvide Sande and Søndervig at the Danish west coast (both plans were adopted in 2020). Earlier in his career, Pasgaard worked for the architectural offices Schmidt Hammer Lassen Architects and Dorte Mandrup A/S.

Hanna Rodewald completed her B.A. and M.Ed. at TU Dortmund University, Germany studying English and American Studies, Fine Arts and Educational Science. In 2013/14, she taught German as a Teaching Assistant at the University of Iowa, United States. In 2018 Rodewald completed her Master of Education and thesis on "Urban Complexity: The Representation of Harlem in Ann Petry's The Street." At the American Studies Department in Dortmund, Rodewald continues to teach courses on fields such as American Art and Urban Cultural Studies. She is also actively engaged in organizing academic conferences including the annual Ruhr PhD Forum or the research symposium in Detroit on Transatlantic Rust Belts in 2021. As a doctoral researcher, she is part of the Graduate Research Group Scripts for Postindustrial Urban Futures: American Models, Transatlantic Interventions (2018-2022) at the University Alliance Ruhr (Bochum, Dortmund, Duisburg-Essen) which is funded by the Volkswagen Stiftung in Germany. The group explores imaginative strategies and future narrative scenarios for deindustrializing cities of the German Ruhr Area and the American Rust Belt. Looking into narratives of the creative class in post-industrial cities from a transatlantic perspective, Rodewald particularly focuses her analysis on the creative city script. In the course of her research, she has completed a practical year at the Museum Ostwall at the Dortmund U and is now part of the cooperative project Page 21 which experiments with digital narration and artworks within a virtually immersive setting. As an artist she is also part of the art collective Salon Atelier based in Dortmund where she participated in performative group projects such as Saloon (2019) or Viva BVB (2020).

Alia Sherif holds a master's degree from Brandenburg University of Technology (BTU) in Cottbus, Germany and Alexandria University in Alexandria, Egypt, after completing the double masters' program Urban Design: Revitalization of Historic City Districts in 2020. In 2017, Sherif graduated from the American University in Cairo (AUC) with a Bachelor's Degree in Architectural Engineering. Sherif started her career as a teaching assistant at AUC for a design course. The design course was centred around contemporary Egyptian architecture and developing an architectural language that is contextually relevant. Sherif complemented her academic interest with practical experience working as a junior architect at a design office (Raef Fahmi Architects, Maadi, Cairo). She was involved in designing multiple residential, commercial, and recreational projects in Cairo and Alexandria, on an architectural and urban scale. Throughout her academic years, Sherif has participated in a number of international workshops. Through these workshops she addressed and challenged different urban issues and contexts including Egypt, UK, and Netherlands. Most recent of these workshops is (Re)cycle Limburg workshops in Maastricht, Netherlands (2019) which was focused on investigating the role and meaning of public spaces and how they can be a catalyst for social cohesion, healthy lifestyle, and well-being. She also participated in RIBA's design workshop in London (2017), where the New Urban Agenda was explored and how it can be applied to tackle urban issues in the historical city, the informal city, and the city from scratch. She also contributed in "Cairo and the Nile" workshop organized by Cairo University and UC Berkeley (2017), proposing urban solutions to revitalize the Nile front as an inclusive public space. Presently, Sherif is working with Turath Conservation Group (TCG) on a revitalization project in Souq al Silah street in Historic Cairo.

Yiming Wang is an Assistant Professor at the College of Architecture and Urban Planning, Tongji University, and an Associate Research Fellow at the Institute of Elaborated Governance for Megacity in Shanghai, China. He completed his PhD at University of Technology Sydney, Australia in 2018 and held a Post-Doctoral Research Fellowship at the College of Architecture and Urban Planning in Tongji University during 2018 and 2021. He is an architect-urban designer with research interests focusing on Chinese urbanism, urban regeneration, transformation, and governance of the urban commons. Selected publications include *Pseudo-Public Spaces in Chinese Shopping Malls: Rise, Publicness and Consequences*, Routledge, 2019. He is an additional author of the UN-Habitat report: Net Zero Carbon Village Planning Guidelines for the Yangtze River Delta Region in China (2019). His research outputs have been widely published in leading international and Chinese journals including URBAN DESIGN International, American Journal of Economics and Sociology, Norwegian Journal of Geography and Urban Planning Forum. International conferences include the 56th ISOCARP World Planning Congress (online virtual conference, December 2020); China Urban Development (London, 2017); the 21st Construction; Building and Real Estate Research Conference for RICS (Sydney, 2015); and the 9th International Symposium on Architectural Interchanges in Asia (Gwangju, 2012). He has received research grants from the China Postdoctoral Science Foundation and Shanghai Pujiang Program. Wang has also participated in a number of important urban development projects including Urban Design of the CBD Area of Jiangbei New District, Nanjing, China. As project team member, he received various design accolades including the highly coveted architectural design Luban Award in China.

Abbey Wuu graduated from Curtin University with a Bachelor of Applied Science (BAppSc) in Architecture and a Master of Architecture (MArch). At Curtin University Wuu developed an interest in public design and urban spaces, and how this informs behaviour and experiences. She is also interested in how different groups of people form diverse relationships with the built environment. After graduating, Wuu began working freelance in design, project management and planning on commercial projects including restaurant fit-outs, interior refurbishments and pop-up stores, and residential work involving house expansions. Wuu is presently engaged as a client-side planner and project manager for the coordination of airport infrastructure. A selection of the projects Wuu has worked on include calculating passenger forecasting trends, deciphering the trends into area capacity requirements, developing existing airport processes, and working on infrastructure and technology redevelopments and expansions. Wuu is also researching passenger interactions and engagement within the airport through observation as an infrastructure planner. Wuu is also involved in internal and external stakeholder engagement with various companies. Related to this she is focusing on developing her knowledge of understanding human interactions and social norms within the city's shifting cultural landscape.

Aliaa Zidan is a PhD student in the department of Architecture Engineering in Menoufia University since 2018. Her dissertation title is" Regeneration of Traditional Crafts as an approach for the Sustainable Development of Historic Cairo." The aim of her thesis is to identify a more efficient system for managing the historical city, as well as strengthening the local economy in the region. The objective is to achieve sustainable development goals (SDGs) before 2030, through developing the cultural industries and traditional crafts. Zidan completed her master's thesis "Preserving Intangible values in Cultural Heritage Sites: A Study on the Mosque of Al-Sayyid Al-Badawi in Tanta," (2016) in which she studied the means to value and preserve intangible heritage, through the celebration of the birthday of Al-Sayyid Al-Badawi in Tanta (Mulid al-badawi). Relating to this research she was able to make a comparative analysis between local events with international celebrations, such as the one of Santiago de Compastela in Spain. Zidan graduated from the department of Architecture in Menoufia University in 2013. She is an Associate Researcher on "The creative sustainable city: application on regeneration of traditional crafts in historic Cairo." She is also an Associate Researcher in a paper titled "Intangible heritage as an approach for the urban preservation and local community development." In January 2018 she won the first prize in the competition of regeneration of the urban space in front of Hamam Bashtak - Al-Darb Al-Ahmar, Cairo. She has also contributed to numerous workshops since 2016 which focused on the sustainable development of historic Cairo and shared experiences. She is a member of "Establishment of Traditional Craft Revitalization and Training Centre in Old Cairo" project which is funded by the Embassy of Japan in Egypt. Zidan is a teaching assistant at Higher Institute of Engineering and Technology in Tanta. She is also an architect in the TCG "Turath Conservation Group," working on conservation projects in Egypt. She is presently a research assistant and member of the "Managing Libya's Cultural Heritage" project.

Introduction:
The social and the built: cities, complexity, and Jane Jacobs

Caroline Donnellan

Boston University Study Abroad London, UK

The abandoned city

The COVID-19 pandemic lockdowns in 2020 saw cities around the world experiencing the same phenomenon of abandoned streets, buildings, and transport hubs. What had been familiar became overnight strangely familiar.[1] The shared mass experience declared itself so vividly because the city is the product of "social evolution" — a human settlement — which in its elemental form is a large, densely populated conurbation.[2] With the absence of people, it becomes a ghost city and, in a smaller configuration, a ghost town. The irony is that when the city becomes populated and expands, it is perceived as if it is a problem to be solved. The post-war solution was to demolish older buildings, sites, and sometimes entire areas. The developments that replaced them and the speed at which they were constructed were the result of a heady mix of capitalism and modernity that knew no bounds. Marshall Berman asserts: "Modern environments and experiences cut across all boundaries of geography and ethnicity, of class and nationality, religion and ideology."[3] In creating a new vision of the city, the planners promoted the benefits of their new designs, and how they would invariably improve on the existing models. An example of this type of planning on a national scale was the implementation of the Interstate Highways in the US.

The initiative began when the National Highway Users Conference, overseen by General Motors and other stakeholders, lobbied the US government for tax money to build a major transport network. The proposed development was unveiled at the Futurama installation at New York World's Fair in 1939. The exhibit revealed a system of Interstate Highways which connected cities by slicing through their downtown areas, regardless of their existing social networks. The Interstate Highways became a reality under President Dwight D. Eisenhower. Earlier, in 1919, when Eisenhower was on a military convoy from Washington DC to San Francisco, the journey on the Lincoln Highway took 62 days. Today, the journey takes approximately 1 day and 17 hours to drive on the Interstate Highways. What galvanized Eisenhower's vision to build better roads was "his observations of the German autobahn network of freeways" during World War II which instilled in the future President the desire to build a superior transport network for the US.[4]

The Federal-Aid Highway Act (1956) provided the legislation to construct a 41,000-mile network, with a funding provision of $26 billion out of which 90% was paid by the federal government and the other 10% by each State. The arrival of the Interstate Highways in the 1950s invoked the American Dream of the 1930s in providing physical and social mobility, which ran in tandem with the remaking of the road map of America. The building of the Interstate Highways and the demolition of downtown city areas were further promoted as providing large-scale federal slum clearance. The reality was that these areas were torn down regardless of whether they were slums or not, which, in going against their residents' wishes, destroyed their "networks of social interaction."[5] During this period Jane Jacobs was an associate editor of the Architectural Forum. In response to the destruction of these inner-city areas she published *Downtown is for People* (1958) which was effectively a manifesto to save American cities. "This is a critical time for the future of the city. All over the country civic leaders and planners are preparing a series of redevelopment projects that will set the character of the center of our cities for generations to come."[6] The breaking up of these areas saw their former communities dispersed as they were forced to leave their homes and neighborhoods, with many of them being relocated into the new residential developments being built on the city outskirts.

The idea of major residential developments outside of the city centre was first introduced in England with Ebeneezer Howard's *To-morrow: A Peaceful Path to Real Reform* (1898). What he proposed was a utopian vision of communities living harmoniously within "a healthy, natural and economic combination of town and country life."[7] The book reprinted as *Garden Cities of To-morrow* (1902) included a postscript which emphasized the idea of a bonded community whose aim was "to secure the best interests of all its inhabitants."[8] The Garden City Movement was conceived in response to crowded and unsanitary inner city living. What was envisioned were smaller city-like developments with zoned residential, civic, and industrial areas, surrounded by a protective green agricultural belt. This vision was realized with the establishment of Letchworth Garden City in 1903. Further Garden City developments followed, as did green suburban initiatives. These included Hampstead Garden Suburb from 1907, created as a semi-rural idyll with the nearby London Underground Station of Golders Green opening the same year. Further developments were realized inside and outside of Britain including in the US. They were not welcomed by Jacobs who wanted to live inside the city, unlike Howard who wanted to live outside the city. For Jacobs, the new suburban developments were an anathema to city living. "They will be spacious, parklike, and uncrowded. They will feature long green vistas. They will be stable and symmetrical and orderly. They will be clean, impressive, and monumental. They will have all the attributes of a well-kept, dignified cemetery."[9]

Ignoring complexity

The creation of the suburban housing projects, and the demolition of inner-city areas led to Jacobs' seminal work *The Death and Life of American Cities* (1961). The problem was compounded for Jacobs because the planners reduced the city to single issues. "The simple needs of automobiles are more easily understood and satisfied than the complex needs of cities, and a growing number of planners and designers have come to believe that if they can only solve the problems of traffic, they will thereby have solved the major problem of cities."[10] While the Interstate Highways responded to the issue of providing an effective transportation system, there was no recourse as to their negative impact. The person responsible was Robert Moses who oversaw the construction of 13 expressways with the aim to reduce traffic congestion. In doing so his expressways destroyed historic areas, buildings, and communities, and brought with them pollution and noise. A less publicized fact was the vast profits that the developers were making from the new developments. The Trans-Manhattan Expressway (originally known as the George Washington Bridge Expressway) now cuts through the northern end of the borough of Manhattan. The project was originally driven by "rewarding developers and raising property values south of the park, where he [Moses] had already razed a swath of Greenwich Village for redevelopment."[11] The other planned developments of the Cross Harlem Expressway and the Mid-Manhattan Expressway did not go ahead.

After the Mid-Manhattan Expressway failed, Moses was keen to push through the Lower Manhattan Expressway where he came head-to-head with Jacobs. The plan was also unsuccessful due to the weight of opposition spearheaded by Jacobs because for her it would have destroyed Greenwich Village (including her own home) and changed the entire appearance of the area. Her core argument was that it ran contrary to "how cities work in real life" which for Jacobs was about people and communities.[12] With her unwavering position Jacobs came under opposition during and after her lifetime. One issue to emerge was (and is) concerning the areas she rescued from demolition which has since led to their gentrification. The original community that lived in Jacobs' Greenwich Village has long gone but preserving the area's identity through its buildings and streets has turned it into architectural heritage, and very expensive real estate. The other question concerning Jacobs is that she had the agency to fight the planners in New York and later Toronto whereas other cities did not have the same kind of voice representing them. The point is

Jacobs believed she had a voice and used it. Ground-breaking or flawed, Jacobs' determination impacted on the world she lived in, and continues to inform the debate today between the social and the built city. Ricky Burdett outlines the basis of these underlining positions. "Despite the increasing complexity and specificity of the global urban condition, the old "bottom-up versus top-down" model still frames the debate about how cities should be planned, managed, and governed."[13]

While the bottom up (social) versus the top down (built) dichotomy is ongoing, Stefano Moroni and Stefano Cozzolino propose that this "complexity is due mainly to the fact that the core element of cities is multiple *action*."[14] Cities are about multiple action(s) through their shifting positions, identities, and visions, whether real or imagined. When these positions, identities, and visions are mediated in literature, film, the internet and other media, cities can be idealized and romanticised, or dehumanized and brutalized. In this way the city becomes the site of many projections, and once it is "*narrated*" it cannot be un-narrated, Roland Barthes claims it then becomes performed.[15] Through this narration, and performance, the visitor (reader) assigns the city with a set of their own ideas and associations — this is the point where the idea of place is created. Steven Feld and Keith Basso explore how "people encounter places, perceive them, and invest them with significance."[16] In the same way, this book acknowledges the relationship between people and place, and what it offers them. It recognizes the many ways of encountering the city, which can be an intensely personal or shared collective experience. It understands the city as being a place of connection and disconnection, as well as intentness and withdrawal. In doing so, it facilitates these multiple positions within the social city approach and the built city method. While they can appear adversarial and antagonistic, they are also reciprocal and interdependent because they are constituent parts of the same (whole) city — Pierre Bourdieu explores this same dichotomy within human action.

> The union of contraries does not destroy the opposition (which it presupposes), the reunited contraries are just as much opposed, but now in a quite different way, thereby manifesting the duality of the relationship between them, at once antagonism and complementarity, *neikos* and *philia*, which might appear as their own twofold "nature" if they were conceived outside that relationship.[17]

What Bourdieu identifies is the juxtaposition between the argumentative and feuding *neikos*, and the friendly and affectionate *philia* in this "marriage of contraries."[18] The duality identified by Bourdieu, amongst others, informs the ideas in this book concerning what cities engender, how they function and why they continue to act as catalysts for different kinds of interactions. It is this marriage of contraries that underpins the rationale for the chapters in this book, which evolved from papers presented at *The City and Complexity – Life Design and Commerce in the Built Environment* conference, 17-19 June 2020. The online event was organized by City, University of London, and the international research organization AMPS (Architecture, Media, Politics, Society), and marked the 50th anniversary of Jane Jacobs' *The Economy of Cities* from when it was published in the UK by Jonathan Cape in London in 1970. The book was originally published by Random House in New York in 1969. *The Economy of Cities* explores how (major) cities act as command-and-control centres of exports, and as depots for goods. While these cities usually are no longer depots, they remain at the nodal point of trade, transactions, and communications. "What we abstractly call the dissemination of cultures consists of many exports, some of them amazingly complex, that were first developed within the local economies of cities."[19] In Jacobs summation, cities are interconnected, economic, social, and cultural networks.

The Economy of Cities was at the forefront of a new kind of urban literature. What she develops is the idea of an integrated urban and social economics. The book returns to the themes of complexity, uncertainty, non-linearity, and unpredictability which were originally explored in *The Death and Life of Great American Cities*. The main tenet of her work is that cities are more complex networks than modernism could advocate for. With its severance from the past, modernism isolates buildings from their surroundings. In the same way modern developments create mono-functional zones, which in reducing them to their constituent parts negates the possibility of facilitating more varied and interesting urban environments. Ignoring a city's past and present, for Jacobs, contributed to the "central problem of planning for cities."[20] This position influenced writers and theorists on cities, including those working in the field of architecture. The American architect Robert Venturi's seminal work *Complexity and Contradiction in Architecture* (1966) discusses the position of modernism.

The core problem, for Venturi, was modernism's self-belief that it was not only the standard bearer of the new, but saw its further role was to eradicate what it envisioned as the traditional, the outdated, and the obsolete. Underpinning the belief that modernism had the ability to make things better was the forward pincer movement towards the idea of progress, and betterment. Modernism became the designated style for post-war American design, and the ideological tool for political and economic dominance. In questioning modernism's rhetoric, and its resistance to history, (and other cultures), Venturi proposes an alternative way of thinking about design. In advocating for inclusion rather than exclusion Venturi argues that buildings should not have to confirm to any one orthodoxy and can instead have a "messy vitality over obvious unity."[21] For Venturi, postmodernism was always more than a design style and the look of things, it was about interrogating the ideological basis of modernism and its promotion of "a sense of new possibilities."[22] Similarly to Jacobs' approach, in rejecting the principle of how things should be, Venturi forwards the case of how things are, which does not necessarily fit within a clearly definable niche. In this way, Venturi moves away from something less reductionist, and advocates for complexity and contradiction in design.

Interpretative framework

The interpretative framework of this book similarly draws on the complexity and the contradiction of cities which understands them as dynamic changing networks, as Gert de Roo asserts: "Discontinuous change is the only constant factor in the world we are part of, and what seems stable to us is actually nothing more than a temporary period of persistence, a frozen instant within a dynamic world, [...] there is no permanent stability."[23] The one thing that the COVID-19 pandemic has taught is that the *frozen instant* of stability has thawed. What appeared predictable (although it never was) is no longer predictable. In responding to this constant flux, cities have had to become "complex adaptive systems [that] evolve and co-evolve, internally and externally, either slowly and in incremental steps or rapidly [...] that give expression to developments that keep the system far from a state of equilibrium."[24] It is in this lack of equilibrium, that these chapters present singular case studies and comparative assessments through different voices, and perspectives. The international writers aim to be robust and rigorous, as well as explicit and transparent in preferencing clear prose in place of theoretical grandstanding. The objective is to address the city as a centre for development and sprawl, creativity, and conflict, and regeneration, and urban withdrawal. What binds the chapters together is that cities are understood as being dually sites of socio-political import and as physical built spaces and are examined with these distinctions in mind.

The social city chapters explore a set of initiatives in the historic cities and surrounding areas of Cairo, Athens, Shanghai, Dortmund, Essen, and Chongqing which focus on human interactions, and shifting communities, and the places they inhabit. The built city chapters examine the planning, development, and lack of, in Canberra, Perth, Copenhagen, London, Melbourne, and Wellington. They focus on their cities' urban and topographical features, and information technology, through policy, planning and development. The aim of both sets of chapters is to identify the complex alternating processes between the social and the built, in the knowledge that they are divergent viewpoints that should be treated as such rather than grouping them together as if they are one unified voice. A further factor is that these issues are identified and responded to with working solutions. At the same time, the idea of conflict is not necessarily negated and boxed into the solution as a resolution format. Conflict is a necessary ingredient of the city which can produce creativity, innovation, and resourcefulness, and is why some positions are left unresolved. In conclusion this book is arranged according to the Geddesian principal that the city is the result of social evolution. As the thought (the social) comes before the action (the built) this book follows the same principle.

The Social City

Chapter 1. Alaa El-Habashi, Aliaa Zidan, and Alia Sherif's *Re-clustering historic Cairo through the creative economy: A Study of the revitalization of the traditional carpentry along Souk Al-Silah Street* considers the older Islamic city within the context of the modern metropolis. Fourteenth-century Cairo emerged as the cultural centre of the Islamic world. When UNESCO conferred on Cairo the status of a World Heritage Site in 1979, its Islamic heritage was officially venerated for its culture through its mosques, madrasas, hammams and fountains, while other historic areas were being abandoned.[25] When Cairo expanded in the nineteenth century the neighbourhood quarters of the *haras* went into decline due to "changes in cultural views and traditional lifestyles."[26] The twentieth century saw the *haras* being lost within the new developments which were unable to accommodate their traditional ways of life. As Kristof Van Assche, Raoul Beunen, and Martijn Duineveld assert: "Modernist planning did not exhibit much self-awareness [...] It also tended to ignore the presence of other, alternative forms of knowledge and expertise, other experts, and non-experts, making it hard to really draw on local knowledge and to discern local interests."[27]

Following the anti-government protests and insurrections in the 2010s that affected Arab countries, change began to gradually impact on their cities. "With the Arab spring in 2011 in Egypt, new experiences, new debates and new approaches started" which led to the re-appraisal of their cities.[28] One impact saw the Souk Al-Silah Street community-centred revitalization program re-establishing the original footprint of the *hara* in this part of the Egyptian capital. The aim of the project has been to reconnect the local community with its cultural heritage, and to provide social and urban cohesion. In this case study El-Habashi, Zidan, and Sherif assess how this socially focused regeneration strategy is providing a holistic solution to urban fragmentation. They assess how the re-implementation of traditional joinery within the craft focused *hara* is reconnecting the community and is also contributing to the local economy. In doing so the core questions to be addressed are — is cultural clustering an effective solution to urban sprawl and what is the implication of the reintroduction of a craft orientated *hara* in promoting continuity with the past?

Chapter 2. Edna Langenthal's *Agōn (Ἀγών) in ancient Athens and conflict in the modern city* examines how the ancient Greek city-state that has long been associated with the arts, learning, and philosophy gave rise to a different legacy. According to Greek myth, following the contest between the goddess Athena and god Poseidon for Attica, the land under the Acropolis was named after the victor. The Panathenaic Games were part of the Panathenaic Festival and were to honor the victor and their patroness, Athena. The Panathenaic Games were more than competitions within a stadium — they were about ritual, ceremony, and performance. What emerged from the Games was the idea of *agōn* which instilled in Athenian culture the idea of public contestation. Mark Wenman identifies how "the term agonism comes from the Greek *agōn* meaning contest or strife" and contains three basic elements: "(i) a conception of constitutive pluralism, (ii) a tragic vision of the world, and (iii) a belief that conflict can be a political good."[29] As a political and social concept agonism accepts conflict as a necessary constituent of its practice. Langenthal applies this same principle to the city and argues that agonistic encounter became a recurring cultural trope in fifth century Athens and remains a characteristic of the contemporary city. Her point is that conflict should not be viewed through the lens of neo-liberalism, that seeks to resolve internal tensions. In this way, cities should be understood as "organized complexity" in their ability to facilitate oscillating binary positions including reciprocity and competition.[30]

In this chapter, Langenthal explores a range of positions revolving around the theme of *agōn*. These include how global capitalism has increased the need to re-examine the city which can be better reassessed through the idea of *agōn*. She considers how diversity should be valued as an important contribution to the life of the city and examines the issues that emerge from not belonging to it when marginal populations are pushed out to its fringes. The problem in removing these communities and individuals from the city (centre) is that they lose their own sense of competition. As cities are shaped by human action, and communities and people are influenced by the spatial conditions in which they live, the divergence between social experience and the built environment should not be removed. If these differences are taken away there is no innovation and no point of transformation, which is why the city needs to remain the site of new and challenging experiences. Peter Carnevale discusses the potential effects of these interactions. "If creativity is applied to the handling of differences, the outcome might very well be a mutually beneficial, integrative agreement."[31] Within this mutually beneficial agreement, Langenthal follows a similar trajectory and considers the questions — what is the role that conflict plays in the city's development and what is the relationship between the city as a social settlement and the people who inhabit it?

Chapter 3. Shuang Fei's *Public Space in the West Bund, Shanghai* examines the changing identity of the Xuhui waterfront. In the nineteenth century Shanghai became one of five treaty ports forced to open to European trade after the First Opium War (1839-1842) which enabled it to develop its foreign as well as domestic trade. By the 1930s the city emerged as a primary commercial hub. After the Second Sino-Japanese War, and the taking over of the mainland by the communists in 1949, this resulted in trade becoming restricted to other socialist countries which saw the city's position decline. Following this period, the wider urban situation was also compromised. "During the 10 years of the Cultural Revolution (1966 to 1976), China's urban landscape was in an extremely undesirable condition and its urban development virtually stagnated."[32] Change began with Deng Xiaoping's economic liberal reforms in the 1980s which took effect in the 1990s. The economy grew, with Shanghai replacing Singapore in 2010 as the world's busiest container port. The extent the Chinese Communist Party was willing to support the new economic policies was demonstrated through its "surge of culture-led urban regeneration efforts."[33]

The post-industrial Shanghai waterfront — the Bund — was assigned as a protected historical district and became the focus of a major urban renewal program. The redevelopment on both banks of the Huangpu waterfront saw the Bund emerging as a new-style contemporary Chinese city in providing financial services, technological innovation, and a cultural hub. The strategy involved using the services of international as well national architects which became part of a changing vision to promote Shanghai's rebranded global identity. The aim was "to compete, and possibly surpass, global cities such as New York, London, Singapore, and Tokyo in terms of economy, image, and quality of life."[34] Contributing to this vision is the West Bund which, as the new cultural quarter, facilitates museums and exhibition spaces within its repurposed industrial and contemporary buildings. What is addressed in this chapter is how the public interacts with the West Bund. The focus of Fei's research is on the intersection between the government's involvement with the West Bund, the contemporary Chinese art scene, the collectors, and the people who use it. She argues that the relationship between art, power, commerce, technology, social media, and notably We Media has enabled these cultural spaces to become more open forums than was originally envisioned by the government. The questions she raises are — what kinds of spaces have emerged in this restyled Chinese city, and what effect have they on the public that use them?

Chapter 4. Hanna Rodewald's *Creative frontiers: Germany's Ruhr area as a space of polyrational possibility* explores how this former industrial region has been transformed into a site for social and economic diversification. The regeneration initiative has been supported by substantial public investment with the aim to preserve regional identity by building on Ruhr's industrial heritage. One of the major sites is the former coal-mining UNESCO-listed Zollverein Coal Mine Industrial Complex which facilitates the Ruhr Museum. In stimulating culture and education, it represents some of the services on offer in this area. In exploring the changing identity of the Ruhr, Rodewald examines the cities of Dortmund and Essen through the framework of the frontier as a place of transitional space, changing expectations, and "a point of convergence and connection."[35] With examples ranging from art, city branding, and urban planning, Rodewald draws on the idea of frontier imagery to explore the shift from the postindustrial into the new social and cultural landscape. Christian Zuidema identifies this point as where "conceptions of stability and linearity are replaced by those of dynamically interacting social and physical systems."[36] Rodewald fuses the idea of the frontier in conjunction with Benjamin Davy's polyrational theory of planning and its multiple "insular, opportunistic, kinship, collaborative, corporate, structural, container, and environmental" land uses.[37]

The issue with repurposing postindustrial sites which are subject to traditional planning and restricted land uses, is that with major cash injections and directives this significantly alters their socio-economic complexion. The newly regenerated urban developments attract a more upwardly mobile demographic, which sees the existing community moving out. The problem with gentrification is that it redefines the area's social geography. The paradigm nineteenth century example was Baron Georges-Eugène Haussmann's Paris. When Prefect of the Seine, Haussmann's massive demolition of the old city made way for the new boulevards and public works, which redefined its social and economic geography. As Neil Smith asserts: "If Baudelaire, Engels and Berman (1982) all saw the Haussmannization of Paris as one defining moment of a capitalist modernity, can we see in gentrification a defining geography of postmodernity?"[38] Within this geography of postmodernity there is the potential for pluralism that encompasses opposing positions, including gentrification and displacement. As postmodernism does not work in absolutes, it can provide a holistic approach to city planning. In the same way, postmodern planning informs Rodewald's research in relation to the frontier as a space for spatial (and mental) possibilities and polyrational land uses. Within this framework, Rodewald addresses the questions — how does this benefit the reimagined Ruhr cities, and how can it provide an effective, alternative, and imaginative approach to designing future cities?

Chapter 5. Jie Chen and Yiming Wang's *Power relations in industrial land redevelopment and loss of industrial heritage in Chongqing, China* addresses the complex issue that has arisen due to a lack of conservation by the Government. As one of the four municipalities, Chongqing has at its core a "vast, explosively expanding, industrial metropolis."[39] The city's fortunes changed when it was awarded provincial city status in 1997 which saw it make "remarkable progress in economic and social development."[40] The city realigned its identity as a successful financial trading area, a transportation hub, and a major modern manufacturing center. With Chongqing's "population mobility and policies" it has been subject to unprecedented urbanization and lauded for a seemingly more socially aware urban plan.[41] "Since 2010, when the urbanization rate of Chongqing City had exceeded 50%, the city has shifted its focus from pure economic growth to living quality improvement. Urban planners began to focus more on community-based interventions within the city context that called for a better quality of life and a new and more people-oriented type of urbanization."[42] The program of urbanization, however, is having a detrimental effect on older sites, and notably on manufacturing developments which are being demolished without any regard for their conservation.

In this chapter, Chen and Wang examine Chongqing Steel Factory's redevelopment to assess how top-down power structures have impacted on the deterioration of the site's industrial heritage. The problem has been spurred on by the wave of entrepreneurialism which has contributed to the increasing value of land. The result is that older obsolete buildings have been and continue to be demolished without any regard for their heritage value, to make way for new residential, commercial, and modern industrial developments. As Chen and Wang argue, the Government State-Owned Enterprises redevelopment strategy has resulted in the targeted loss of the industrial historic landscape. A further conundrum is that the situation has been exacerbated by an absence of grass roots-level activism. What the authors identify is a lack of top-down social responsibility from the Government concerning its industrial historic environment. If positive action were undertaken for conservation, this would preserve the area's industrial heritage. It would also demonstrate a stronger bond between the government and its citizens, while providing new jobs, that would create less waste, in an improved environment. As the situation in Chongqing has not been resolved, the core question addressed by Chen and Wang is — what solution can be sought to address the removal of China's industrial heritage through land redevelopment?

The Built City

Chapter 6. Viktoria K. Holmik's *Developing a Collage City Methodology: A Case Study of Canberra* addresses the issues surrounding the planning and development of the Australian capital. On 24 May 1911, the American architect Walter Burley Griffin was appointed to create a plan to build the new city of Canberra. In the blueprint which he developed with his wife Marion Mahony, the architects incorporated significant elements of the natural landscape, as well as zoned areas which echoed the ideas of the Garden City Movement. "At the heart of Griffin's plan was the use of topography as an integral design feature and as a setting; a symbolic hierarchy of land uses designed to reflect the order and functions of democratic government; a geometric plan with the central triangle formed by grand avenues terminating at Capital Hill."[43] What resulted was a plan that lacked cohesion which contributed to a strained relationship with the Australian authorities. With an ongoing lack of funding, this meant by the time the Griffins were removed from the project in 1920 little real work had been undertaken on the development.

One point that the Griffins and the Australian authorities might have agreed on is that planning is a complex process, and planning an entire city is especially complex, as Susa Eräranta states: "Planning processes are messy and complex and should be researched as such."[44] On this basis, Holmik approaches Canberra as a complex, incomplete development, and proposes a way to resolve the areas that lack cohesion. To do so Holmik draws on Colin Rowe and Fred Koetter's *Collage City* (1978) which develops the idea of an assemblage, and specifically an aggregation of forms that creates something new and more complex. This design concept is as much about what is left out, as what is left in. For the authors it is the "method of paying attention to the left-overs of the world, of preserving their integrity and equipping them with dignity, of compounding matter of factness and cerebrality, as a convention and a breach of convention."[45] By drawing on collage city theory, Holmik considers how vest pockets (small intersections) are a useful way to connect the city and its spaces. In arguing for a more holistic and desirable (utopian) vision of Canberra, Holmik considers the question — how can the vest pocket strategy be applied to create a more joined-up holistic city?

Chapter 7. Emil E. Jonescu, Abbey Jia Wuu and Khoa Do's *A case for a multi-dimensional development grid for Perth, Western Australia* considers an alternative approach to mapping the multi-ethnic city. The authors identify how the root of the problem is historic. The physical demarcation was created by the railway lines built between the suburb of Northbridge and the business district on the other side of the tracks. When Chinese immigrants began arriving in Northbridge from the late 1800s, they were later followed by Greek and Italian immigrants. The outcome was that Northbridge emerged as an "ethnic neighbourhood."[46] Northbridge has since been defined as a lively cultural quarter with its art galleries, restaurants, bars, clubs, and boutiques. What defines Northbridge is community and difference that revolves around its multiculturalism. While the wider position of the Australian government earlier adopted an "official cultural policy of multiculturalism" this was not reflected in city planning and contributes to why in Perth there is an implied ethnic border which has created mono-functional precincts. [47]

In this chapter Jonescu, Wuu and Do propose an alternative approach to Perth's planning. As traditional zoning does not allow for multiplicity, and therefore for conflict and chaos, they propose a different kind of urban model. To do so they draw on Frei Otto's multi-dimensional organic grid plan, which enables multicultural communities to co-exist within the same space. Their research reverberates with Stefano Moroni and Stefano Cozzolino's proposition that "complexity also depends on the fact that multiple actions take place within a multi-layered ontology of plural conditions of actions, some of which emerge unintentionally."[48] Along the same trajectory Jonescu, Wuu and Do apply a set of concepts that advocates for a more imaginative approach to city planning in proposing a fully integrated multi-layered city. In their re-evaluation of Perth's built environment, they advocate for an alternative urban plan. The core question they address is — what are the potential implications for implementing a more organic, three-dimensional, and user-centred urban development strategy?

Chapter 8. Jens Christian Pasgaard, Karen Olsen, Tom Nielsen, and Morten Daugaard's *The Unsmart City: Pitfalls of Predictability — Copenhagen* examines the consequences of information technology on its users within the urban environment. The context for the smart city began after Copenhagen went into economic and urban decline in the 1980s. "Central-city development was characterized by a set of eroding processes that included de-industrialization, suburbanization, high unemployment rates, high welfare costs, an outdated housing market, strong segregation and various other factors."[49] By the 1990s "the term *smart city* was first used" which saw the city shift towards a service and knowledge-based economy.[50] During this period, the Municipality of Copenhagen adopted a forward-thinking planning approach by working with the city's dense urban fabric, surrounded by its green space, through the implementation of a highly sustainable, energy efficient, and smart technology framework. In this chapter, Pasgaard, Olsen, Nielsen, and Daugaard address how a progressive Danish society was willing to embrace digital technology which saw the rise of smart cities coupled with "unprecedented urbanization and the need for sustainability."[51] The new network-oriented service economy, with its push to digital, made the city more efficient, more resilient, less resource-consuming, and provided a way of protecting the environment and for saving money.

This chapter assesses the impact of smart city technology on its users by considering its benefits and drawbacks through the framework of supporting technological development, good urban design, and interesting city spaces. The research focus examines how imperceptible smart city technology affects people's experiences and liveability concerning their physical and mental wellbeing in relation to sustainability. As Duncan Maclaren asserts: "The city's vision frames the idea of liveability around sustainability and how urban space can create opportunities for people to partake in unique and varied urban activities."[52] Concerning the potential issues that have arisen from imperceptible smart technology this chapter considers the questions — what is the real cost of the smart city, and how effective is smart city technology when faced with the unpredictability of urban contexts?

Chapter 9. Caroline Donnellan's *Bankside, SE1 — A central London concerted waterfront regeneration strategy?* assesses how this area on the south bank of the River Thames underwent a sustained period of major redevelopment from the mid-1990s. Post-millennium Bankside emerged as a concerted waterfront regeneration strategy — except there was no concerted waterfront regeneration strategy. The reinvention of Bankside was not the result of a major funded masterplan but was due to a self-organizing set of circumstances, interconnecting interventions, forces, and perspectives. Prior to this point Southwark Council set out its planning policies in 1995 which identified Bankside as a site for regeneration and invited funding proposals. There was no substantial investment initiative, nor masterplan forthcoming.[53] What is notable is that the Mayor of London's development strategy *The London Plan* (2004) did not even mention Bankside despite Shakespeare's Globe opening in 1997 and Tate Modern in 2000. These institutions were at the vanguard of other cultural organisations, creative industries, as well as businesses opening in Bankside.

While the official bodies failed to recognize Bankside's potential, it was nonetheless able to organize its own urban renaissance. This chapter, therefore, examines how Bankside developed its own urban vision by initially outlining its development, and that of the wider Southwark area, in relation to the City of London. It discusses how the later post-industrial area underwent a process of renewal which was spearheaded by its "cultural infrastructure."[54] The research considers how Bankside was recast as a central London waterfront location in its ability to "attract people, events, functions and investments and to produce quality, environmental sustainability and social cohesion."[55] It discusses how Bankside's various enterprises created a diverse mix of urban strategies, and with the repurposing of the built environment began "the integration of places, people, economies and traditions."[56] On this basis, this chapter considers the question — how did Bankside create its own independent concerted waterfront strategy in the absence of an official top-down planning initiative?

Chapter 10. Angela Foster's *A comparative study of the barriers and opportunities for urban development in Wellington, New Zealand and Melbourne, Australia* addresses how different factors have impacted on these two harbor cities. A core difference between them is that Wellington unlike Melbourne has witnessed a decline in building. Wellington City Council stated in 2015 there has been a "loss of many head offices" due to the haemorrhaging of the corporate sector.[57] This dilemma remains unresolved. Various factors are contributing to this situation including a depleted city brand identity, despite it being the hub of a thriving film industry. One reason is due to Wellington being New Zealand's capital and hosting the more mundane buildings of state including its governmental offices. Wellington is also not attracting new residents as the housing market is witnessing a drop in property prices. By contrast Melbourne is the fastest growing and most densely populated city in Australia, that has minimal public housing. The impact has created a high demand for rental housing which has affected its urban development. The ongoing urban challenge is summarized by Michael Buxton, Robin Goodman, and Susie Moloney: "Melbourne is expanding extensively outward while also growing upward through vast new high-rise developments in the inner and, to some extent, middle-ring suburbs. At the same time, medium-density development continues in earnest in the middle and established outer suburbs."[58]

In Foster's professional capacity as an architect having worked in Wellington and Melbourne, she assesses their planning and development's barriers, and opportunities. One practical solution she proposes as a solution to the issues that can arise is through a Tinder style design app which enables all stakeholders to have a voice in the planning process. This means the public is already on board prior to the consultation period, which has the potential to alleviate some of the later social problems, as well as additional costs that can occur. What she signposts is that city planning must deploy "the highest level of complexity and variety in order to be able to cope with unpredictable changes in the physical and social environments."[59] Foster's work illustrates that planning, and development are complex processes and should be treated as such. To alleviate the potential pitfalls that can ensue, Fosters proposes ways of improving the planning process through a framework of questions which address — how can urban design be adapted to promote sustainable and good living environments, and how can design proposals engender positive urban growth? The issues outlined by Foster, and the other contributors signpost similar dilemmas facing councils, planners, designers, and city dwellers.

Conclusion

What the chapters identify are the same themes of how we inhabit cities, how we make plans for them, and how at times we ignore them entirely. With over 50% of the world's population living in cities, the process of urbanization is ongoing. As cities' importance and numbers continue to grow, they remain at the focus of social, economic, and political interest, as well as of national and international compliance, and challenging circumstances. It is for this reason that cities emerge as complex dynamic platforms, which share the ongoing challenge of unpredictability. During the pandemic this was witnessed through the international media networks screening images of empty city streets, buildings, and transport hubs. What was experienced was the same uncanny and global phenomenon of cities without people, which highlighted an eerie absence within this chain of "social evolution."[60] This was further evidenced when the global news networks from 24 February 2022 began screening the Russian invasion and destruction of Ukrainian cities. The following month President Volodymyr Zelenskyy declared: "They continue to ruin our infrastructure, our life, which we have built, and our parents, and grandparents, many generations of Ukrainians."[61] When Jane Jacobs wrote *The Death and Life of American Cities,* she also lamented the destruction of her own cities albeit for different reasons. At the same time, Jacobs celebrated the vitality of cities and their street life, which is why she vehemently opposed the new suburban developments which she regarded as having "all the attributes of a well-kept, dignified cemetery."[62] In the final analysis, cities with their sinewy social and built networks can only be challenging and contradictory, because they are neither dead nor inert spaces. In acting as the crucibles for explosive, and creative, exchanges, they continue to develop even when they are expunged, because cities are our lives built by us.

Bibliography

Abouelfadl, Hebatalla, Dalila ElKerdany, and Christoph Wessling. Introduction to *Revitalizing City Districts: Transformation Partnership for Urban Design and Architecture in Historic City Districts.* Edited by Hebatalla Abouelfadl, Dalila ElKerdany, and Christoph Wessling, vii-viii. Cham: Springer, 2017.

Andersen, Hans Thor, and Lars Winther. "Crisis in the Resurgent City? The Rise of Copenhagen." *International Journal of Urban and Regional Research* 34, no. 3 (September 2010): 693-700. https://doi.org/10.1111/j.1468-2427.2010.00984.x

Bao, Helen X. H., Ling Li, and Colin Lizieri. "City profile: Chongqing (1997-2017)." *Cities* 94, no. 1 (November 2019): 161-171. https://doi.org/10.1016/j.cities.2019.06.011

Barthes, Roland. *The Death of the Author.* London: Fontana Press, 1977.

Berman, Marshall. *All That is Solid Melts Into Air: The Experience of Modernity.* London and New York: Verso, 1983.

Bjørner, Thomas. "The advantages of and barriers to being smart in a smart city: The perceptions of project managers within a smart city cluster project in Greater Copenhagen." *Cities* 114, no. 7 (July 2021): 137-143. https://doi.org/10.1016/j.cities.2021.103187

Bourdieu, Pierre. *Outline of a Theory of Practice.* Cambridge: Cambridge University Press, 1977.

Burdett, Ricky. "Designing Urban Democracy: Mapping Scales of Urban Identity." *Public Culture* 25, no. 2 (March 2013): 349–367. https://doi.org/10.1215/08992363-2020638

Buxton, Michael, Robin Goodman, and Susie Moloney. *Planning Melbourne: Lessons for a Sustainable City.* Clayton: CSIRO Publishing, 2016.

Carnevale, Peter. "Creativity in the Outcomes of Conflict." In *The Handbook of Conflict Resolution,* edited by M. Deutsch, P.T. Coleman, and E.C. Marcus, 414-435. San Francisco: Jossey-Bass, 2006.

Carta, Maurizio. "The Fluid City Paradigm: A Deeper Innovation." In *The Fluid City Paradigm: Waterfront Regeneration as an Urban Renewal Strategy*, edited by Maurizio Carta and Daniele Ronsivalle, 1-19. Cham: Springer, 2016.

Comunian, Roberta. "Rethinking the Creative City: The Role of Complexity, Networks and Interactions in the Urban Creative Economy." *Urban Studies Journal Limited* 48, no. 6 (September 2011): 1157-1179. https://doi.org/10.11 77/0042098010370626

Davy, Benjamin. "Polyrational property: rules for the many uses of land." *International Journal of the Commons* 8, no. 2 (August 2014): 472-492.

den Hartog, Harry. "Shanghai's Regenerated Industrial Waterfronts: Urban Lab for Sustainability Transitions?" *Urban Planning* 6, no. 3 (July 2021): 181-196. https://doi.org/10.17645/up.v6i3.4194

Eräranta, Susa. "Social complexities in collaborative planning processes." In *Handbook on Planning and Complexity*, edited by Gert de Roo, Claudia Yamu, Christian Zuidema, 171-185. Cheltenham: Edward Elgar Publishing Ltd, 2020.

Feld, Steven, and Keith H. Basso. *Senses of Places*. Santa Fe: School of American Research Press, 1996.

Flowers, Benjamin S. *Skyscraper: The Politics and Power of Building New York City in the Twentieth Century*. Pennsylvania: University of Pennsylvania Press, 2009.

Fournier, Colin. "Cities on the Edge of Chaos." *Architectural Design* 85, no. 6 (November 2015): 128-133. https://doi.org/10.1002/ad.1990

Freud, Sigmund. *The Penguin Freud Library*. Vol. 14, *Art and Literature*. Harmondsworth: Penguin Books, 1990.

Geddes, Patrick. *Cities in Evolution: An Introduction to the Town Planning Movement and to the Study of Civics*. London: Williams & Norgate, 1915.

Gitlin, Jay, Barbara Berglund, and Adam Arenson. "Introduction Local Crossroads, Global Networks, and Frontier Cities." In *Frontier Cities: Encounters at the Crossroads of Empire*, edited by Jay Gitlin, Barbara Berglund, and Adam Arenson, 1-8. Philadelphia: University of Pennsylvania Press, 2013.

Howard, Ebenezer. *To-Morrow: A Peaceful Path to Real Reform*. London: Swan Sonnenschein & Co., Ltd. 1898.

Howard, Ebenezer. *Garden Cities of To-morrow*. London: Swan Sonnenschein & Co., Ltd. 1902.

Huang, Ling, Junhang Luo, and Xiang Peng. "Three Stages of Urban Community Development and Regeneration Planning in Chongqing (2010-2020)." In *Chinese Urban Planning and Construction: From Historical Wisdom to Modern Miracles*, edited by Lanchun Bian, Yan Tank, and Zhenjiang Shen, 133-155. Cham: Springer, 2021.

Jacobs, Jane. "Downtown is for People." In *The Exploding Metropolis*, 140-167. New York: Doubleday Anchor Books, 1958.

Jacobs, Jane. *The Death and Life of Great American Cities*. New York: Vintage Books, 1961.

Jacobs, Jane. *The Economy of Cities*. New York: Vintage Books, 1970.

Jordan, Kirrily, and Jock Collins. "Symbols of Ethnicity in a Multi-ethnic Precinct: Marketing Perth's Northbridge for Cultural Consumption." In *Selling Ethnic*

Neighborhoods: The Rise of Neighborhoods as Places of Leisure and Consumption, edited by Volkan Aytar and Jan Rath, 121-137. New York: Routledge, 2012.

Maclaren, Duncan, and Julian Agyeman. *Sharing Cities: A Case for Truly Smart and Sustainable Cities.* Cambridge, MA: MIT Press, 2015.

Lemos, Gerard. *The End of the Chinese Dream: Why Chinese people fear the future.* New Haven and London: Yale University Press, 2012.

Mayor of London. *The London Plan: Spatial Development Strategy for Greater London: Consolidated with Alterations since 2004.* Greater London Authority, 2008.

Moroni, Stefano, and Stefano Cozzolino. "Action and the city. Emergence, complexity, planning." *Cities* 90, no. 1 (2019): 42-51.

Moroni, Stefano, and Stefano Cozzolino. "Conditions of actions in complex social–spatial systems." In *Handbook on Planning and Complexity,* edited by Gert de Roo, Claudia Yamu, Christian Zuidema, 186-201. Cheltenham: Edward Elgar Publishing Ltd, 2020.

OECD. *Urban Renaissance: Canberra, A Sustainable Future.* Paris: OECD Publications, 2002.

Ortman, Scott G., José Lobo, and Michael E. Smith. "Cities: Complexity, theory and history." *PLoS ONE* 15, no. 12 (December 2020): 1-24. https://doi.org/10.1371/journal.pone.0243621

Pira, Saeid. "The social issues of smart home: a review of four European cities' experiences." *Pira European Journal of Futures Research* 9, no. 3 (2021): 1-15, https://doi.org/10.1186/s40309-021-00173-4

de Roo, Gert. Introduction to *Handbook on Planning and Complexity.* Edited by Gert de Roo, Claudia Yamu, and Christian Zuidema, 1-18. Cheltenham: Edward Elgar Publishing Limited, 2020.

de Roo, Gert "Spatial Planning and the Complexity of Turbulent, Open Environments - About purposeful interventions in a world of non-linear change." In *The Routledge Handbook of Planning Theory,* edited by Michael Gunder, Ali Madanipour, and Vanessa Watson, 314-325. London and New York: Routledge, 2019.

Rowe, Colin, and Fred Koetter. *Collage City.* Cambridge, MA, and London, England: MIT Press, 1978.

Sedky, Ahmed. *Living with Heritage in Cairo: Area Conservation in the Arab–Islamic City.* Cairo & New York: The American University in Cairo Press, 2009.

Sepe, Marichela, "Urban history and cultural resources in urban regeneration: A case of creative waterfront renewal," *Planning Perspectives* 28, no. 4 (October 2013): 595-613. http://dx.doi.org/10.1080/02665433.2013.774539

Smith, Neil. *The New Urban Frontier: Gentrification and the Revanchist City.* London & New York: Routledge, 1996.

Southwark Council. "Southwark Unitary Development Plan (1995) Policy R.2.1." Report presented at the London Borough of Southwark Council, London 1995.

Sun, Xuan, Yunxia Liu, Tao Sun, Sihang Yu, Chenguang Li, and Lie Zhai. "Land Cover Changes and Urban Expansion in Chongqing, China: A Study Based on Remote Sensing Images." *Environment and Urbanization Asia* 12, no. 1 (March 2021): 39S-58S. https://doi.org/10.1177/0975425321998035.

Turner, Graeme. "The cosmopolitan city and its Other: The ethnicizing of the Australian suburb." *Inter-Asia Cultural Studies* 9, no. 4 (November 2008): 568-582. https://doi.org/10.1080/14649370802386487

UNESCO. "Historic Cairo." Accessed April 14, 2022. https://whc.unesco.org/en/list/89/

Van Assche, Kristof, Raoul Beunen, and Martijn Duineveld. "Strategy in complexity: the shaping of communities and environments." In *Handbook on Planning and Complexity*, edited by Gert de Roo, Claudia Yamu, and Christian Zuidema, 151-170. Cheltenham: Edward Elgar Publishing Limited, 2020.

Venturi, Robert. *Complexity and Contradiction in Architecture*. New York: The Museum of Modern Art, 1977.

Wainwright, Oliver. "Street fighter: how Jane Jacobs saved New York from Bulldozer Bob." *The Guardian*, April 30, 2017. https://www.theguardian.com/artanddesign/2017/apr/30/citizen-jane-jacobs-the-woman-who-saved-manhattan-from-the-bulldozer-documentary

Weingroff, Richard F. "The Man Who Changed America, Part 1." *Public Roads* 66, no. 5 (2003): 20-35.

Wellington City Council. "Wellington Urban Growth Plan: Urban Development and Transport Strategy: 2014-2043." Report presented at the Wellington City Council, Wellington, June 2015.

Wenman, Mark. *Agonistic Democracy: Constituent Power in the Era of Globalisation*. Cambridge: Cambridge University Press, 2013.

Ye, Lin. "Urban regeneration in China: Policy, development, and issues." *Local Economy* 26, no. 5 (July 2011): 337-347. https://doi.org/10.1177/0269094211409117

Zhong, Sheng. "Artists and Shanghai's culture-led urban regeneration." *Cities* 56 (July 2016): 165-171. https://doi.org/10.1016/j.cities.2015.09.002

Zuidema, Christian. "Post-contingency - considering complexity." In *Handbook on Planning and Complexity*, edited by Gert de Roo, Claudia Yamu, and Christian Zuidema, 66-84. Cheltenham: Edward Elgar Publishing Limited, 2020.

President Volodymyr Zelenskyy. "Breaking!" 0:24-0:33. Twitter, March 6, 2022. https://twitter.com/i/status/1500472014452273157

Part 1:
The Social City

Chapter 1

Re-clustering historic Cairo through the creative economy: A study of the revitalization of the traditional carpentry along Souq al-Silah Street

Alaa El-Habashi

Menoufia University, Egypt

Aliaa Zidan

Menoufia University, Egypt

Alia Sherif

Brandenburg University of Technology, Germany;
University of Alexandria, Egypt

Abstract

Cairo's historic living economy, along with religious, trade, and social attributes, shaped the city's spatial urban fabric. The city was structured to embody coexisting economies in what is referred to in Arabic as "*hara*," an urban cluster specific to a certain type of activity, for ethnic or familial groups. Over time, the *haras* have disintegrated into a huge conglomerate of urban and social problems. This chapter reflects on Cairo's historical creative *haras*, especially those related to crafts, the different developments along the city's history, and their effect on the *hara*. Souq al-Silah Street is taken as a case study where the re-clustering approach could be adopted to achieve physical as well as socio-economic regeneration through the revitalization of a traditional joinery system that is particular to Cairo. The aim is to rethink the notion of the *hara* to reflect on a modern cluster that would boost a local creative economy.

Keywords: Cairo, historic Cairo, clustering, creative clusters, traditional crafts, revitalization, joineries

***

Introduction

Modern Cairo is inextricably connected with ancient Egypt and its historic environment. The Giza plateau on the west bank of the Nile contains the three iconic tall pyramids which were built 4,500 years ago as royal mausoleums. West of the Nile River delta are the archaeological remains of Memphis, the former city and capital of ancient Egypt which was designated a UNESCO World Heritage site in 1979. On the East Bank is a further UNESCO World Heritage site also listed in 1979, now known as Historic Cairo, Medieval Cairo, and Islamic Cairo. The area includes the site of a Roman-era fortress and Islamic settlements which pre-date the official founding of Cairo in 969 AD, that contains one of the largest and densest concentrations of Islamic architecture in the world. While the expansion of Cairo began in the nineteenth-century by the late twentieth-century it had turned into a sprawling metropolis. With a city population of 21.3 million, Cairo as the capital and largest city in Egypt has to balance its social, political, economic, cultural, and religious life along with its history and burgeoning urban redevelopment. A strategy to avoid the city's fragmentation is cultural clustering.[1]

This chapter assesses the efficacy of this kind of cultural clustering and focuses on the revitalization of traditional carpentry along Souq al-Silah, one of the main streets in Al-Darb-al-Ahmar neighborhood which dates to the Mamluk era (1250 AD-1517 AD). To undertake this investigation, the research method draws on planning theories and first-hand observational analysis. On this basis, our work as researchers has involved working with a local NGO, the Nile Palace Charity Foundation, whose main objective is to support local artisans. This approach proceeds on the basis that the city is a social space that has developed through the society that lives and works in it and should continue to do so.[2]

Cairo's international recognition

The UNESCO Creative Cities Network (UCCN) was established in 2004 with the aim to promote cooperation with and among the cities that have identified creativity as a strategic factor in their sustainable urban development. Cairo acquired this listing in 2017 when it was included in the Creative Cities' Network in the area of folk art and crafts. With this official UNESCO recognition and the World Heritage Site listing, historic neighborhoods associated with traditional crafts were considered as catalysts for socio-economic development. The international recognition of traditional crafts has helped to promote creativity, sustainable development, and civic identity. Prior to receiving the awards, cultural clustering was already seen as a valuable tool for redevelopment due to its historic role in binding the urban fabric of the city.[3] Urban cultural clustering was intended to complement the city's traditional structure that embodied coexisting economies in what is referred to in Arabic as a *hara*, meaning a traditional urban quarter that facilitates certain kinds of activities for its inhabitants. The *hara* is equivalent to the western idea of a neighborhood but with more distinct urban, architectural, social characteristics and community activities.

The issue emerged when traditional urban structures were disregarded in modern re-development plans. What was overlooked was the efficacy of the *harat* (plural of *hara*) which could have counteracted the effects of the city turning quickly into a homogenous and conglomerated megalopolis. The question this raises is — can the *harat* be restored and specifically those associated with traditional crafts to counteract the effects of a planning system that has formerly paid little attention to the social impact this has had on the built environment? A further question is that if the *harat* are restored, what scale and size would they need to be to accommodate the scale of the burgeoning contemporary city? Evidence shows that the re-introduction of this kind of clustering provides an effective and holistic solution to urban sprawl. Lewis Mumford argues in *The Culture of Cities* (1938) that urban planning should emphasize the organic relationship between people and place: "Organic planning and building, [is] not for show but for defense, civic association, the expression of common values."[4] Another approach taken directly to scattered neighborhoods is Jane Jacob's *The Death and Life of Great American Cities* (1961) who asserts that urban renewal does not take into account the rights of its urban dwellers, and that a solution is through the clustering of either communities or neighborhoods.[5]

The idea of clustering was reflected in many practical global applications, including the American city Philadelphia. As the largest city in the U.S. state of Pennsylvania and the sixth-most densely populated U.S. city, Philadelphia has seen cultural clusters replacing districts which have a high historic value, that in the 1990's were regarded as valueless slums.[6] Philadelphia's new clusters are currently hubs of growing developments, as they are not only preserving a historic urban structure but are promoting its inhabitants' sense of belonging to their neighborhoods, their heritage and are actively taking a positive role in their sustainability.[7] When Historic Cairo became a World Heritage site, it was one of the first Arab cities on the list because of its tangible historic urban and architectural attributes. The conundrum was that, as a designated World Heritage site, this ostensibly cut off parts of these historic areas from the real life of the city. When Cairo was registered as a creative city in the field of Folk art and crafts, this meant that its cultural identity and economy were dually recognized.[8] The local economy depends mainly on the city's crafts, which constitute 80% of its cultural activities.[9] While culture, heritage and economy are fundamental components of the identity of the city and its inhabitants, their intrinsic value, however, is underestimated in modern developments. Re-clustering can therefore become an effective means of socio-economic and urban revitalization.

Souq al-Silah: A potential cluster for traditional carpentry

The preliminary survey of traditional carpentry workshops, artisans as well as specific urban characteristics in Al-Darb-al-Ahmar guided the choice of a case study site, where the re-clustering approach could be adopted to achieve physical as well as socio-economic revitalization. The specific site within Al-Darb-al-Ahmar is Souq al-Silah Street and some urban nodes branched from it, an urban area where the traditional carpentry intensely exists and has a potential for a dedicated *hara* to be reconfigured. The selection of the nodes was based on the following criteria: 1) Existence of a unique activity or craft that is practiced by the community; 2) Existence of historic attributes in the selected urban context that express the value of what such activities or craft have produced throughout the history; 3) Existence of pockets with related interests within urban fabric upon which the proposed re-clustering plan can be integrated.

During the Ayyubid period (1171 AD-1250 AD) the street was named after its function as a weapons market, which was lined with workshops for spears, swords, and shields. Nowadays, all that remains of the street's history is the name of the street. What has since evolved is a carpentry and furniture production hub with several pockets of workshops located along the main spine of the street, with further activities spilling into the public domain of the street (figure 1.4). Towards the south of the street, which is more accessible to motorized vehicles, there is a concentration of 2 main workshop pockets. Within each pocket, each group of workshops performs a certain stage in the production of the piece of furniture; carpentry, carving, gilding and upholstery. On the other hand, towards the northern part of the street activities are more inclined towards storage and heavy industry, which causes noise and congestion.

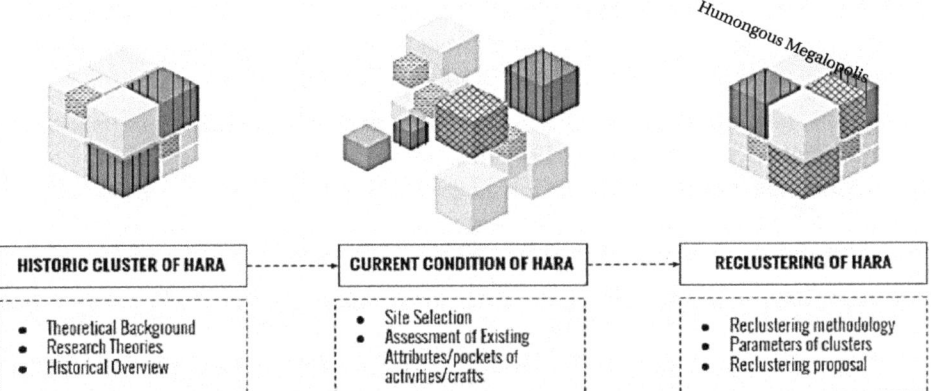

Figure 1.1 Research structure and objectives diagram. Image Credit: Authors ©

In figure 1.1, the first diagram illustrates the historic urban cluster of the *hara*. The middle diagram illustrates an exploded cube representing how the *harat* are presently dispersed and fragmented within the city structure, losing their distinct characteristics. The tangible and intangible attributes of the *harat* are still visible in specific sites which includes traditional carpentry practiced by artisans. The third diagram represents the proposed reassembled cube whose components aim to provide a balanced structure for the reimagined *harat*. To address this problem Souq al-Silah Street, provides a paradigm example of how revitalizing traditional wooden joinery acts as a cohesive measure in linking the social life of the city with the built form through this kind of re-clustering.

Historic Cairo and the *hara*

The morphology of Cairo's urban fabric and the distribution of functions was affected by the city's socio-economic structures at two different levels. The first is in the nomenclature of streets and neighborhoods, whose names reflect the occupation, religion, or ethnic background of the residents such as Al Nahhassin (coppersmiths) neighbourhood, Haret el-Yahud (*hara* of Jews) or Al Magharba (the Moroccans).[10] Names of areas and streets were also attributed to influencing patrons such as Yakaniyya, referring to Yakan family, or to a commercial activity such as Souq al-Silah (weapons market). Secondly, the different hierarchies of streets and distributions of functions reflected different levels of privacy and social interactions.[11] Urban blocks were composed of a network of *harat*, where "a group of town people practicing the same occupation and headed by a shaykh (master or leader)" worked and resided.[12] In this public and private exchange, the *hara* emerged as an organic extension of inner private courtyards of houses, acting as a semi-public spaces for the residing community to interact, at least during certain hours of the day.[13] The *harat* had defined boundaries that included gates to ensure the privacy of its inhabitants, holding specific unique characteristic, which were related to a certain craft, religious background, or some commercial activities whether permanent or periodical.[14]

Public assets and spaces were mostly managed by the members of its local community with different level of interferences from the state, depending on the situation throughout the history of the city.[15] A director acted as a mediator between the community and the authorities, cooperating to assure security, and apply urban city affairs within his domain, such as cleaning and lighting the city and participating in decisions related to city management, such as moving harmful crafts outside the city.[16] The *harat* were products of their communities and were never stagnant but rather an evolving urban feature within the city. In that respect, several neighboring *harat* would merge, and a large one would subdivide into many. This historic urban dynamism, however, is still to be studied and explored.

Historic Cairo and crafts

Crafts and the creative industry were one of the most distinguished and dominant types of activities within the *hara*. It included a specific craft guild *(Ta'ifa Hirafiyya)*, where its citizens were able to professionally connect.[17] Each guild had its apprenticeship system to enable the apprentice member (*sabi* or *sanay'i*) to be a teacher (*usta* or *mu'allim*) after a graduation ceremony qualified him to set up shop on his own.[18] The guild master (*shaykh al-ta'ifa*) and the *hara* director (*shaykh al-hara*) was usually the same person who would be responsible for solving efficiently and autonomously problems and conflicts. The nature of the crafts, the size of its production and its importance to the community played an important role in the distribution of crafts workshops within the urban fabric and shaped the physical and social structure of the *hara.*[19] Crafts were distributed in a hierarchical manner; light industries were located in the heart of the neighborhoods and heavy industries were situated along main streets outside the city's center for mobility and accessibility reasons.[20] Pollutive and noisy production processes were pushed out of the city's center close to or outside the city walls.[21] It is important to note however that Cairo was and still is a city that is in constant development and expansion since medieval times, therefore the borders and streets that defined the outside and the center have always been dynamic and constantly changing.

With the *hara* related to crafts, there was a natural correlation between the residence of the artisans and their workshops, creating efficiency in function and circulation within the city. In the eighteenth-century, the average distance between the workshop and the residence was never more than 400m.[22] This relationship began to change in the nineteenth-century due to the deterioration of the urban fabric of the city, and the changing nature of work patterns. The impact saw residents being pushed outside the historic city center. The housing patterns were also determined according to the social and economic bearing of the artisans. The local bourgeoisie residence was in the area near the downtown markets, which were clustered around the *qasaba*, the main central spine of Fatimid Cairo on which major commercial activities and public buildings were located.[23] Collective housing of more modest groups allowed residence in the areas closest to the city center can be categorized into the following typologies. Caravanserais (*khan*) were originally for housing merchants and their goods, but also served as places for trade, storage, transactions and other commercial activities. The row-houses (*rab'*) were for housing craftsmen in the upper floors and workshops in the ground floor. The *waqf* system emerged as a charitable endowment system by which profits from the ground floor shops were used to maintain the upper floors of the building, that enabled the buildings to operate efficiently and independently, and to be maintained periodically.[24]

Remains of the *hara*

At the turn of the nineteenth-century, Napoleon's troops in their expedition of Egypt complained about the *hara* gates, as they concealed behind them a large population ready to attack the French soldiers.[25] The troops could not differentiate the *hara* gates from those of the houses. The map of Cairo drawn by the French cartographers during Napoleon's expedition demonstrated that the cartographers drew the city through the public spaces they were able to access. Gated *harat* were not mapped, confirming that those semi-public spaces were exclusive for the community and that outsiders must be admitted for entering. In August 1798, orders were issued to demolish the *hara* gates.[26] In his chronicles, Jabarti pointed to three consecutive phases that such demolitions followed and wondered on how the regulatory system that once balanced the state's mandates with the needs of the local community would be managed.[27] Jabarti was visionary, as such a balance was never since restored.

Cairo underwent three major consecutive stages of development that led to the *harat* being dissolved and the ongoing urban sprawl. The first stage occurred during the reign of Khedive Ismail, who planned celebrations of the opening of the Suez Canal in 1869 and adopted Haussmann's Parisian avenues in Cairo. Ismail created new neighborhoods and effectively established a modern city to the western side of the historical city. The city expanded for the first time toward the west side of El Khalig El Masry (the Egyptian bay), an artificial canal branching from the River Nile delineating the western edge of the historic city. New neighborhoods included Nasiriyah in the west and south of Azbakeya

Park, and Shubra and Fagala in the north of the city. Additionally, new roads linked the old city with the modern city through Muhammad Ali, Clot Bey and al-Azhar Streets.[28]

The second stage of Cairo's development at the beginning of the twentieth-century included the establishment of new districts or suburbs such as Zamalek, Maadi and Garden City which was inspired by garden suburbs in England and was designed for the upper social classes with large open green spaces.[29] New streets and axes were developed to connect the suburbs with the city center. Organically growing informal areas developed along the fringes of the city where land was much cheaper, filling the gaps between the city and the new suburbs.[30] This informal growth, led by private actors, became a solution for the housing needs of the lower and middle classes, which was triggered by the migration to Cairo with huge numbers from other cities and from the countryside.[31]

The third stage of development was triggered by the overcrowded conditions the capital had reached. In the 1970s, President Sadat adopted the idea of liberal economy and announced a program to establish thirteen new satellite cities in the desert surrounding Cairo. The aim of establishing these cities was to decrease the density and congestion of the city by attracting approximately two million residents outside of Cairo. This, however, was not achieved due to insufficient services, infrastructure and job opportunities.[32] These expansions promoted further informal sprawls to marginalize the historic core and led to further congestions.[33]

After the 2011 revolution, the country went through a period of civil and political unrest during the transitional period following the removal of President Mubarak from the presidency. The political instability saw attention diverted from planning which led to unprecedented urban sprawl.[34] Informal buildings and developments were rapidly built that included demolishing buildings within the historic city. The impact of the new informal neighborhoods can also be interpreted as natural growth that maintains the social aspect and natural clustering through residential and commercial activities. Historic neighborhoods such as Al Hattaba and Ein al Seera are examples of neighborhoods that maintain some of their historic integrity but have been categorized as informal. Organic and naturally growing patterns created resemblance between the historic fabric and informality. This has led to legal threats which are created by confusing the recent growth, usually with poor urban and architectural qualities, with the historic fabric. The notion of informality has dominated legal categorization of any organic fabric that is not following a grid pattern with challenging security, infrastructure, and civil defense.[35]

1930 2019

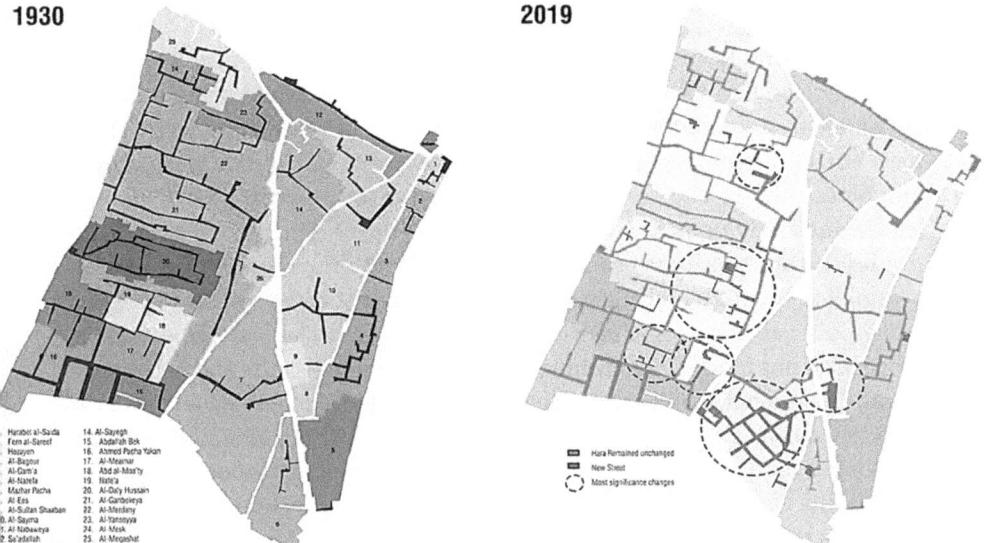

Hrabit al-Saida 14. Al-Sayegh
Fem al-Saref 15. Abdallah Bek
Hosayen 16. Ahmed Pacha Yakan
Al-Bagour 17. Al-Meamar
Al-Dam'a 18. Abd al-Maa'ty
Al-Natefa 19. Nafe'a
Mazhar Pacha 20. Al-Daly Hussain
Al Ees 21. Al-Garboeya
Al-Sultan Shaaban 22. Al-Merdany
0. Al-Sayma 23. Al-Yanssya
1. Al-Nabawenya 24. Al Mesk
2. Sa'adellah 25. Al-Megashat
3. Zara al-Nawa 26. Al-Mabayyd

Hara Remained unchanged
New Street
Most significance changes

Figure 1.2 Al-Darb-al-Ahmar 1930 and 2019. Image Credit: Ramirez and El-Habashi ©

At the historic *hara* scale, the challenges were amplified through the continuous demolition of historic buildings to make way for modern apartment buildings which were incompatible with the existing built environment. The effect has been to disfigure the urban and architectural values of the historic city. Visual, physical, and environmental implications have been caused by changes in building heights and density. Furthermore, changes in street widths and patterns to accommodate modern traffic have disrupted the homogeneity and hierarchy of the historic *hara* structure. This urban disfiguration can be exemplified through some detailed assessments of selected historic urban areas. The maps in figure 1.2 illustrate the differences that occurred in the historic urban fabric of Al-Darb-al-Ahmar, a district in Historic Cairo, since 1930. The map to the left indicates the closed structure of the old urban fabric that was still maintained with its unity and autonomy. With the consequences of the third phase of city's development and the associated informal growth, modern streets have pierced through the interconnected *hara* system and disrupted its homogeneous structure. Among the remaining physical attributes of the *hara* are the different types of gateways that no longer have their door leaves. Intangible remains can still be perceived, especially those which include religious ceremonies expressed in the moulids (celebrations of religious saints) or traditional educational system, which was held in the courtyard of Al-Azhar mosque. Other forms including residential neighborhoods, commercial activities, and crafts can still be assessed but with no clear managerial framework.

Wooden joineries and the Cairene *hara*

A major activity in the *hara* was the role of traditional carpentry which was dependent on an interlocking joinery system.[36] Due to wood being scarce in Egypt, local carpenters have mastered techniques to reuse and recycle small pieces of it to create large products such as the traditional Islamic Mashrabiyya (a type of window enclosed in intricate wooden latticework), doors, cabinet leaves, mosque's pulpits, and screens for churches.[37] For durability of such products, the techniques were developed to not employ nails nor glue in assemblies, but rather relying completely on a sophisticated system of tongues and grooves, to allow for expansion and contraction of the material especially those used outdoors.[38] The technique was developed in Cairo, and became an identity associated with local carpentry in conceiving distinguished architectural wooden pieces.[39] A recent preliminary survey of what remains from that traditional craft indicates that Al-Darb-al-Ahmar neighborhood still entails most of the workshops that are still operating side by side with many historic buildings that demonstrate objects of such crafts. The survey also assessed the compatibility of the existing built fabric with existing traditional crafts.

An example of result of this survey is the detection of the spread of some workshops with no consideration of the products' sizes and hierarchy of the traditional craft. Transferring raw materials, whose size is incompatible with the city fabric, exacerbates the mobility problem. In addition, many workshops threaten the stability of the historical buildings because of the use of heavy modern machineries. Furthermore, many of the artisans no longer live next to their workshops but moved outside the historic city, adding further pressure on traffic, and transferring the economic bases outside of the historic fabric, and with it the correlations with the *hara* has been dispersed. As for the traditional assembly technique described above, the survey concludes that there are less than a dozen practicing it among more than sixty carpentering workshops surveyed, indicating that the traditional joineries are no longer in demand. Abo-Zaid, a local family famous for traditional carpentry since the sixteenth century in historic Cairo, is among those who are holding on to practicing the historic interlocking technique. However, only five elders from the family are running the business with no young generations considering carrying on with it (figure 1.3).

Figure 1.3 Traditional interlocking joinery practitioners. Image Credit: Authors ©

Figure 1.4 Carpentry workshops along Souq al-Silah Street. Image Credit: Authors ©

The urban fabric in and around Souq al-Silah Street is rich with the attributes of traditional wood crafts. These architectural elements are considered an open exhibition along the area's heritage buildings. Moreover, the Islamic Art Museum, within walking distance from the street, has many masterpieces transferred from Souq al-Silah, such as the Wooden Qur'an box and table inlaid with ivory and ebony brought from the madrasah of Umm al-sultan Sha'ban.

Re-clustering historic Cairo

Drawing from the historic clustering of the city, re-clustering is a potential strategy to revitalize different parts of the historic city according to its historic significance, whether it is related to crafts, markets, religion or education.[40] In the case of Souq al-Silah, the vision for the area is to activate its creative economy by reorganizing and re-integrating the existing pockets related to the historic craft of interlocking joinery into a proposed urban cluster as a model. The hope is that this prospective cluster would incite other pockets with compatible and related activities to merge and form neighboring clusters causing the city to reform its historic structures based on the principles of the *hara*. In the case of the Souq al-Silah street cluster, a guideline to evaluate compatibility of workshops is developed based on criteria such as size of workshop, nature of the activity and tools and machinery being used. Workshops deemed incompatible according to these criteria would then be relocated outside the boundaries of the historic city, to allow for integration of more appropriate workshops that would add value to the area.[41]

Unused historic buildings and monuments are considered assets that can play an important role in re-clustering and revitalization of crafts. According to their historic and architectural values, a scheme for the adaptive reuse of buildings such as *rab'*, *Sabils*, remains of palaces and historic courtyard houses such as Bayt Yakan and Bayt al Razzaz could be developed to host functions such as museums, markets, and training centers for traditional interlocking joinery; functions which would offer means for sustainability and economic growth. In implementing these measures along with the creation of crafts unions, a modern interpretation of the historic guilds would re-consolidate the *hara* as an interconnected urban entity that is economically and socially sustainable. The framework the proposal follows is to consider the tangible and the intangible values entailed in attributes within the historic urban fabric of the city and propose an urban re-structuring of the city fabric based on the concept of clusters, that is culturally accepted and inspired by the system of historic *harat*. This process follows specific parameters that would determine the identity of the cluster as well as its scale.

The scale of the cluster guarantees an effective interaction with the neighborhood and the city. It should allow an active role for the local community in managing the cluster but at the same time have an acceptable legal boundary for the state to recognize and support it with the required infrastructure. The prospective scale entails common interests and the vision for the inhabitants, allowing an active environmental role to support the overall eco-system of the city. This scale shall also allow efficient accessibility to and from the cluster for various means, and all the categories and types of the inhabitants. Applying these parameters along the street of Souq al-Silah and its surroundings results in identifying two clusters (figure 1.5). The first is the carpentry cluster (*hara al-Nijara*) located towards the South. The second is the cluster of the carpenters specialized in interlocking Joinery (in Arabic *Hara Najarrin al-Jam'yiya*), which is located towards the lighter section in the North.

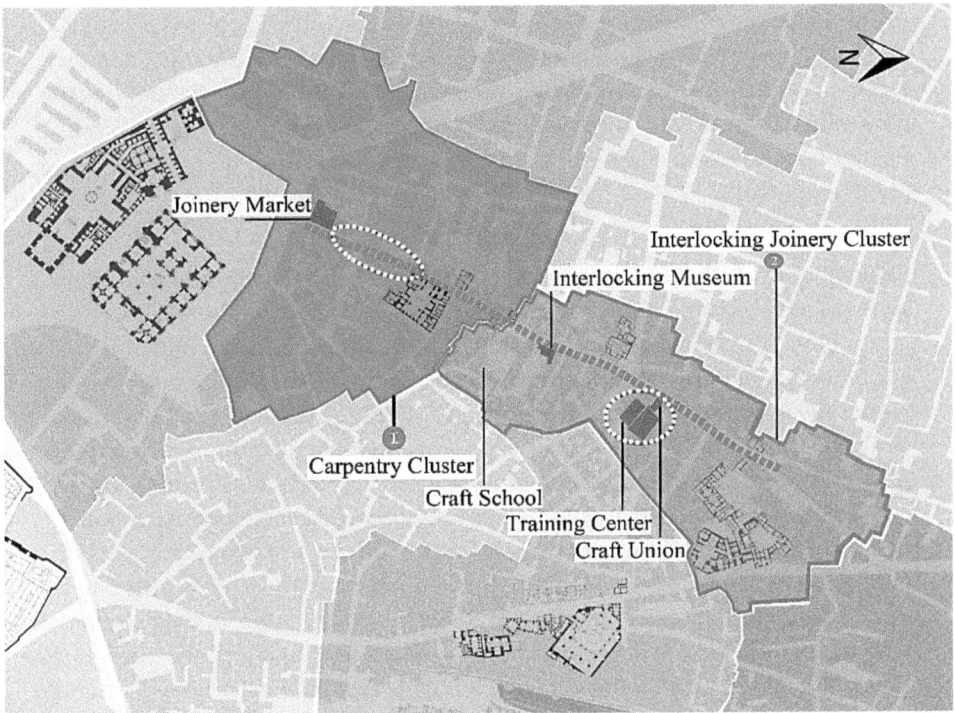

Figure 1.5 Proposed clusters. Image Credit: Authors ©

The northern cluster deals with the making of wooden objects, including the headquarter of the artisans' union that is about to be established, as well as the proposed training center, craft school and museum where the local artisans would exhibit distinguished pieces that would explain the complexities and the lengthy making process.[42] The southern is the commercial front of the first. It is where all the manufactured objects are exhibited in showrooms or in a market that is being negotiated to be established within the ruins of a gate of a medieval palace (the Manjak al-Salihdar gate). *Hara al-Nijara* benefits from the wide front it has on one of the major streets of Cairo, Muhammed Ali Street to the east, and one of the most widely frequented squares north of the fifteenth-century Mosques of Sultan Hassan, and the nineteenth and twentieth centuries al-Rifa'i mosque. The borders of each of those two clusters are carefully selected to fulfill the parameters indicated above, leaving those lines as proposals which shall be better shaped and indicated by the local members of the community. Each of the two clusters has a heart, or rather a center through which it houses a community-based body that oversees the administrative matter and acts as a liaison between its inhabitants and users and the State. For this vision to materialize, a series of actions were designed, which are considered as initiatives to encourage the communities, investors, artisans and other interested personnel and parities to get involved. Some of those actions have already started in the form of workshops and support groups for the artisans, and the hope is to assess the progress continuously in order to update a management plan to be presented to the local community as well as the authorities.[43]

Conclusion

Reflecting on the historic interconnection of the urban, social and economic layers of the *hara*, this research proposes the use of creative/cultural clustering as a tool for the revitalization of Historic Cairo's urban fabric as well as for its cultural and economic regeneration. The proposal of Souq al-Silah street as a case study illustrates how crafts, specifically interlocking joinery, could be used as a catalyst for the re-clustering process, ensuring that it is community based. The re-clustering of the street into two distinct but interlaced clusters is based on existing pockets of activities as well as social networks. The proposed borders delineate clusters and can be considered as a planning tool that requires active community participation to be implemented. Those borders are drawn based on assessments that might have missed all the dynamics of the local community with the urban fabric. What is important is that these lines are neither fixed nor final but are simply a guiding point to initiate the re-clustering process. The aim is that each cluster is formulated on its historic identity.[44] It also should not be impeded by a rigid planning process but one that would instead celebrate the city's outstanding values.[45] In demonstrating the positive social impact on the existing urban fabric, cultural clustering should become an essential part of the planning process in Cairo. The reason is that cultural clustering improves the city's management as it provides a clear framework, it strengthens the feeling of belonging for its citizens, and helps to promote the city's cultural and historic value as a World Heritage center.

Bibliography

Abd El Rahman, Ahmed, and Samah El Khateeb. "Mapping Informal Areas in Egypt Between the Past Interventions and Next Urban Revolution." *Journal of Urban Research* 21, no. 1 (2016): 116-129. https://doi.org/10.21608/jur.2016.89852

Al-Jabarti, Abd al-Rahman. *The Marvelous Compositions of Biographies and Events.* Beirut: Dar al-Faris, 1970.

ARCHiNOS Architecture. "Wood Working Crafts." Hands On: Traditional Crafts in 'The City of the Dead' in Cairo. Accessed June 2, 2020. https://www.undeadcrafts.com/carpentry

Celebi, Evliya. *SEYAHATNAMESI: Misir, Sudan, Habes 1672-1680.* Translated by El-Safsafe Ahmed Al-Qattory. Cairo: The National Center for Translation, 2010.

Chalcraft, John T. *The Striking Cabbies of Cairo and Other Stories: Crafts and Guilds in Egypt 1863-1914,* State University of New York Press, 2005.

Dobrowolska, Agnieszka. *The Building Crafts of Cairo: A Living Tradition.* Cairo: The American University in Cairo Press, 2005.

El-Habashi, Alaa el-Din Elwi. "Athar to Monuments: The Intervention of the Comité De Conservation Des Monuments De L'Art Arabe." PhD dissertation. University of Pennsylvania, 2001.

El-Habashi, Alaa, and Aliaa Zidan. "The Creative Sustainable City: Application on the Regeneration of Crafts in Historic Cairo." Paper presented at the tenth Conference of Sustainable Environmental Development, Sharm El Sheikh, Egypt, March 16-20, 2019.

Fahim, Ali. *Al nigara al 'amalia* (the practical carpentering). Cairo: al-tawfiq press, 1914.

Ghazaleh, Pascale. *Masters of the Trade: Crafts and Craftspeople in Cairo 1750-1850.* The American University in Cairo Press, 1999.

Haridi, Salah. *Al-Hiraf wal-sina'at fi 'ahd Muhammad 'Ali (Crafts and Industries in the Age of Muhammad 'Ali).* Cairo: Dar al-ma'arif, 1985.

Jacobs, Jane. *The Death and Rise of Great American Cities.* New York: Random House, 1961.

Jomard, E. F. *Wasf Madinat Al-Qahira (Description of the City of Cairo).* Translated by Ayman Fu'ad al-Sayyid. Cairo: Maktabat al- khanji, 1988.

Lane, Edward W. *An Account of the Manners and Customs of Modern Egyptians, Written in Egypt during the Years 1833-1835.* London: W. Clowes and sons, 1860.

Le Grand, Napoleon. Plan Général de Boulaq, du Kaire, de l'Ile de Roudah, du Vieux-Kaire et de Gyzeh. In: Description de l'Egypte ou Recueil des Observations et des Recherches qui ont été faites en Egypte pendant l'Expedition de l'Armée Francaise. Paris: L'Imprimerie Impériale, Environs du Kaire, 1809.

Mommaas, Hans. "Cultural Clusters and the Post-industrial City: Towards the Remapping of Urban Cultural Policy." *Urban Studies* 41, no. 3 (March 2004): 508. https://doi.org/10.1080/0042098042000178663.

Mommaas, Hans. "Spaces of Culture and Economy: Mapping the Cultural-Creative Cluster Landscape." In *Creative Economies, Creative Cities: Asian-European Perspectives,* edited by Lily Kong and Justin O'Connor, 45-59. Dordrecht, Netherlands: Springer, 2010.

Mubarak, Ali Pasha. *Al-Khitat al-tawfiqiyya al-jadida li Misr al-qahira wa muduniha wa biladiha al-qadima wal-shahira*. Vol. I. Cairo: General Egyptian Book Organization, 2014.

Mumford, Lewis. *The Culture of Cities*. New York: Harcourt Brace Jovanovich, 1938.

Nadeem, As'ad. *Traditional Arts and Crafts from Cairo*. Cairo: Egyptian Archives for Folk Life and Folk Traditions, 2014.

Piffero, Elena. "Beyond Rules and Regulations: The Growth of Informal Cairo." In *Cairo's Informal Areas Between Urban Challenges and Hidden Potentials*, edited by Regina Kipper and Marion Fischer, 21-27. Cairo: The Egyptian-German Participatory Development Programme in Urban Areas, 2009.

Ramírez, Natalia, and Alaa El-Habashi. "reGREENeration of Historic Cairo: Hara al-Nabawiya and Bayt Madkour in al-Darb Al-Ahmar." *The Journal of Public Space* 5, no.1 (2020): 51-74. https://doi.org/10.32891/jps.v5i1.1251

Raymond, André. *Artisans et commerçants Au Caire XVIIIe Siècle*. Damas: Institut français de Damas, 1973.

Raymond, André. *Grandes villes arabes à l'époque ottomane*. Paris: Sindbad, 1985.

Riad, Mohamed. *Cairo: The people fabric in space and time and their problems in the present and future*. Cairo: General Egyptian Book Organization, 2007.

Sayyid, Ayman F. *The Topography and Urban Evolution of CAIRO*. Cairo: General Egyptian Book Organization, 2015.

Séjourné, Marion. "The History of Informal Settlements." In *Cairo's Informal Areas: Between Urban Challenges and Hidden Potentials*, edited by Regina Kipper and Marion Fischer, 17-19. Cairo: The Egyptian-German Participatory Development Programme in Urban Areas, 2009.

Stern, Mark J., and Susan C. Seifert. "Cultural Clusters: The Implications of Cultural Assets Agglomeration for Neighborhood Revitalization." *Journal of Planning Education and Research* 29, no.3 (January 2010): 262-279. https://doi.org/10.1177/0739456X09358555

UNESCO. "Creative Cities Network." Accessed April 24, 2021. https://en.unesco.org/creative-cities/cairo.

UNESCO. "Urban Regeneration Project for Historic Cairo (URHC) Team." In *The Outstanding Universal Value of Historic Cairo-draft URHC proposal*. Cairo: URHC, February 2013.

Viney, Steven. "The state of urban planning and informal areas after the Egyptian Revolution." *Egypt Independent*. March 17, 2013. https://egyptindependent.com/state-urban-planning-and-informal-areas-after-egyptian-revolution.

Wiet, Gaston. *Al-qahira madinat al-fan w-al-tegara (Cairo, city of art and commerce)*. Translated by Mustafa Al-'Abadi. Cairo: General Egyptian book organization, 2015.

Chapter 2

Agōn (Ἀγών) in ancient Athens and conflict in the modern city

Edna Langenthal

Ariel University, Israel

Abstract

This chapter develops a new perspective on Athens concerning the ancient Greek concept of *Agōn - Ἀγών*, which is usually translated as competition or constructive conflict. *Agōn* was an integral part of ancient Greek life, particularly in the polis for which competition was an essential characteristic. The essay focuses on ancient Athens on the Greek Attica Peninsula, which was revealed as a strong city-state and had a focus for the arts, learning and philosophy. Although *agōn* seems to contradict our contemporary desire to dissolve and eliminate conflict in the city, this essay suggests thinking of conflict not as an aberration or an exceptional condition of public space but as an essential characteristic of urbanity. *Agōn* is used to reveal the lineage between the polis of the ancient Greek world and the modern city since conflict is inextricable from both phenomena.

Keywords: Athens, *agōn*, conflict, architecture, Plato

***

Introduction

Agōn was a motive power… the general leavening element that, given the essential condition of freedom, proved capable of working upon the will and the potentialities of every individual.[1]

Ancient Athens on the Greek Attica peninsula emerged as a powerful city-state and a locus for the arts, learning and philosophy as exemplified in Plato's Academy. While the cultural and political influence of the city continues to reverberate across the western world, a very different legacy emerged relating to the Panathenaic Games (from 566 BC to the 3rd century AD). A feature of the athletic competitions was the idea of *agōn* meaning contest. *Agōn* later took on the meaning of struggle and conflict which as a phenomenon can also be understood in terms of conditions of living in the modern city. This research focuses on how the concept of *agōn* is an unavoidable dynamic that runs the gamut of the city. The main thrust is that it should not be analyzed through the lens of modern liberal political ideology, which seeks to resolve its internal tension, but rather in its usefulness in becoming "more capable of survival, diffusion and reactivation." [2] Foremost, this chapter addresses how *agōn* is an essential component of the social life of the polis (city) which rather than being avoided should be embraced. While this research focusses on Athens, it considers the phenomenon of *agōn* as an essential quality of all cities. The core research question is — what is the relationship between the city as a social settlement and the people who inhabit it, and how does the conflict enable its development? To discuss this question, the research draws on philosophical enquiry notably in Plato's Republic, architectural history, and urban studies. Plato's Republic will allow to discuss the human soul as an agonistic structure that connects it to the city.[3] Turning to the architectural history of Athens I will point out the way the urban historical space reflects the perception of the ancient Greek on *agōn*.[4] Finally, urban studies will allow to convert those ideas to the 21st century.[5]

Cities are shaped by human action, and people are influenced by the spatial conditions in which they live. The influence of the built environment on human experience, should not be underestimated. This relationship can be traced back to the polis of ancient Greece where *agōn,* which is translated as competition or constructive conflict, was used to describe the relationship between the polis (city) and its inhabitants. The dynamics of *agōn,* this "motive power" profoundly affects human behavior.[6] Although it was integral to various aspects of Greek life, this chapter focuses on its significance to the polis, which was founded on the ideal of competition. The role of conflict in the modern city can be understood in in relation to the concept of *agōn.* While the modern city differs from the ancient Greek polis, they are both shaped by human phenomena. The notion that the polis is the progenitor of the modern city became prevalent in the early twentieth century when attempts were made to define the relationship between concentrations of wealth and population. This phenomenon cannot be measured quantitatively because such definitions are incomplete. The emphasis on a single dimension – the quantitative – with a purely physical conception of the city results in an elusive impression.

The lineage from the ancient polis to the modern city can be understood by examining *agōn* which is integral to the urban dynamic – both ancient and modern. The reorganization of political life that arose in ancient Greece began as a local deviation from mainstream political culture and ultimately changed the trajectory of world history. This view does not limit Greek political culture to the invention of democracy, but rather situates it within the general framework of the polis. The political institutions of archaic Greece were built in absolute contrast to the Middle Eastern pattern of centralized power. By breaking away from the political framework that had previously been accepted without challenge throughout the Mediterranean, the Greeks initiated a comprehensive cultural revival and expansion of social activities which prevented the consolidation of exclusive centers of power. This led to multiple expressions of the polis and internal pluralism within each polis. The dynamism and autonomy of the political sphere rose beyond its borders, eventually leading to a multifaceted process of cultural innovation – which included the development of epic poetry, tragedy and philosophy. These innovations liberated logic and the imagination. Thus, from the end of antiquity, classical heritage has "been fashioned and understood as a counter-culture and a refuge from the dominant world-view."[7] The city is a space that accommodates shared experiences and radical diversity, that inevitably lead to conflict. Ethnic and national identities are not only associated with sovereign forces and political systems but also with cultural practices and activities.

Architecture and the social fabric of the city are part of this relationship, which Jane Jacobs characterizes through the urban experience as offering multiple forms of existence.[8] Jacobs sought to make sense of the complexity, conflicts, and apparent chaos of the urban space, while countering the prevailing view that overcrowding and urban density, and the conflicts they create, are inherently problematic. Jacobs turned her critical eye to the social injustices that characterized the city and critiqued government efforts to support particular economic, or cultural interests while neglecting others. Since conflict is a fundamental aspect of the city, it should not be thought of as a phenomenon that needs resolution. Rather than trying to unequivocally resolve and erase it from the urban space, conflict should be re-conceptualized as constitutive of the urban condition. The built environment is both the background and the essence of the conflict. The cultural homogenization brought about by global capitalism increases the urgency to reexamine the pluralism inherent in the dialectical agonism and practical rationality of the polis. In discussions of urban and contemporary architecture, the classical tradition can serve as a counter-cultural example that emphasizes and celebrates heterogeneity, which is a crucial aspect of the Greek political imagination. The willingness of the Greeks to preserve diversity and competition in the city in spaces such as racetracks and theatres contrasts with the modern inclination to resolve urban conflict. In many contemporary cities, marginal populations are pushed to the suburbs, far from the competition of the city center. Urban conflict has always existed, and cities experiencing conflicts can be valuable sources for revealing urban paradigms.

The soul of the polis

In Book 2 of the *Republic*, Socrates continues the discussion of justice which was central to his dialogue with the sophist Thrasymachus and orients his investigation by posing the question: "Is it always, without exception, better to be right than wrong?"[9] Socrates proposes a new methodology of investigation that adjusts the focus from the individual soul as the primary framework for examining the essence of justice to the urban space. This methodological change reveals Socrates' understanding that the human soul and the polis are identically structured and that their relationship is analogical.[10] To illustrate this point, Socrates uses the metaphor of big and small letters to emphasize how the city can be used as a lens to study the soul.[11] Hagi Kennan proposes that Socrates' analogy works in both directions, and, furthermore, that he uses it "to elaborate a conception of the city that is autonomous and is discussed completely in and of itself."[12] Socrates' analysis of the constitution of the polis offers a paradigm for theorizing the city, one that internalizes the human as its essential measurement.

Within the dialogue Plato discusses the soul, arguing that it consists of three constantly interacting parts: appetite, spirit, and reason, which are engaged in a constant state of struggle. Each state has its own set of motivations, which push and pull in different directions for control of the soul. For Plato, the question of the just soul is connected to the question of what constitutes a balanced soul. He concludes that the soul is balanced when logic takes control. However, it is important to remember that this rarely takes place since the three parts of the soul are engaged in a constant state of struggle. Multiplicity and plurality are essential characteristics of both *agōn* and the Platonic soul and can be characterized by their components, whose many forces are engaged in a never-ending conflict for dominance. Like the soul, the city is inhabited by a plurality that struggles against the tension inherent to otherness. For this analogy to work, the city cannot be understood as a neutral container in which each function has a planned and defined place. Rather, the city must be understood as lacking totality and as engaged in a continuous struggle that forces it to constantly change.

Place

Place plays a significant role in forming and influencing human identity. According to Martin Heidegger's analysis of the basic structure of existence in *Being and Time* (1962), being-in-the-world means being in place. For Heidegger, the way a human being is situated in the world is different from how objects are situated spatially. Objects are situated in relation to other objects in space. Examples of being in space include such things as water in a glass or clothes in a drawer. The distinction between place and space can be understood by examining the difference between two contrasting definitions of the preposition in. The phrase, in space, signifies a relationship of existence in which two bodies are in space. In other words, they are related to one another by their location in the space where they are situated. The objects in the previous examples, the water and the glass and the clothes and the drawer, are in space in the same way.[13] While these relations of containment are appropriate when describing things which are objectively present in space, they are not fit to describe human existence or "being-in-the-world." Humans are not simply in a particular space; they are in a place. Heidegger describes what it means to be in a place in terms of dwelling. When people dwell in a particular space, the space is not an object for them. It becomes a part of them and penetrates the way they relate to other objects in the world. Heidegger traces the preposition in back to the word *innan* in old German which means dwelling, habit, and custom.[14] Therefore, the way to understand being in the world is through the way people are involved with and relate to things and meanings.[15]

In order to clarify Heidegger's analysis of "being-in-the-world" in terms of dwelling, it is necessary to examine the relation between things and meanings. Heidegger understood dwelling as constituted by the notion of care (e.g, *colo*, I care) and respect.[16] Care or respect can only be experienced vis-à-vis the other. "Being in" in terms of dwelling is, therefore, constituted by a relationship. In other words, the Heideggerian conception of dwelling is relational, and this has important implications for the nature of being-in-the-city. Urban dwellers are not situated in the city as if they were objects in a container. They are located in relation to the city and the others that inhabit it. As dwellers, they are competitors in place, and *agōn* characterizes this competition or conflict, which is an expression of the plurality that constitutes the city. It is necessary to differentiate between two conceptions on the role of otherness in urban conflict. It is a common mistake to think of the city as a structure in which conflict occurs. According to this conception, the city is either a container for otherness or the context in which otherness takes place. As a result, otherness becomes a retrospective quality, something that follows or comes after the establishment of the city. Although the city is not a container for conflict, it cannot exist without it. It is important to emphasize that it cannot be separated from it, as it is an integral part of the structure of the city. As a consequence, conflict should be understood as constitutive of the city, and *agōn* should be recognized as one of its essential characteristics.

The body of the polis

The discussion relating to agonistic spaces can be seen in the close and intricate relations between the public space, political transformation and the appearance of the democratic mode of governance. These relationships transpired at a particular and decisive historical time – at the end of the sixth century BCE – and at a particular and decisive historical place – ancient Athens. The ultimate result of these factors was the emergence of democracy in the Greek city-state (polis). The spaces that created the conditions for the emergence of democracy appear in the intentional choices that were made in constructing lived experience in ancient Athens. These choices can be seen in archaeological and historical documentation of the era.

Two specific and important examples of agonistic spaces in the Greek polis are the Agora and the Acropolis in the upper city. In democratic Athens, physical public spaces, and the buildings within them often function as arenas. Some of them were purposely designed to accommodate discussion and conflict, and others were created for different situations, but took on their political role as time passed – for example the Theater of Dionysus. The success of Athenian democracy depended on the various venues, particularly the open spaces, and they facilitated planned and improvised meetings as well as a variety of interactions. They often functioned as arenas that generated discussion and action. Examples of such arenas include the Agora, the marketplace and civic heart of the polis, the council house for the Boule, the side of the Pnyx Hill which functioned as the gathering place of the popular Assembly and the theatrical areas.

The democracy within the Agora is thought of in its simplest sense as a rule by the people. Moreover, it is assumed that an etymological examination of the word supports this definition. The word democracy comes from the Greek *dēmokratia* means popular government. The prefix *dēmos* means "common people" and the suffix *kratos* means "rule or strength."[17] To understand how *agōn* (as a place of contest or conflict) is related to the etymology of the word democracy, proper weight must be allocated to the second part of the word. Placing the emphasis on *kratos* indicates that the meaning of the word is not just rule or strength, since in ancient Greek the original meaning of *kratos* is overpowering. This original definition implies a sense of struggle or conflict. In Nicole Loraux's *The Divided City: On Memory and Forgetting in Ancient Athens* (2002), Loraux adds to this perception and claims that the meaning of the word *dēmokratia* is the division of the city into two parts.[18] As a result of the conflictual struggle brought on by this division, one part of the city must be victorious over the other. In order to claim this victory, the more powerful side must gain a plurality of votes. By emphasizing the kratos of democracy, it becomes clear that it is an agonistic form of government, since the people, the demos, must struggle to overpower their opponents in the political field. That is to say, it emphasizes the competitive and conflictual situation in the Agora in which someone takes a stand that is not necessarily acceptable in the eyes of another party.

As a starting point we must recognize the basic importance of controversy in the city. This understanding was adopted by Solon, who was an Athenian statesman, lawmaker and poet. He is best remembered for his efforts to legislate against political, economic and moral decline in archaic Athens. Solon's democratic constitution, written in 594 BCE, contains an extraordinary law that asserts the primacy of conflict for democracy. He observed that the state was often in conflict and that certain citizens would concede without taking a stand. In response to this observation, he wrote that anyone who does not take a stand may lose his citizenship and even be deported from the polis.[19] Solon's laws were written on wooden boards known as *axones*, and they were positioned on a revolving mechanism near the Agora, in the seat of the government of ancient Greece, the Prytaneion.[20] Solon's wooden boards served as a reminder that democracy requires participation. It requires taking a stand. The political arena grew out of the controversies that arise in the polis and the understanding that the structure of the polis is essentially conflictual, it is agonistic. In other words, the struggle cannot be resolved.

The population of the polis was diverse, yet it had the ability to cultivate and promote a common identity. This diversity is evidenced in the *Republic* by Plato who emphasizes the multiplicity of the city's population: "if you deal with them as one you will altogether miss the mark."[21] A common identity was usually achieved by creating rivalry and competition among its inhabitants. Yet, the individual identities of the groups that inhabited the polis were maintained.[22] The polis, therefore, can be said to have consisted of a coherence of the non-identical.[23] The polis cultivated a mutual recognition of difference in its inhabitants, which was necessary for incorporating diversity within a common space. Moreover, political power in the Greek polis was not concentrated among a particular group. Rather, it consisted of institutions open to rivalry and debate for which *agōn* and logos were substantial components.[24] The Agora, which was located in an area of Athens that gradually slopes upward to the south, was the center of activity in the polis. It was related to *agōn* since it was a place where citizens gathered to engage in debates.

Figure 2.1 Model of the Agora and northwest Athens in the 2nd century CE looking along the entire course of the Panathenaic Way from the Dipylon Gate (bottom) to the Acropolis (top) view from the northwest. Image Credit: American School of Classical Studies at Athens: Agora Excavations ©

The conflict found its expression in social, commercial, ritual, and political functions as well as in architecture and the urban fabric that it formed. As an architectural project, the agonistic perception of space was realized at various points throughout the polis. This allowed for multiple definitions of the civil sphere. The center of all activity in the polis, the agora, was connected to *agōn*. It was a place for gathering, but also for debate and competition.[25] *Agōn* was perceived as a process, but also as a result that expressed opposing interests. The result of *agōn* was realized in terms of social, political, ritual and commercial functions, and by the architecture and the urban texture that embodied them. Already during the sixth century BCE a series of political events demanded the creation of a public space. In order to meet this demand, the state expropriated an area of the city for the creation of the Agora, which means assembly or open space. At the time of its construction, the spatial configuration of the polis was not yet as well defined as it would become in its later periods. The first public buildings faced west, attached to the Kolonos Agoraios Hill. They were not constructed in any particular order, and before them stood a large open plaza.

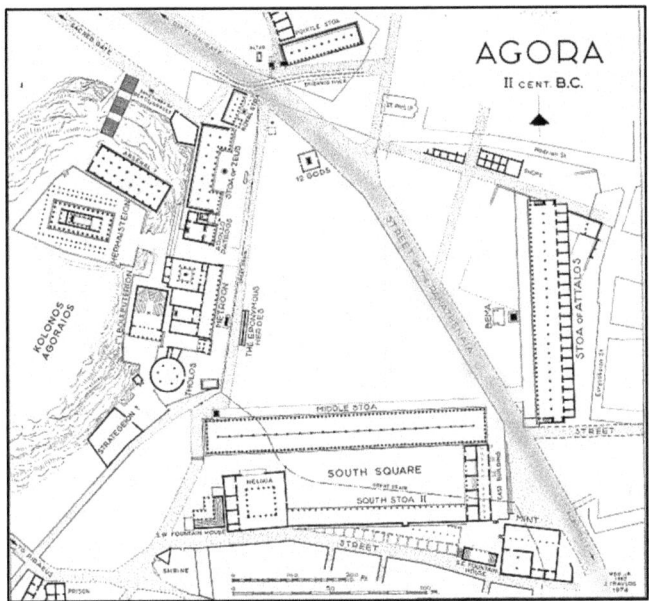

Figure 2.2 Overview of the agora (700-480 BC) Highlighted: The Panathenaic way where game celebrations started. Image Credit: American School of Classical Studies at Athens: Agora Excavations ©

Research dedicated to the agonistic aspects of the Greek Agora demonstrates the ritual importance of the competitions that were held there.[26] In the eposes, Homer describes the Agora as a place where competitions, political gatherings and judgments occurred on the occasion of festivals.[27] In "Agōnes on the Greek, Agora between Ritual and Spectacle: Some Examples from the Peloponnese," (2010), Rachele Dubbini claims that earlier scholarship has drawn on the Homeric text for evidence of the development of civic games, but it has not focused on the localities made available for them.[28] The importance of the *dromos* the race-track and *choros* the path or the route or direction orchestra and their topographical relationship to the Agora have been overlooked. She adds that already in the Homeric text it is obvious that the *dromos* and *choros* should not be understood as permanent structures. They appear to be particular areas of the Agora that were prepared on the occasion of an agonistic event. The starting line was the only fixed element of the racecourse, while there is no mention of any structures set up for the audience. The judges of the *agōn* stood inside the space for the choruses and prepared the *choros* by levelling the ground. Moreover, the spectators were not permitted to gather inside a permanent structure. Rather, they were forced to watch the action from within an unpaved area of the Agora that was so sparsely constructed that it did not even have a platform for the spectators to stand on.

Athens' most important festival took place every four years in honor of Athena, the city's patron goddess. The festival consisted of athletic and equestrian contests, music and rhapsody competitions as well as other sports and festivities. Dubbini suggests that in order to understand the agonistic setting (i.e., the physical setting of the competitions) it is useful to refer to the architectural form used for choral performances, the orchestra. Through a reference to Photius, she claims that this term initially indicated the structure located in the agora of Athens, and later came to mean the hemicycle of the theatre.[29] The orchestra is thus the area reserved for action (in this case choral performances), while the spectators occupy the *theatron* (seating area) which are temporary structures built as necessity required. The *orchestra* can be understood as an architectural form that was often surrounded by spectators and which was defined conceptually as *choros* and architecturally as *orchestra*. Archeological excavations of ancient Greek sites such as the Agora in Corinth reveal the importance of structures used in competition, for example excavations uncovered *dromos* which were used as the starting line in races and the *choros* which were not only the place where the orchestra performed, but also the place where judges of competitions sat.[30] The use of race tracks and theaters in agonistic rituals brought fierce and sometimes violent competition to the center of the Agora.

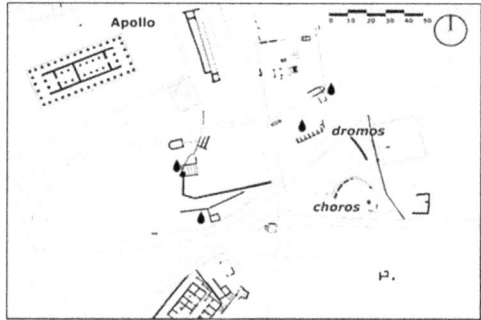

Figure 2.3 The Agora in Corinth. "The agora of Corinth in classical time."
Image Credit: Rachele Dubbini ©

The Acropolis

Unlike the Agora which can be considered as an organic space that has been continuously used throughout history, the entrance to the Acropolis was initially created as a monument designed to guide the visitors but was adopted and adapted to new political requirements over time. Transferring the Agora from the old part of the city, which was located to the east of the Acropolis, to its classical location - northeast of the Acropolis - strengthened the connection between the Acropolis and the general plan of the city center (*astu*).[31] The route of the Panathenaic Way passes through the classical Agora to the western entrance of the Acropolis. This change in the location of the Agora, from the central market and the political center of the city to a holy area, increased the communication and movement between them.[32]

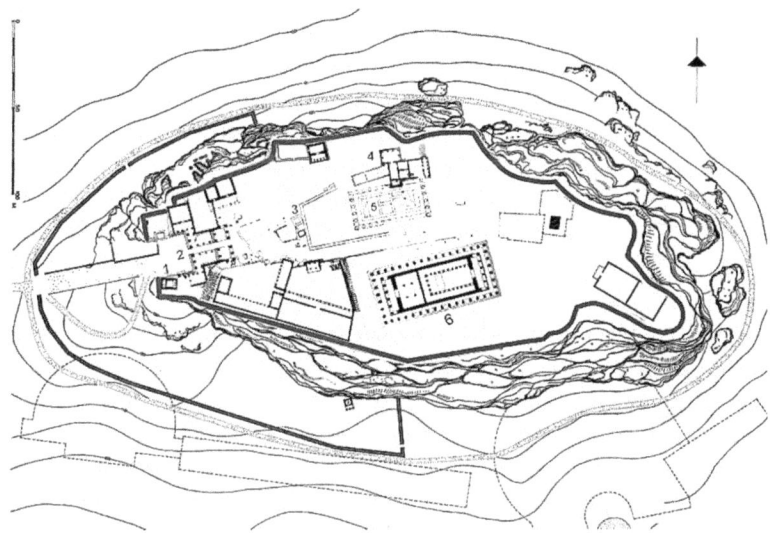

Figure 2.4 Plan of the Acropolis 1. Temple of Athena Nike 2. Propylaea 3. Statue of Athena Promachos 4. Erechtheion 5. Old Temple of Athena 6. Parthenon.
Image Credit: Archive of Archaeological Society at Athens ©

For approximately 30 years, since the expulsion of the last tyrant Hippias by the Spartans in 510/511 BCE and the Persian invasion in 479/480 BCE - the Acropolis was a site of siege and conquest. In 507 BCE Kleisthenes was elected to start the democratic reformation of Athens. Two decades after this reform, monumental development work was undertaken at the entrance to the Acropolis. Parts of the Bronze Age fortifications were dismantled, a front entrance courtyard was erected and became the focal point of the great rampart by which the Acropolis could be ascended. New plans were started to create a new gate from the old Propylon, which was a marble structure that stood near to the remains of the cyclopic construction and created an impression of strength, power, and defense. Together old Propylon and the Athena Nike Sanctuary demarcated the space of the front courtyard. At the side of the lustral basin in the forecourt is a columned structure believed to be used for ritual water cleansing.

There were probably other structures, including possibly votive dedications such as the Boiotian and Chalkidian (design styles in ancient Greece) as well as a pre-Mnesiclean cistern which was installed in the post-Marathon period.[33] The construction of the front courtyard with the terraced theater area underlines the possibility that this area was used for the purpose of gatherings and was also a place that connected the overall area of the space. Undoubtedly these architectural changes, even though they are incomplete, indicate an intentional effort to create a large-scale entrance to the most important holy area in Athens; a place that could accommodate a large assembly of people and, in particular, would be able to hold the 500 members of the Citizens' Council.[34] In "Contested Space at the Entrance of the Athenian Acropolis" (2017), Jessica Paga argues that the entrance to the Acropolis is a space that was changed in the early democratic period in order to serve as a site for exchanging opinions and protesting. This area was the setting of many foundational historical events associated with the early democracy, and it adapted and assisted the emerging political regime by means of its functionality.[35]

Since the Bronze Age, the main entrance to the Acropolis was on the western side (figure 2.4) as it is an accessible area in the steep rock where the Acropolis is located. This area has remained the only point of entry since the thirteenth century. There are four elements - the Bronze Age fortifications, the old Propylon, the ramp, and the bastion of the Sanctuary of Athena Nike - which constitute the monumental components of the entrance to the Acropolis during the late Archaic period. Numerous studies of the entrance area have been produced since the late nineteenth-century excavations of the site; however, they are beyond the scope of this paper.[36] The Acropolis, which is located on a mountain that is higher than the rest of the city, emphasizes that the accessibility and the size of the entrance are connected to its visibility as well as its ability to link two parts of the city.

The Athenians who survived the Persian attacks were able to look up from their location in the Agora and see the remains of the Sanctuary of Athena and the Parthenon as symbols of survival and victory. It is possible that during the siege of 507 to 508, people in the Agora would have been able to see and possibly hear the large crowd of the demos barring the entrance to the Acropolis.[37] In many ways, the entrance space itself became a symbol of struggle and Athenian success. This is expressed in Aristophanes' *Lysistrata*, produced in 411 BCE.[38] In the first choral ode, old men discuss besieging the women on the Acropolis. The historic siege of 507 to 508 BCE describes how the elders, and the inhabitants of Athens created the gate of the Acropolis; it is a moment of reflection on the glorious moments of early democracy, when the demos, the people, opposed the Spartans and defeated them and the tyrant Isagoras. The play indicates the fact that a historical event, which had taken place about a century before the play was written, was preserved in the hearts of the citizens, and indicates that the entrance area to the Acropolis was a place of *agōn* (contest), competition and conflict.

The monument and reconstruction of a new space for the entrance area is now understood as being a response to the victory of the Athenians in 508-7

BCE which reinforced the power of democracy. In doing so, this area summarizes the events that occurred at the end of the sixth century BCE and the beginning of the fifth century BCE, making the many victories of democracy concrete: "The democratic ideals of accountability and visibility are written into the physical fabric of the space, with the prominent display of the Hekatompedon Decrees (a limestone temple built in the current location of the Parthenon) and the open, theatral forecourt. The use of new materials and construction of new built elements appear alongside the preservation of the city's Bronze Age past, a reminder of the historic role of the citadel."[39] The entrance to the Acropolis was not just the entrance to the holy area in the city of Athens but to a vibrant and dynamic space in which many conflicts took place, and the Greek *agōn* was expressed; this was a place where the Athenians expressed their perception of *agōn* as the definer of the polis.

A return to the present

In the contemporary, post-political world, it is difficult to theorize or imagine the public sphere. This difficulty arises from the rationalistic and individualistic attitude underlying most contemporary liberal thought. It is not immediately apparent how the agonistic conception of the polis can inspire the contemporary city, since contemporary liberalism rejects the pluralistic and conflictual nature of the social world. Despite this rejection, these conflicts are ever present. Since they have no rational solution, inhabitants of urban spaces must learn to embrace the agonistic dimension of human society.

Plato's *Republic* can be read as a model for city planning. Plato understood that otherness is inherent to the urban structure and that its essence is therefore conflictual. This is evident in the analogy between the city and the human soul. Both consist of pluralities, and each element of these pluralities is in a constant state of conflict. According to this model, urban spaces are unsaturated and given to transformation. They exhibit a flexible grammar, capable of new syntaxes, new harmonious developments and new integrations, which do not contradict previous ensembles. *Agōn* is an important concept in twentieth-century political theory.[40] Moreover it appears in philosophy and is pertinent for understanding ethnic and national conflicts. [41] *Agōn* is associated with pluralism, where the identical and the different are radical forces, creating a conflict which usually cannot be resolved. It has a dialectic structure, and is evolving constantly, since it is not based on an extreme polarity, but rather on mutual differences and similarities. The distinction between mutuality and polarity is significant, since polarity does not exist within the *agōn*, rather outside it, in the antagonism. In the *Democracy Paradox* (200), Chantal Mouffe cites antagonism as existing between adversaries, where adversaries are not respected or legitimate, while in agonism there is an agreement through conflict, even if it cannot be solved.[42]

In contemporary political theory, *agōn* (and conflict more generally) is not perceived as having ideological value, rather it is thought of as a means of enabling reforms in democratic systems. These theories discuss *agōn* as an abstract system and sometimes as a radical system of understanding and action. Such a discussion dislocates *agōn* from its roots in the urban structure. And indeed, in most of these discussions, the city is not a necessary element.[43] *Agōn* in its ancient form cannot be directly applied to the postmodern city, and it is clear that competitions such sporting events conducted in the heart of cities plagued by conflict will not solve their problems. However, when *agōn* and its connection to the polis is closely examined, a foundational idea, which can be applied to the contemporary urban experience, emerges: Public life does not only support difference, it is created by it. Therefore, participation in the public sphere is an important means of expressing and dealing with difference.[44]

It is important for a city to adopt an agonistic form of politics and to create compatible public spaces in which *agōn* can manifest itself in a controlled manner. Otherwise it is difficult to constructively deal with the various conflicts that emerge in all urban spaces. Without agonistic political spaces that provide a controlled forum for conflict in the public sphere, urban conflicts tend to erupt violently. Are citizens of liberal democracies such as the United States able to express disagreement in ways that are necessary for democratic life? This conflict, as well as other historical examples, erupted antagonistically rather than agonistically. The latter accepts and leaves room for a kind of pluralism of values that cannot be reconciled. This notion is very different from the pluralism found in liberal thought that strives for a harmonious state of political consensus, which, in reality, is impossible to achieve. Once the possibility of an agonistic perspective is recognized, the legitimacy of the other's demands is also recognized.

Inhabitants of the city must recognize that when they do not agree, it may be impossible for their views to be reconciled. This should include the realization that the other has the right to hold a different position. This phenomenon of mutual and respectful disagreement that cannot be neatly reconciled with consensus is compatible with the democratic societies of the ancient Greek polis in general and Athens in particular. Contrary to the current view that tries to find ways to create consensus, the main task in a democracy is not to reach an agreement but to manage dissonance and create political forms that allow for coexistence. From a social standpoint, agonist politics emphasize the importance of recognizing that the other is not an immoral or wicked enemy. If this view is taken, politics becomes a sphere where opposing groups aim for the elimination of their enemies, which is a result that is not compatible with the policies and ideals of a democratic state. If conflicts cannot be expressed using political vocabulary, they will be expressed in other forms, which are not manageable by democratic institutions. It is therefore important to offer clear expressions of political differences, even if they offer contradictory alternatives from which the public must choose.

Cities are by their very nature spaces of conflict and offer potential grounds for expressing the daily role of agonism and the formation of an agonistic public space. Calling for the right to a city is interesting because it is a way in which a common struggle can be expressed. In other words, the city must offer agonistic spaces where groups of different people can come together and discuss their competing perspectives and ideologies in the public sphere. In conclusion, when considering Tschumi's remarks on architecture in general and his project Parc de la Villette in particular, it becomes clear that defining a space architecturally means defining the spatial borders in which events can occur.[45] Architecture should create the conditions of occurrence for a non-hierarchical or non-traditional society by creating an environment that nurtures the relationship between space and events. Creating an architecture that fosters civic pluralism, like that which was found in the Greek polis, could transform our cities, our environment and the structures of power in which we live. As we discussed in the case study of Athens, there is a correlation between the structure of society as pluralistic and conflictual, and its physical places - the Agora and the Acropolis. These places inhabit spaces where society can build itself through debate and discussion. Therefore, architects should look at the multiplicity of public spaces, whether they are places dedicated to events, or to gatherings and meetings. Through participating in the public space, we can develop a civil sphere, informed by the antagonism which is inherent to human relations.

Bibliography

Arendt, Hanna. *The Human Condition*. Chicago, IL: University of Chicago Press, 1958.

Aristophanes. *Lysistrata*. Translated by Jack Lindsay. New York: Hartsdale House, 1920.

Aristotle. *Politics Books I and II*. Translated by Trevor J. Saunders. Oxford: Clarendon Press, 1995.

Aristotle. *The Athenian Constitution; The Eudemian Ethics; On Virtues and Vices*. Translated by H. Rackham. Cambridge, Mass. Harvard University Press, 1935.

Arnason, Johann P., and Peter Murphy. Introduction to *Agōn, Logos, Polis: The Greek Achievement and its Aftermath*, 7-14. Stuttgart: F. Steiner Publishing, 2001.

Bundgaard, Jens A. *Mnesicles: A Greek Architect at Work*. Copenhagen: Gyldendal, 1957.

Burkhardt, Jacob. *The Greeks and Greek Civilization*. Translated by Sheila Stern. Edited by Oswyn Murray. London: Harper Collins Press, 1998.

Dubbini, Rachele. "Agōnes on the Greek Agora between Ritual and Spectacle: Some Examples from the Peloponnese." In *Body, Performance, Agency, and Experience*, Volume II. Edited by Angelos Chaniotis, Silke Leopold, Eric Venbrux, Jan Weinhold, and Axel Michaels, 157-81. Wiesbaden: Harrassowitz, 2010.

Eiteljorg, Harrison. "New Finds Concerning the Entrance to the Acropolis." *Athens Annals of Archaeology* 8 (1976): 94-5.

Finlayson, Alan. *Democracy and Pluralism: The Political Thought of William E. Connolly*. London: Routledge, 2011.

Gill, David W. J. "The Decision to Build the Temple of Athena Nike ('IG' I³ 35)." *Historia: Zeitschrift Für Alte Geschichte* 51, no. 3 (2001): 257-78.

Heidegger, Martin. *Being and Time*. Translated by John Macquarrie and Edward Robinson. New York: Harper & Row, 1962.

Huizinga, Johan. *Homo Ludens: A Study of the Play Element in Culture*. London: Maurice Temple, 1970.

Jacobs, Jane. *The Death and Life of Great American Cities*. New York: Vintage Books, 1992.

Kastrissianakis, Konstantin. "From Antagōnistic Politics to an Agōnistic Public Space. Interview with Chantal Mouffe." *Cities in Turmoil, Special Issue, Re-Public* (2010).

Kenaan, Hagi. "Human Cities and the Space of Conflict," In *Human Cities: Civil Society Reclaims Public Space*, edited by Rafaella Houlstan-Hasaerts, Biba Tominc, Matej Nikšič, and Barbara Goličnik Marušić, 37-40. European Project Human Cities, 2012.

Kolb, Frank. *Agora und Theater. Volks- und Festversammlung*. Berlin: Gebr. Mann Verlag, 1981.

Loraux, Nicole, *The Divided City: On Memory and Forgetting in Ancient Athens*. Translated by Corinne Pache and Jeff Fort. New York: Zone, 2006.

Mattingly, Harold B. "The Athena Nike Dossier: IG I3 35/36 and 64 A–B." Classical Quarterly 50 (2000): 604-6.

Mouffe, Chantal. *The Democracy Paradox*. London and New York: Verso, 2000.

Mouffe, Chantal and Markus Miessem. *The Space of Agōnism*. Berlin: Sternberg Press, 2012.

Paga, Jessica. "Contested Space at the Entrance of the Athenian Acropolis." *Journal of the Society of Architectural Historians*, vol. 76, no. 2 (2017): 154-74.

Plato. *Phaedrus*. Translated by Alexander Nehamas and Paul Woodruff. Indianapolis: Hackett, 1995.

Plato. *Republic, Book 2* in *The Collected Dialogues of Plato Including the Letters*. Edited by Edith Hamilton and Huntington Cairns. Translated by Lane Cooper. Princeton: Princeton University Press, 1962.

Papadopoulos, John K. "The Original Kerameikos of Athens and the Siting of the Athenian Agora." *Greek, Roman, and Byzantine Studies* 37, no. 2 (1996): 107-128.

P. E. Van 'T Wout. "Solon's Law on Stasis: Promoting Active Neutrality." *Classical Quarterly* 60, no. 2 (2010): 289-301.

Robertson, Noel. "The City Center of Archaic Athens." *Hesperia: The Journal of the American School of Classical Studies at Athens* 67, no. 3 (1998): 283-302.

Tanoulas, Tasos. "The Pre-Mnesiclean Cistern." *AM 107* (1992): 160.

Tomlinson, R. A. "Review of The Sanctuary of Athena Nike in Athens: Architectural Stages and Chronology, by Ira Mark." *Journal of Hellenic Studies* 115 (1995): 238.

Tschumi, Bernard. *Architecture and Disjunction.* Cambridge, MA: MIT Press, 1994.

Wenman, Mark. *Agōnistic Democracy: Constituent Power in the Era of Globalization.* Cambridge: Cambridge University Press, 2013.

Wenman, Mark. "'Agōnistic Pluralism' and Three Archetypal Forms of Politics." *Contemporary Political Theory* 2, no. 2 (2003): 165-86.

Chapter 3

Public space in the West Bund, Shanghai

Shuang Fei

University of Copenhagen, Denmark

Abstract

Under the leader Deng Xiaoping, radical economic reforms shifted the People's Republic of China towards a more economically neo-liberal climate. The government later began the implementation of a comprehensive development project in central Shanghai which had been occupied by dilapidated factories and a post-industrial port. At the World Expo 2010, the Xuhui waterfront emerged as the showpiece of redevelopment in connecting urban renewal with a cultural strategy. At its hub, the Bund provided a new urban waterfront and landscaped areas with buildings for 1) cultural innovation, 2) technological innovation and 3) financial services. This chapter investigates the process of spatial transformation within the cultural quarter of the West Bund and the new ways the public is interacting within this new, more western-style environment. The research argues that diverse relations of power have prevented it from becoming a tool for purely financial gains, which has seen a new kind of Chinese public emerge.

Keywords: Shanghai, public, space, government, culture, quarter

***

Introduction

At the midpoint of China's eastern coastline and at the mouth of the Yangtze River is Shanghai, which has served as a transportation and commercial hub for over a millennium. The city's strategic geographic position has enabled Shanghai to play a major position in the Chinese economy. After the People's Republic of China (PRC) was founded in 1949, Mao Zedong (Chairman Mao) announced that Shanghai would be "central to the socialist economy."[1] Under the leader Deng Xiaoping in 1978, radical economic reforms shifted the PRC towards a more economically neo-liberal climate. The impact saw Shanghai emerge as the "center of Yangtze River Economic Belt in China" and a "socialist modern international city."[2] A large number of new commercial complexes sprang up at an unprecedented rate from the late 1980s. With the later rise of online shopping, the commercial complexes increasingly featured some form of art exhibit, performance, or activity as an added attraction. Using culture as an economic driver but also as an urban strategy was taken to another level following the Shanghai Expo 2010. In the area close to the Huang Pu River in Shanghai's Xuhui district the former hub of the city's iron, coal, grain, and oil industries of the West Bund underwent a major programme of urban regeneration. Following the government renewal programme from 2012 the area was turned into a new kind of place and public space for a Chinese city spanning 8.95 kilometres and 500,000 square meters. The waterfront strategy was underpinned by three approaches — culture and creativity, technology and innovation, and business and finance.

The West Bund emerged as the new face of China in reflecting how the government was responding to the idea of a more culturally aware city. A further, and more unexpected, outcome has been that the West Bund has enabled its visitors to behave in a different way than had previously been the case in the rest of the city, acting in a slower, relaxed and in more social way. This research explores the West Bund through its public spaces, and cultural initiatives including its museums along the Xuhui waterfront and considers the new kinds of social interactions that have been produced. It further considers the role that social media plays in articulating a particular identity for this area. The research is taken from an interdisciplinary range of literary sources from cultural studies to urban sociology. The methods drawn on are observation, data collection, and interviews conducted with architects, artists, security staff, museum managements, governmental institutions, and the general public. The chapter looks initially at Shanghai and its historic position through the area of the West Bund. Thereafter, it examines the political reforms in China from 1979 and how this affected the urban landscape in the 1980s and the 1990s. It focuses on how the changing climate facilitated a new way of thinking about public space, culture, and commerce at the West Bund. The key question it explores is — how has the West Bund changed the way the Chinese public is responding to the new kinds of public spaces that have been produced within this new cultural quarter?

A new vision for Shanghai

Shanghai is in the unique position of having a strong European imperial influence while maintaining its eastern Chinese identity. The reason was due to its location as a seaport and network of rivers which connected it to the hinterlands and made it an important coastal city. At the same time, with the impact of foreign dominance and "the flowering of treaty port business," Shanghai accelerated in its economic power which put it at an advantage compared to other Chinese cities.[3] Due to the demand for financial services, the area near to the waterfront known as the Bund, meaning embankment, became occupied by Western style buildings, foreign consulates and banks. The Bund emerged as an international symbol of prosperity in the nineteenth century.[4] In the period after the last Imperial Government of the Qing Dynasty, China suffered a long-term period of war and civil war which led to Shanghai's stagnation. After the PRC was created, the economy transferred the control of business from the private sector to the public sector. This changed with Xiaoping's neo-liberal economic reforms and opening-up of the state, which began to stimulate China's economy later repositioning of the state to business. The impact of public state intervention on a "well-established capitalist economy typical to most treaty port cities at the time" had major repercussions for Shanghai.[5]

The impact of the new directives "in China has seen the construction of a particular kind of market economy that increasingly incorporates neoliberal elements interdigitated with authoritarian centralized control."[6] From 1990, the Chinese Government launched a new vision for Shanghai as an international port city which was delivered through a new urban programme. The state provided massive funding for improving the urban infrastructure, which included modern traffic networks, water facilities, telecommunication projects, and new sources of energy. One important project in the Pudong New Area, later named Lujiazui Central Business District, was launched in 1993. With attractive policies for investors, the project signalled that Shanghai was open for massive overseas investment. Economic reforms, followed by a series of spatial restructuring measures and institutional reforms, helped Shanghai to achieve "a double-digit growth for 15 consecutive years since 1992" to become "the fastest economic growth of any mega-city since the early 1990s."[7] What emerged in Shanghai was a hybrid economic political modern that was essentially "neoliberalism with Chinese characteristics."[8]

The politico-economic background for the complex

The establishment of commercial complexes from the 2000s is closely tied to three important periods. The first of these stems from the reforms within the Chinese economic system. The Chinese Communist Party (CCP) began building a socialist economy, that as discussed saw business transfer from the private to the public sector. The post 1978 economic reforms began as "a gradual expansion of the role of the market and a reformist approach toward the ownership issue" and to "reform its state sector while permitting the "relatively unconstrained growth" of the non-state sector."[9] Some state-owned businesses were turned into private companies, moving towards a more market-oriented economy. The second period relates to reforms since 1994, which were in response to the government's serious fiscal crisis. The reforms cleared the rules for distributing different categories of taxes to central and local governments. The amendment to policy ensured that the central government took over a large proportion of fiscal revenue to invest in infrastructure, whereas local governments sought to raise local finances. The central government permitted local governments to sell land to private enterprises for urban development, which led to a boost in property markets, and to a programme of rapid urbanization. In order to restrain real estate development from purely generating profits new measures were implemented. The government created policies to link investment in shopping malls, hotels, offices buildings, museums, and renewal projects.

Since the 1990s, state-owned enterprises became involved in massive infrastructure development. They became instrumental in dominating urban development in 2008 when the central government undertook measures to manage the impact on China concerning the international financial crisis. One of the important measures was known as the Four Trillion plan, which granted huge loans from the central bank for infrastructure development, that included affordable housing, rural infrastructure, transport systems, technological innovations, the environment, and medical, cultural, and educational services. The land development process consisted of first-level and second-level developments. The first-level development included land acquisition, demolition, resettlement, and compensation as well as the urban infrastructure put in place for the second-level development, operated by the government and its authorized state-owned enterprises. The second-level development refers to a process of developing the land to be traded in the market through landowner transfers, leasing, or mortgages, by private developers. These policies and measures boosted the development of complexes and initiated new ways of thinking about public spaces.

West Bund

The Chinese Government made a bid in 1999 for the World Expo at the 126th meeting of the Bureau of International Expositions (BIE) and was successful. Shanghai used the "World Expo 2010 as a catalyst to regenerate its main waterfront along Huangpu Riverbank and enhance its culture sector."[10] Notably, it became the engine for the urban renewal project at Xuhui Waterfront which was renamed "West Bund Culture Corridor" after the 9th Party Congress of Xuhui District and is now known as the West Bund.[11] The government began the implementation of a comprehensive development project for both banks of the Huangpu River in 2010. The scope of the project includes the sites for World Expo 2010 and the Xuhui waterfront which was occupied by dilapidated factories and a post-industrial port. West Bund indicated that Shanghai was mapping out an ambition to be an international center of the cultural and creative industries (CCI) that referenced other developments including London's

South Bank and notably the area of Bankside with its mixture of reclaimed new developments and repurposed industrial buildings.[12]

The vision of the West Bund was to provide a world-class urban waterfront and landscaped areas with buildings for three major tertiary sector areas 1) cultural innovation, 2) technological innovation, and 3) the financial services. The West Bund has over twenty cultural institutions including museums and galleries along the 8.4 km shoreline. Along with the museum quarter there is also an emerging theatre cluster, which will make it the largest cultural zone in Asia. The other projects in development include West Bund Media Port, West Bund Smart Valley and West Bund Financial Centre. While the financial sector plays a major role in the West Bund, its identity is culture and creative-led. These areas are interlinked at the West Bund as CCI is generating substantial economic returns. In 2017, Shanghai's local Government projected that the value of the CCI sector will rise to eighteen percent of the gross municipal product by 2030, and that by 2035 West Bund will become an international center of CCI.[13] How CCI is supported at the West Bund is through its riverside public space, Art Museum Avenue, the Culture and Art Pilot Zone and the three Complexes: "One Port, One Valley, One City" (a Media Port, an AI Valley, and a Financial City).[14]

The Riverside Public Space and Art Museum Avenue was the first development created by the government authority. The specific government bodies responsible for the development were the Shanghai Xuhui Waterfront Area Comprehensive Development, the Construction Management Committee and a state-owned enterprise called Shanghai West Bund Development (Group) Co., Ltd (WBG). The impact of their work saw the public space of the riverfront being revived through incorporating landscape designs and sports facilities. On the site of Art Museum Avenue and the Culture and Art Pilot Zone, dilapidated industrial buildings were renovated and transformed into art museums, exhibition halls, and creative clusters. The aim was to become "the largest art zone in Asia."[15] The three complexes are attracting private investment for the culture industry, the artificial intelligence industry, and the digital currency industry. The profits and tax from land sales have compensated the investments and ensured the ongoing operation of the art museums, the artistic activities and the creation of the public spaces.

Shanghai urban space art season (SUSAS) and camp 3399

The launch of the international contemporary art fair Shanghai urban space art season (SUSAS) cemented the West Bund as a new cultural urban quarter. One of the main draws of SUSAS is the regenerated industrial heritage of the site which helped to attract the press and media who paid as much attention to the renovations as to the art on display. SUSAS emerged as a series of cultural and artistic activities initiated in the autumn of 2015 which ran for three months in the West Bund that was organized by a combination of architects, curators, artists, urban planners, critics, media, WBG and the local government. The objective was to motivate the public by engaging them in a series of cultural activities. These included art exhibits, urban planning exhibits, and seminars which took place in the renovated buildings, and in the waterfront open space. "From Chen, the director of West Bund's industrial cultivation department, "culture-led" never became a strategy until the landing of three iconic projects: (1) Long Art Museum (2) Yu Deyao Museum, and (3) Shanghai Dream Center."[16] The privately owned Long Art Museum and Yu Deyao Museums acquired the option to renovate existing buildings on the site. The Shanghai Dream Center also transferred to the Media Port when it turned into a commercial complex that was supported by the cultural, media, and information and communication industries.

SUSAS attracts huge gatherings that includes fashion icons, dancers, bloggers, skateboarders, and others. Through SUSAS they can display their personalized lifestyles on social media including We Media. The global innovation agency, publisher, studio and incubator for networked knowledge and culture, We Media allows its users to spread information independently, and is not reliant on the centralization of information. We Media also enables internet journalism so that its users can play an interactive role in reporting news and disseminating information. In doing so, the information that it helps to generate attracts people events such as SUSAS, the art museums, and the public spaces at the West Bund. The success and profits generated by the first SUSAS motivated the organizers to hold the event biennially. The main exhibition site for SUSAS in 2015 was the West Bund Art Center. The theme was urban renewal that had three strands. The first was to explore ways of solving urban problems. Secondly, it also looked at how to accelerate the sustainable development of the regional economy. The third strand was to improve the quality of society. The interdisciplinary exhibition threaded together urban studies, policy and practice with planning, design, traffic, housing, infrastructure, political economy, cultural industry, sustainable development, social organization, and public welfare.

The following SUSAS events also had an urban theme that were hosted in different sites. In 2017, SUSAS was presented at the Pudong Riverside, and in 2019, was held at the Yangpu Riverside. What is interesting about SUSAS is that it focuses on informing rather than consulting, and in this way, it limits the relationship between the visitors, the events, and the organizers. It is foremost a platform for artists, architects and urban scholars where they can express their ideas and articulate their feelings. They also provide their professional knowledge on what they are seeing and experiencing. The issue is that this exchange is one way, as the public has less of a platform to express themselves and to give their own feedback. The other issue is that cultural and artistic activities need to be ratified by the authorities through a one-way decision-making procedure which creates its own issues concerning free speech. Despite its limitations, SUSAS nonetheless has created a new kind of platform that encourages more public speech than is the norm in Chinese cities.

Next to the SUSAS site is Camp 3399 which was established to provide individuals with a place of self-organized activities. Originally part of the Xuhui riverside development area and called Xuhui Riverside Public Open Space) this is an event space that has grown into its own creative hub which was renamed to Camp 3399. The turfed area facilitates basketball courts and a skate park, it has also hosted festivals, markets, music performances, and festivals, as well as interactive dance. The site was originally state reserve land awaiting commercial development. The local government and the WBG received suggestions from a group of architects requesting to transform it into a temporary green space in 2017. Since that point Camp 3399 has emerged as a popular forum that presents more bottom-up cultural, artistic and related activities. Many of the activities have been organized by non-governmental organizations, communities, and small companies within the cultural industry. They have provided their own publicity and also relied on social media. The Dianping app is the popular Chinese social media application for collecting consumer reviews. The data identifies how people's leisure practices are mostly limited to having picnics or walking dogs. On this basis, there has been less enthusiasm for cultural activities which has meant that the West Bund had to ensure a way of attracting visitors to its museums and public spaces.

Art at the West Bund

What is important is to identify is that how art and culture are perceived in China, is different from in the west. In modern China, presenting art and culture through urban forums makes it more accessible. Related to this, Henri Lefebvre asserts: "To put art at the service of the urban does not mean to prettify urban space with works of art [...] Leaving aside representation, ornamentation and decoration, art can become praxis and poiesis on a social scale: the art of living in the city as work of art."[17] Building on this proposition, Benjamin Fraser proposes that to put "art at the service of the urban" is to reunite it with the urban phenomenon.[18] In this way, art affects the way that people encounter public space, while Robert Layton asserts that "art should focus on the social context of art production, circulation, and reception, not on the evaluation of particular works."[19] On this basis, art, and more broadly, culture, depends on the social context in which it is presented. Accordingly, the West Bund, through its art museums, places for co-creating artistic activities, transnational art programs, and other resources changes the way its visitors use this new kind of public space.

The relationship between public space and people extends to power and knowledge, Michel Foucault asserts that power cannot be completely understood as a group of institutions or mechanisms with an aim for a citizen to obey and yield to the state.[20] He reiterates that power is considered as a capacity of "structur[ing] the possible field of action of others."[21] Foucault turned the focus from the subject or outcome of power to the technically mediated process of power.[22] Drawing on this proposition this relationship between power and public space is explored in the following three West Bund examples: (1) the public art museum Xian Museum; (2) the private art museum Long Museum; and (3) the West Bund Art Center and the Culture & Art Pilot Zone. While these three projects have been established and funded by WBG, the spaces they have created are also affected by visitor's responses and interactions within these settings.

The Xian Museum is located in the riverside area of the West Bund and is regarded as a premier venue on Art Museum Avenue. Designed by the English architect David Chipperfield and his team, the new space is for art exhibitions and for public educational events. It opened to the public in 2019 with a joint cultural program between Paris and Shanghai which is supported by both governments. Under the five-year joint exhibition programs from 2019 to 2024, the flow of shared cultural resources became possible through the Xian Museum. The aim has been to provide an educational role for families with children who are attracted by its facilities as well as the outdoor public space. The Long Museum was founded by Yiqian Liu and Wei Wang. Liu is the chairman of Sunline Group, a Shanghai-based investment company and along with his wife is also a prominent art collector. Yichun Liu, a renowned Chinese architect was asked to design the building from the former industrial site of Beipiao Wharf which was used for loading and storing coal. The redesign has turned the coal-hopper unloading bridge into a connection between the inside and the outside of the museum. After opening in 2014, the fusion of its industrial heritage and modern design attracted a younger art-going audience. Within the space they are able to display their fashion tastes and everyday lifestyles through various self-designed activities which are mostly represented on social media. These kinds of activities are encouraged by the Long Museum due to the publicity this generates in the virtual world.

The West Bund Art Center and the Culture & Art Pilot Zone have also been designed by Yichun Liu and stand on the site of the obsolete Shanghai aircraft factory which is across the road from the Xian Museum. The West Bund Art Center is a large exhibition hall that has been renovated from the major aircraft hangar that provides space for brand activities, government events and those relating to culture, art, design and fashion, and technology innovation. The Culture & Art Pilot Zone is a creative cluster renovated from the older factories on the site, bringing together artists, architects, and design and cultural organizations. This site was planned to serve professional and elite's cultural activities and the art trade. It exhibits various art shows and one-off events. The three projects present different power relations between governmental cooperation and family education, and the private institutions and the public's everyday lives. Located at the southern end of the West Bund is Fine Art Storage that is the leading domestic art logistics service provider that can operate outside the Shanghai Free Trade Zone. It is the first project in China that is jointly developed with an internationally renowned artwork storage company, Singapore Freeport Management Co., Ltd.

Bodily interaction with the setting

The use of the public space is determined by the waterfront, the museums, and its cultural activities. The accumulative effect impacts on the nature of the spaces and also on the public, in how they cerebrally and physically interact with what is presented to them. As John Pløger asserts, "by people sensing space bodily, where spaces are recognizable for a culturalized body shaped by the taken-for-granted deep culture of society."[23] What this means is that how people respond to what they see is already culturally determined. On this basis, cultural forums enable individuals to experience an altered setting through the art works on display, through the buildings and through the public space. Notable in the West Bund, the public are less enthusiastic than expected to participate in the well-planned artistic events arranged by SUSAS. Conversely, they engage and interact more with the unplanned events of Camp 3399. This raises the question of whether the artistic events empower people to take actions to express themselves and to interact with the settings in different ways.

Considering China's political system, Meiqin Wang's argument is that this may be "attributable to the authoritarian approach of urban governance that denies the right of ordinary citizens to participate in the development and transformation of their cities."[24] What this research proposes is something more fluid concerning the long-term effects of Chinese culture on people's consciousness concerning their rights and responsibilities. Fei Xiaotong proposed the term "social circles" to describe the character of Chinese society which emphasizes relations among people.[25] Xiatong uses the metaphor of water rippling from the center to symbolize relationships falling further or closer to the center (e.g. to the self). His thesis is that in the unspoken rules of relationships, one's rights and obligations to one another are related to favors returned over a period of time to maintain close relationships.[26] This reveals that a person considers his or her obligations and rights in a collective with social relationships centered on himself, herself, or themself and that one's rights and obligations are maintained with expected returns. Approaches for expressing and getting feedback through art practice are essential to building an individual's consciousness of their roles in creating public space.

Reflections on the effects

While multiple power relations change the ways of using public space, if the Chinese public is not motivated to interact with the settings and gain enjoyment of the space, there is the risk of the West Bund becoming solely an economic driver to "[sell] the image of the city as a cultural center and tourist destination."[27] People have diverse interactions with public spaces that are determined by many agencies including different cultural influences, whereas activities like jogging, walking dogs, or having a picnic are more similar. This research argues that more diverse socio-material relations prevent culture and its spaces from becoming a tool for purely financial gains. On this basis, it becomes a benefit for improving the quality of public space and of the enjoyment of it. According to the Global Public Space Toolkit, published by the United Nations Human Settlements Programme (UN-Habitat), "The quality of public-space enjoyment is tied to rights and duties. The right to enjoy adequate public spaces involves the duty to contribute to this goal through adoption of responsible individual or collective behavior to be involved in initiatives of active citizenry."[28] In the Chinese context, the individual's power of changing public space affects rights and obligations. It also impacts on their approaches to expressing themselves and on the feedback and returns they might gain to these cultural exchanges.

Conclusion

Considering the complexity of cities, it is evident that urban development is no longer a singular project solely reliant upon politico-economic factors. It is a multifaceted process that changes through different agencies involvement. In the West Bund, the role of cultural practices in effecting a public space empowers people to interact and behave in a particular manner. Based on the findings of this case study, what can be posited is how the combination of strategies has turned this Xuhui District of Shanghai into a rapidly developing leisure area, financial center and innovation incubator. Within the waterfront strategy a new place and space was created, and so was a new kind of Chinese public. What has been created is a new kind of assemblage the new with the old coal wharf, cement factory and giant fuel tanks that contribute to what is the West Bund. Colin McFarlane identifies this as an "emergence, becoming, processuality, turbulence and sociomateriality of phenomena."[29] What has happened at the West Bund is that over the past ten years, the Huangpu River waterfront of Xuhui has been transformed from a site that was previously cut-off from the rest of the city with its disused walled-off collection of factories. The advent of this new public space benefits nearby residents, and also attracts a large number of visitors that has turned it into a popular tourist destination. For visitors and residents alike, what is evident is that the new spaces of the West Bund have changed the way that the Chinese public respond to them, and to art and culture in urban places.

Acknowledgements

I am grateful to Ulrik Ekman, my supervisor, who has provided me with her valuable comments for improving my chapter. I also appreciate the information about the case study provided by Liu Yichun. I am also grateful to the editor and anonymous reviewers for their work.

Bibliography

Arkaraprasertkul, Non. "Power, Politics, and the Making of Shanghai." *Journal of Planning History* 9.4 (2010): 232-259.

Chen, Yawei. "Making Shanghai a Creative City: Exploring the Creative Cluster Strategy From a Chinese Perspective." In *Creative Knowledge Cities: Myth, Visions and Realities,* edited by Geenhuizen Marina van and Nijkamp Peter, 437-64. Cheltenham, Northampton: Edward Elgar, 2012.

Chen, Yawei, Qiyu TU, Ning Su. "Shanghai's Huangpu Riverbank Redevelopment beyond World Expo 2010." Paper presented at the annual conference AESOP 2014: From Control to Co-Evolution, Utrecht/Delft, The Netherlands, July 9-12, 2014.

Fei, Xiaotong. *From the Soil: The Foundations of Chinese Society.* Translated by Gary G. Hamilton and Wang Zheng. Berkeley and Los Angeles, California, London: University of California Press, 1992.

Foucault, Michel. "The Subject and Power." *Critical Inquiry* 8.4 (1982): 777-795.

Fraser, Benjamin. *Toward an Urban Cultural Studies: Henri Lefebvre and the Humanities.* New York: Palgrave Macmillan, 2015.

Harvey, David. *A Brief History of Neoliberalism.* Oxford: University Press, 2007.

Herrmann-Pillath, Carsten. "Fei Xiaotong's Comparative Theory of Chinese Culture: Its Relevance for Contemporary Cross-disciplinary Research on Chinese 'Collectivism'." *The Copenhagen Journal of Asian Studies* 34.1 (2016): 25-57.

Information Office of Shanghai Municipality. "Suggestions for Accelerating Development of Culture and Creative Industries in Shanghai." Modified December 15, 2017. http://www.shio.gov.cn/sh/xwb/n790/n792/n989/n1027/u1ai14603_K318.html.

Jos, Gamble. *Shanghai in Transition: Changing Perspectives and Social Contours of a Chinese Metropolis.* London: Routledge Curzon, 2003.

Klauser, Francisco, Till Paasche, and Ola Söderström. "Michel Foucault and the Smart City: Power Dynamics Inherent in Contemporary Governing Through

Code." *Environment and Planning D: Society and Space* 32 (2014): 869-885. doi:10.1068/d13041p.

Lardy, Nicholas R. *China's Unfinished Economic Revolution.*Washington, DC: Brookings Institution, 1998.

Layton, Robert. "Art and Agency: A Reassessment." *Journal of the Royal Anthropological Institute* 9.3 (2003): 447-464.

Lefebvre, Henri. "The Right to the City." In *Writings on Cities,* edited and translated by Kofman Eleonore and Lebas Elizabeth, 63-181. Oxford: Blackwell, 1996.

Lynch, Richard A. "Foucault's Theory of Power." *Michel Foucault: Key Concepts,* edited by Dianna Taylor, 13-26. London, New York: Routledge, 2014.

McFarlane, Colin. "Assemblage and critical urbanism." *City* 15.2 (2011): 204-224. doi: 10.1080/13604813.2011.568715.

Pløger, John. "Foucault's Dispositif and the City." *Planning Theory* 7.1 (2018): 51-70. doi: 10.1177/1473095207085665.

Qiu, Yichun. "Stakeholders and Partnership in Urban Regeneration: The Case of Shanghai West Bund." Master Thesis. Columbia University, 2019.

The State of Council The People's Republic of China. "Reply of the State Council on the Genneral Urban Plan of Shanghai Municipality." Modified December 25, 2017. http://www.gov.cn/zhengce/content/2017-12/25/content_5250134.htm.

United Nations Human Settlements Programme (UN Habitat). "Global Public Space Toolkit: From Global Principles to Local Policies and Practice." Accessed June 3, 2020. https://unhabitat.org/global-public-space-toolkit-from-global-principles-to-local-policies-and-practice.

Wang, Meiqin. *Socially Engaged Participatory Art Practice in Contemporary China: Voices from Below.* New York: Routledge, 2019.

West Bund. "District Overview." Accessed May 5, 2020. http://www.westbund.com/en/index/ABOUT-WEST-BUND/Area-Overview/District-Overview.html.

West Bund. "Industry Landscape." Accessed May 5, 2020. http://www.westbund.com/en/index/ABOUT-WEST-BUND/Industry-Outline/Industry-Landscape.html.

West Bund. "West Bund History." Accessed May 2, 2020. http://www.westbund.com/en/index/ABOUT-WEST-BUND/History/West-Bund-History.html.

Chapter 4

Creative frontiers: Germany's Ruhr area as a space of polyrational possibility

Hanna Rodewald

TU Dortmund University, Germany

Abstract

From the transatlantic perspective of an American Studies scholar, Rodewald's analysis is on how processes of creative urban renewal in the German Ruhr Area are scripted through the American frontier narrative. Her comparative reading between its American origin and its application in matters of post-industrial redevelopment in cities of the Ruhr works out the complex implications of this myth for processes of urban change. As a polycentric region of post-industrial cities and smaller towns, the Ruhr Area functions as a case study to illustrate how frontier qualities of progress and future-oriented transformation are applied to further economic, spatial and sociocultural advancement. With examples from fields ranging from art to city marketing or urban planning, this chapter illustrates the ambivalent impact of frontier imagery and its promise for creative re-imagination of the status quo. Its use may result in tendencies of gentrification and displacement or a more inclusive approach to city planning which understands the frontier as a mental and spatial space of possibility. In its analysis of the symbolism of the urban frontier in the Ruhr Area, this chapter discusses aspects of both ex- and inclusive social life as well as the collective re-imagination of its post-industrial environment.

Keywords: frontier, Frederick Jackson Turner, urban pioneers, Ruhr Area, post-industrial, creative renewal, gentrification, displacement, urban transformation, space of possibility

***

Introduction

Located in the German state of North Rhine-Westphalia, the Ruhr Area is one of the largest metropolitan areas and economic clusters in Europe. Named after the river Ruhr, which makes up its southern border, the Ruhr Area is home to around five million people in a polycentric conglomeration of cities and smaller towns. This fairly unique settlement pattern resulted from a long history of individual townships that then developed into an economically interdependent network of industrial centers. Today, the larger cities of the Ruhr Area, such as Dortmund, Essen, Bochum, or Duisburg, look back on an image-defining industrial legacy in coal mining and steel production. Since the 1950s, processes of de-industrialization have, however, led to massive job losses, economic decline, and urban shrinkage. Cities going through such forms of structural change have had to adapt to the physical and sociological imprints of their industrial past. Within the urban landscape, a feeling of loss does not only constitute itself architecturally through the abandonment or even demolition of many built structures but was also felt psychologically as a loss of identity, meaning and a sense of self. Former narratives of growth and industrial power were challenged by the severe and long-lasting effects of the post-industrial age.[1] Today the entire region is working towards new economic foundations as well as a cultural redefinition.

With the loss of their life-line industries of steel, coal, and automotive production, as well as the consequences for its landscape and people, post-industrial cities have been and still are undergoing radical processes of urban transformation.[2] The challenge for cities such as Dortmund or Essen, the two major urban centers, is twofold. The first is that they need to find a new economic footing, which has already progressed with technology and logistics companies settling in the area and an official top-down push for the so-called knowledge economy. The region's social structure, however, is until this day influenced by its working class and migration history. The potential dissonance between the traditional inhabitants of the Ruhr Area and the economic direction the region is heading in necessitates the second part of the challenge: Cities of the post-industrial Ruhr region need to create new stories and narratives for an urban re-imagination that builds on representations of the past, that also acknowledges the present and imagines the future. One of the "great promises of narrative forms," Julia Sattler argues, is that they enable us to "play with different possibilities of re-writing, re-configuring, re-inhabiting, and constructing possible futures in a transforming place."[3]

Stories as means of identity formation and cultural expression are therefore an integral part of the ongoing transformative processes and negotiation of meaning in urban frameworks. Through its spatial confinement and the diversity of inhabitants, urban landscapes contain multitudes of stories which consequently shape "inchoate and contradictory cultural processes."[4] Urban narrations are produced and received through various perspectives that depend on issues of class, race, gender, ability, and age. Such complex ensembles of stories consequently result in spatial concepts that are non-linear and multidirectional.[5] As a means of narrating processes of urban transformation, the metaphor of the American frontier has become prevalent in strategies of urban development and city marketing even outside of the United States. The conceptualization of the frontier myth shifted from its original nineteenth-century context of America's westward expansion to a label of distinctly urban phenomenon. Since the 1960s the metaphor of the urban frontier has been utilized to describe attempts to overcome challenges of urban decline and rhetorically push for social progress. More recently, this iconic language has also been applied to cityscapes outside the US as an indicator for innovation and approaches to creative problem-solving.

In various forms of implementation, it has found its way into discussions of post-industrial restructuring in Germany's Ruhr Area. As an area of immense urban transformation due to its deindustrialization, the Ruhr Area in Germany's mid-west seems to be well suited to profit from the inherently creative drive of the frontier narrative. The future-oriented and innovative power for re-imagination of the frontier consequently plays a significant role in reinventing and restructuring de-industrializing cities of this area. The implications of the use of urban frontier logic may imply contradictory outcomes. In the process of current redevelopment strategies of the creative city, the competition for the so-called creative urban pioneers often leads to gentrification, social exclusion, and displacement. At the same time, the narrative framing of the post-industrial urban landscape as having frontier like qualities, can result in innovative and inclusive planning strategies. Consequently, in its analysis of the metaphorical application of the urban frontier in the Ruhr Area, this chapter discusses aspects of both exclusive and inclusive social city life as well as the collective re-imagination of the built environment. From the transatlantic perspective of a German American Studies scholar, I investigate the American frontier as a reoccurring narrative and image used in descriptions of creative urban renewal.[6]

Since Frederick Jackson Turner's speech in 1893, his concept of the frontier has been a central topic not only in American culture but also in the field of American Studies as it has been continuously applied to describe spaces of transition. With its interdisciplinary perspective in the humanities, American Studies can play a pivotal part in analyzing these complex processes of post-industrial urban renewal and identity formation. Focusing on the use of the frontier as a cultural narrative, this analysis that uses the Ruhr Area as a case study in particular deploys the hermeneutic approach of critical cultural inquiry of stories and narratives, that aims to investigate and interpret meaning through textual and visual analysis, and close reading proposed by researchers such as Steph Lawler in her chapter on "Stories and the Social World."[7] After tracing the genealogy of the American origin of the frontier, the following text will touch upon different interpretations of the frontier within city planning, through a comparative reading between its American origin and its application in matters of urban renewal in Germany's Ruhr Area. This research draws on examples from city planning and marketing initiatives and also works of art, to provide an analysis of how the frontier metaphor may lead to urban displacement in creative city planning. The focus of this research counter-argues how the frontier metaphor can equally enable inherently creative spaces of polyrational possibility in Germany's Ruhr region.

The American frontier

In 1893, Frederick Jackson Turner formulated the narrative and metaphorical qualities of the frontier with regard to the settlement of the American West. In his seminal speech, "The Significance of the Frontier in American History," the American historian argued that the settlement was not tied to a specific place or border, but that it instead represented an ever evolving and continually advancing space of development. At "the meeting point between savagery and civilization," as Turner puts it, the frontier created spaces of intervention and ultimately transformed old European conventions into a distinctly American character.[8] Turner describes the frontier's transformative energy as essentially creative when he argues that every pioneer "[e]ven as he dwelt among the stumps of his newly cut clearing, [...] had the creative vision of a new order of society."[9] The American frontier for Turner is an ever-evolving process of cultural intervention shaped by innovative human activity. He consequently predicts that the frontier's creative power of continuous innovation will become an inherent quality of the American character and beneficial for future challenges, when he states:

> [i]n place of old frontiers of wilderness, there are new frontiers of un-won fields of science, fruitful for the needs of the race; there are frontiers of better social domains yet unexplored. Let us hold to our attitude of faith and courage, and creative zeal.[10]

Turner predicts the continued relevance of the individual right to personal opportunity and social democracy.[11] The narrative of the uncharted frontier as a non-defined space for creative re-imagination continuously reappears throughout American history. The philosopher and social critic John Dewey advocated its democratic trajectory as did President John F. Kennedy with his "New Frontier" policy for American cities in the early 1960s. Dewey and Kennedy argued that it had to be recognized as the constant challenge of finding solutions to newly evolving problems. On this basis, when thinking about the future, the frontier became a metaphor for the continuous flow of innovation and social advancement. This approach can be also applied to struggling post-industrial cities today.

Amidst these positive collective as well as individual developments through the frontier, however, the colonizing effects on the indigenous population of the North American continent must be emphasized. It is not surprising that this caveat also applied to its use in modern, urban environments. With regard to the urban frontier, Neil Smith claims that the "term 'urban pioneer' is therefore as arrogant as the original notion of 'pioneers' in that it suggests a city not yet socially inhabited; like Native Americans, the urban working class is seen as less than social, a part of the physical environment."[12] The frontier as a physical and mental space of transition and intervention can result in positive creative progress but also initiate displacement and social exclusion. These complex and ambivalent notions of the frontier narrative can be traced in its applications in the Ruhr Area. As spaces in need of redefinition, post-industrial cities, which have lost their lifeline industries, draw on the frontier narrative for their urban renewal strategies.

The post-industrial frontier

The urban frontier and its symbolic Wild West imagery have emerged in city planning around the globe. In this vein, the European research group Urban Catalyst (2001-2003) has proposed the German term *Raumpioniere*, which they translate as Space Pioneers, in order to describe the positive impact of temporary uses of brownfields.[13] Vast planes of abandoned places and decaying industrial sites were formerly considered problematic and an anathema to the city. These are now scripted as frontier-like spaces entailing creative potential for cultural and economic (re)discovery. The Cultural and Racial Studies scholar, Rebecca Kinney proposes that cities, such as Detroit, have to be framed as postindustrial frontier spaces, in order to "construct the deficiency of the city as changeable. Its problems are thus essential for this narrative, as long as they can be framed as fixable."[14] As a result, Detroit's "landscape of fear shifts to a landscape of possibility."[15]

The cities of Germany's polycentric urban Ruhr region, which was a former powerhouse of coal and steel production, have been heavily invested in finding new meaning and creating new common identities through aspects of the frontier narrative. The International Architecture Exhibition Emscher Park (1989-1999), and the European Capital of Culture (2010) represent only some of the more recent, large-scale attempts to collectively re-imagine and re-appropriate the Ruhr Area. In Spring 2021 the town of Wanne re-branded the empty space of its abandoned properties as a luxurious opportunity for creative spatial and cultural reinvention (*Freiraumluxus*) and as a machine to collect potential (*Potentialsammelmaschine*).[16] In cities of the Ruhr, planning propositions and marketing strategies for a more creative city often narrate their stories of change with the help of the visionary potential of the frontier narrative. Especially in relation to artistic work, this narrative framing stimulates to rethink possibilities of new land use.

Art and its ability to challenge the status quo can help to open up the discussion of the re-use and re-shaping of post-industrial places that might appear forgotten and stuck in time. Christoph Dettmeier's photographic collage series titled Ghostrider (2000-2004) represents such an attempt of artistic renegotiation. In his photos, dark silhouetted cowboys roam the vast wastelands of the deindustrialized Ruhr Valley. On horseback, they appear to search for new opportunities and personal freedom. Dettmeier presents these non-specified places of the Ruhr Region in black and white. Except for the lonely cowboy figures, the scenery seems deserted of any human life which offers a surreal mood of emptiness. There is an absence of any city-ness or human activity. These photographic images refer to the long tradition of American landscape paintings of the Hudson River School or later photographic works by artists like Ansel Adams, which depicted frontier moments of sublime wilderness. What these frontier representations have in common is that they suggest a (re)appropriation of the land shown. But while painters such as Alfred Bierstadt or Thomas Cole depict scenes of supposedly untouched nature, Dettmeier's landscapes are reminiscent of their industrial past. Simultaneously, his Western aesthetic also initiates visions of possible futures that are still to come. Directly connected to Kinney's argument, Jörg Heiser writes about Dettmeier's works, "[r]ather than a way of embellishing existing conditions, the Western myths are a mask, a step towards abstraction that allows existing conditions to be viewed in the first place."[17] In fact, this photographic series seems to engage the viewer to ask whether these spaces have ever been empty or free of meaning? What can one make of their industrial past?

Figure 4.1 Ghostrider, 2002, photocollage. Image Credit: Christoph Dettmeier ©

The first two pages of Ralf Schlüter's article for *Art* magazine from 2010 (see figure 4.2), published in an edition celebrating the Ruhr Area becoming that year's European Capital of Culture, illustrate the urge for reinvention through the metaphoric imagery of the frontier as well as its tendency to omit people and previous meanings from portrayals. Jo Röttger's photograph of the (post-) industrial landscape taken from Essen's Schurenbachhalde represents the Ruhr Valley as a deserted, desolate and bleak landscape. The only sign of human activity are power poles and factory chimneys that pierce the horizon. The foreground shows Richard Serra's rusty sculpture, *Bramme für das Ruhrgebiet* (1998), which has been partly painted over by graffiti. The combination of the photo and the article's allusive title "Der wilde Westen" ("The Wild West"), suggests that within this dull scenery the possibility of reinvention through art, culture and creativity is possible. Alluding to both the American frontier narrative as well as the region's geographical location in the West of Germany, the title plays with the idea that this region displays a rough wilderness both in its landscape and its unusual ideas. By deliberately showing what can be perceived as the deficiencies and the supposed ugliness of this region, the author proposes a landscape of possibility and makes an argument for the need of cultural reinvention. Germany's "Wild West" seems to forebode the formation of a new identity, which succeeds in representing its dusty image of coal and steel production.[18] This equally implies the hope for an economic revitalization of the region, which in turn presents the danger of a commodification of art and culture and puts a heavy burden of economic responsibility onto the creative sector.

Figure 4.2 Schlüter, Ralf. "Der Wilde Westen." *Art* magazine, Feb. 2010, 18-19.
Image Credit: Jo Röttger ©

The two urban development concepts *Claiming Land* (2002-2006) and *Land For Free* (2007-2010) both brought forth by the same collective of artists and city planners (Stefanie Bremer, Dirk E. Haas, Boris Sieverts et al.) address similar questions of repurposing of land and experimental re-imagination scripted through frontier imaginaries. Set in Liverpool and Manchester, two deindustrialized cities in the northeast of England, *Claiming Land* was an initiative in the research project Shrinking Cities. In reference to Thomas Pynchon's novel, *Mason and Dixon*, the project proposed "a 'pioneer-city' which offers new options for usage and ways of living within the empty spaces, thus resulting in a new regional context/connection" between the two cities.[19] With the use of cartography, fictional scenarios of land acquisition and cultural reinterpretation ideas were generated that worked in opposition to the long-standing history of these cities' industrial past.

In the context of the Ruhr Capital of Culture in 2010, *Land For Free* succeeded its British predecessor in offering individual plots of land to applicants with innovative ideas for its use. Geographically located on a 11 sq. m. large island between the river Emscher and the Rhine-Herne canal the project aimed for collective and innovative forms of post-industrial reconfiguration. The frontier character of this project was twofold: in addition to the spatial aspects of periphery, the theoretical laws of planning and aesthetics were equally questioned.[20] The staging of the land as being free of cost questioned prevailing ideas about space as commodity and critiqued the logic of the real estate market. Free of these restrictive regulations, *Land For Free* handed out plots of land in exchange for ideas in order to promote the acceptance of uncertainty and openness within the planning process.

These artistic and open-ended negotiations of post-industrial land use, which apply the frontier metaphor to urban development, can also result in a rather one-sided approach to creative innovation, which ultimately focuses on economic growth. Since the turn of the millennium, ideas about the creative city by Charles Landry (2000) or Richard Florida (2002) have greatly influenced the restructuring of post-industrial cities. In his book *The Rise of the Creative Class*, Florida himself makes use of the frontier metaphor when he asserts "[t]he service sector is the last frontier of innovation in our economy [...]. Creativity is our most precious resource; we can't afford to waste it in any sector of the economy."[21] The promise of revitalization through creativity encourages cities to develop strategies to compete for the creative class in order to raise their economic value and facilitate desired processes of urban change. This year's *Summer of Pioneers* campaign in the small town of Altena, a former industrial city just outside the Ruhr area, clearly follows such an approach as the city aims to attract 20 location-independent workers from the digital or creative economy in order to raise the city's location factor.[22] Frontier characteristics such as a strong notion of personal freedom and the promise of institutional deregulation further such a neoliberal understanding. What has since resulted is a global "war for talent," a term coined by McKinsey & Company in 1998, identifying how economic drivers have impacted concepts of creativity and innovation.[23] The impact has led to the commodification of creativity and the instrumentalization of art and culture as marketable location factors.[24]

When creative city marketing strategies were adopted in Dortmund in 2010 by the city administration, it re-named the neighborhood around the formerly industrial area along the Rheinische Straße as Unionviertel meaning Union quarter. This re-branding strategy identified the Unionviertel as Dortmund's creative quarter. As a result, in 2018, the *Konter City Guide* sponsored by Ruhr Tourism, which highlights hip places throughout the Ruhr Area, claimed the Unionviertel to have a frontier like "air of adventure" which needed to be discovered and explored.[25] With sentences including "[w]e just cannot guarantee what there is to discover," the Unionviertel is staged as being in a state of (economic) unpredictability, which promises the excitement of urban exploration and the possibility of finding something new or forgotten.[26] The heading of this advertising tourist guide lyrically reads "The Awakening of a Sleeping Beauty," which equally underlines the claim that this neighborhood holds an incredible potential, which is about to be brought back to light.[27] It implies that the neighborhood used to be striving before but fell into an immobile state of economic and cultural paralysis. Following the obvious fairytale allusion, the Unionviertel has just recently been kissed awake by a noble prince who is leading it into a bright future. Apparently only a newcomer to this neighborhood can bring out its full potential. This plays right into a claim by urban consultant Richard Florida for the need of the creative class and their young and fresh projects which will revive stagnating neighborhoods.[28] The danger of displacement however, of what has been there all along, asleep or not, seems not be of any concern.

With regard to urban strategies of gentrification, geographer Neil Smith criticizes the exclusionary notion of the frontier logic. In *The New Urban Frontier: Gentrification and the Revanchist City* (1996), Smith states, "the frontier ideology rationalizes social differentiation and exclusion as natural, inevitable. The poor and working class are all too easily defined as 'uncivil,' on the wrong side of a heroic dividing line, as savages and communists."[29] For Smith the frontier is "a style as much as a place."[30] A style that in this case favors a neoliberal ideology of economic profitability and rising real estate values. According to Smith, social conflict is thus displaced "into the realm of myth,

[...] to reaffirm a set of class-specific and race-specific social norms."[31] Similarly to the American settlement era, the application of frontier qualities to cities can be highly problematic. Such a framework often fails to consider that this land has long held both human activity and cultural meaning. Both spatially and mentally, the concept of the frontier is still highly ambivalent, since it always entails processes of intervention and transformation of present circumstances. The frontier language and its implications of its creative energies can be used to describe processes that may lead to entirely opposite outcomes. The urban fabric can either become more socially inclusive or rather quite exclusionary in nature.

The narrative framing of the old and already existing structures as problematic wastelands in need of reinvention may reduce the metaphor of the frontier to one simple argument. Although deindustrialized spaces might appear free of use, they are still assigned with diverse cultural and historical meaning. As Smith has demonstrated, strategies of gentrification and creative city development therefore often result in displacement and social exclusion of marginalized groups. The inclusion of native people who inhabit or are at least emotionally attached to these spaces is thus essential in order to unfold the full creative potential. The creative qualities of the frontier should result in the opportunity for all members of society to take part in processes of urban transformation and to contribute their wishes and needs. In terms of the reconstruction of post-industrial urban landscapes, the creative quality of the frontier can be understood solely economically, but it can also encompass social inclusion and political participation.

The polyrational frontier

The urban planner Benjamin Davy regards the one-sided interpretations of the frontier, which only emphasize a dominant culture, as monorational approaches to the city. Anything that is not in agreement with the dominant way of thinking or planning tends to be neglected. Through the frontier motif, cities however, can come to reflect the complex diversity of their inhabitants through *polyrational* urban planning strategies. In order for city planning to become more inclusive and equitable, he posits the ability to open up to the sometimes-overwhelming complexity of the city. "In the metropolis, everything mixes with everything," he states, "[y]et rarely do we acknowledge the paradox, the irony, the hybrid, the contradiction."[32] What is already evident in the American frontier is that zones of contact and transition always bear confrontations of the new and existing culture. These confrontations engender new ideas and practices and thus new values and identities. In contrast to monorational frontiers, Davy's polyrational frontier results in a truly interactive figure of thought that accounts for the socio-cultural diversity of cities. It entails working with multiple and sometimes conflicting forces from diverse backgrounds. This ultimately leads to the creative coexistence of varying identities which will reflect heterogeneous and complex urban territories. Davy argues that the inclusion of many voices and minds in the re-imagination of a places can lead to productive but oftentimes rather uncomfortable "contradiction and dispute."[33] In this way, urban development becomes more just, flexible and sustainable for future challenges.

Figure 4.3 Former industrial production site of Hoesch in Dortmund, 08.07.2020. Image Credit: Hanna Rodewald ©

The formerly industrial area of the Hoesch Spundwand und Profil GmbH (HSP), which is situated at the northern border of Dortmund's Unionviertel, illustrates the potential of polyrational, creative planning. Originally part of the Dortmunder Union (a mining, iron and steel company), steel walls were produced at this site since 1902. On 17 December 2015 the industrial site, then owned by the Salzgitter AG, closed. In 2016, the real estate company Thelen Holding GmbH bought the 45-hectare area and has since fenced it off from the general public. The area has been abandoned and decaying for several years. Over roughly five years, this postindustrial site has developed into urban wasteland, what Davy might call a petrified space, that is open for creative reinvention. Since its closing, die Urbanisten, an NGO invested in urban development, participation, and sustainability, has collected ideas and future visions for the possible short and long-term reutilization of this vast unused area under the project title *Neue Werk Union*. In reference to the work of Urban Catalyst, they have advertised their project to any type of *Raumpioniere* interested in a strategic staging of a frontier situation. In their attempt of frontier management, they held conferences, invited artists and had multiple open meetings all under the premise of publicly discussing the possibilities of this space and making urban development open for everyone.[34] Their approach brings a staging of the creative frontier and its polyrational possibilities into practice, as they intend to move

> away from classic participation processes and pursue the goals of an innovative planning culture. This is inclusive, grows slowly, integrates

local knowledge in the neighborhood, takes time for self-reflection, constantly rethinks alternatives, and is open to unexpected possibilities.[35]

Die Urbanisten clearly embrace Davy's strategy to plan for uncertainty by including many voices in the process of planning. The Thelen Group and Dortmund's city administration, 21 June 2018, introduced the official development plan under the title *Smart Rhino*.[36] The efforts of the *Neue Werk Union* were not necessarily manifested in this plan, as it did not include a distinct implementation of a creative frontier staging. The current city administration still advocates public involvement and civil participation for their urban vision.[37]

Conclusion: post-industrial frontiers of polyrational possibility

To tackle present and future challenges, the Ruhr area as one of Europe's most prominent postindustrial regions is working towards an economic, material, and image re-definition. This examination of some planning strategy has demonstrated that the language and imagery which accompanies urban design and marketing strategies oftentimes employs frontier imagery. Examples from different kinds of texts, ranging from magazine or marketing articles, to planning texts and critical reflections from urban planning and sociology, have revealed that these various texts might use the rhetoric and imagery of the frontier but interpret it with contradictory outcomes. Both strategies of urban displacement as well as postindustrial renewal through polyrational planning are told through the frontier narrative. Bringing these concepts together in the postindustrial cities of the Ruhr Area, I would like to propose a systematic investigation of the frontier narrative in a post-industrial setting, that offers a less commodified and more holistic approach to the creative urban (re)imagination. Similar to the case of stagnant urban structures *Land For Free*, has to be reevaluated for new purposes. Past values but also new possible visions are especially well detected by artistic investigation and curiosity. By productively transferring this special quality of creative frontier conditions to post-industrial cities, it is important to recognize its sense of *polyrational possibility*, of a constant process of creative reinvention through artistic and democratic forces. This, in turn, implies a radical openness for dialogue and debate of all stakeholders involved as well as the acceptance for a continuous negotiation between the self and the other.

The reflections about modern creative thinking through the metaphor of the frontier, present a new approach to urban planning and place making. It furthers the acceptance that things cannot be planned and defined for eternity. In fact, while the city is in a constant state of flux, urban planning has to facilitate ongoing re-interpretation of conflicting future visions. This means that planners and policy makers have to plan cities with the possibility for uncertainty. As the city is in a constant state of becoming, it is also in need of continuous reinterpretation. The polyrational frontier of possibility is thus an integral part of urban complexity. What has been shown through the example of the Ruhr Area can consequently be exemplary for other urban spaces facing similar challenges. As a metaphor, the frontier aids to think about creative urban reinvention which is not only in favor of economic growth but that tries to factor in the plural and diverse hopes, dreams and needs of many city dwellers.

Bibliography

Bremer, Stefanie, Boris Sieverts, Dirk E. Haas, Päivi Kataikko, Henrik Sander, and Andreas S. Baeing. "Claiming Land, Manchester/Liverpool." *Shrinking Cities.* Accessed May 7, 2021. http://www.shrinkingcities.com/projekte2.0.html

Buchenau, Barbara, and Jens Martin Gurr. "City Scripts Urban American Studies and the Conjunction of Textual Strategies and Spatial Processes." In *Urban Transformations in the U.S.A: Spaces, Communities, Representations.* Edited by Julia Sattler, 395-420. Bielefeld: Transcript Verlag, 2016.

Büros für Städtereisen. "Land For Free." 2007-2010. Accessed May 2021. http://landforfree.blogsport.de/category/about

Davy, Benjamin. "Plan It Without a Condom!" *Planning Theory* 7, no. 3 (2008): 301-317. https://doi.org/10.1177/1473095208096885

Florida, Richard. *The Rise Of The Creative Class, Revisited.* New York: Basic Books, 2011.

Grünzweig, Walter. "Parasitic Simulacrum. Ralph Waldo Emerson, Richard Florida, and the Urban 'Creative Class'." In Urban Transformations in the USA: *Spaces, Communities, Representations.* Edited by Julia Sattler, 83-97. Bielefeld: Transcript Verlag, 2016.

Hankin, Steven, E.G. Chambers, Mark Foulon, Helen Handfield-Jones, and Edward G. Michaels. "The War for Talent." *McKinsey Quarterly* 3, no. 3 (January 1998): 44-57.

Heiser, Jörg. "Speaking through Masks." In *Christoph Dettmeier: Waitin' Around to Die.* Edited by Oliver Zybok, 29-35. Berlin: Hatje Cantz, 2010.

Kinney, Rebecca J. *Beautiful Wasteland: The Rise of Detroit as America's Postindustrial Frontier.* Minneapolis: University of Minnesota Press, 2016.

Krebs, Stefanie. "Landschaften der Piraterie - Eine Ästhetik des Habhaftwerdens." 2007. Accessed May 2021. https://boku.ac.at/rali/ila/veranstaltungen-des-ila/archiv-veranstaltungen/lx-landschaft-denken/l2-24052007/stefanie-krebs

Lawler, Steph. "Stories and the Social World." In *Research Methods for Cultural Studies,* edited by Michael Pickering and Gabriele Griffin, 32-49. Edinburgh: Edinburgh University Press, 2008.

Molotch, Harvey. "The City as a Growth Machine: Toward a Political Economy of Place." *American Journal of Sociology* 82, no. 2 (1976): 309-332.

Neumann, Tracy. *Remaking the Rust Belt: The Postindustrial Transformation of North America.* Philadelphia: University of Pennsylvania Press, 2016.

Ruhrgestalten. *Konter - Free City Guide for Ruhr Area Travel.* Edited by Florian Kolominski, 24-36. Oberhausen: Ruhr Tourismus, 2018.

Sattler, Julia. "Narratives of Urban Transformation Reading the Rust Belt in the Ruhr Valley." In *Urban Transformations in the U.S.A: Spaces, Communities, Representations*, by Julia Sattler, 11-26. Bielefeld: Transcript Verlag, 2016.

Schlüter, Ralf. "Der Wilde Westen." *Art Magazine* (February 2010): 18-27.

Senatsverwaltung für Stadtentwicklung. *Urban Pioneers - Stadtentwicklung durch Zwischennutzung in Berlin*, 36-48. Berlin: Jovis, 2007.

Smith, Neil. *The New Urban Frontier: Gentrification and the Revanchist City*. London: Routledge, 2005.

Stadt Altena. "Summer of Pioneers." Accessed May 05, 2021. https://altena-pioneers.de

Stadt Dortmund. "Mit Wirkung bei der Quartiersentwicklung von Smart Rhino." Accessed February 28, 2021. https://www.dortmund.de/de/leben_in _dortmund/planen_bauen_wohnen/stadtplanungs_und_bauordnungsamt/ nachrichten_spboamt/detailseiten_spboamt.jsp?nid=630144.html

Stadt Wanne. "Freiraumluxus für Kreative: Eine Potentialsammelmaschine für Wanne." Accessed May 07, 2020. https://www.freiraumluxus.de

Thelen Group. "Smart Rhino." Accessed February 28, 2021. https://www.thelen-gruppe.com/portfolio/projekt/smart-rhino/.html

Turner, Frederick J. *The Frontier in American History*. New York: H. Holt and Company, 1920.

Urbanisten. "Neue Werk Union." Accessed February 28, 2021. https://dieurbanisten. de/urbanisten-projekt/kreative-stadtentwicklung-auf-dem-ehem-hsp-areal/.html

Chapter 5

Power relations in industrial land redevelopment and loss of industrial heritage in Chongqing, China

Jie Chen

Tongji University, China

Yiming Wang

Tongji University, China

Abstract

Since the 2000s, redeveloping the deteriorating industrial land occupied by state-owned enterprises in prime urban locations has been an urgent task for the Chongqing authorities. This redevelopment strategy has converted former industrial sites into residential, commercial, and new industrial spaces, but meanwhile brought about the loss of industrial architectural character in Chongqing. This raises a fundamental question about the reasons driving the negative reality of industrial landscapes. The Chongqing Steel Factory redevelopment project provides the ideal opportunity to examine it as a case study in reference to the issue of power structures in industrial land redevelopment and their impacts on industrial heritage conservation. It argues that the loss of industrial heritage in Chongqing is not just simply attributable to the pursuit of the state-capital coalition for land values but also shaped by the missing cultural power of local grass-roots heritage voices in demanding to retain the historic industrial buildings.

Keywords: Industrial heritage, adaptive reuse, industrial land redevelopment, power relations, Chongqing

***

Introduction

Chongqing is the largest city in inland China, with a population of over 31 million, 28.7% more than Shanghai, and an administrative scope area of over 82,400 square kilometers, nearly 13 times bigger than Shanghai in 2018.[1] Given that the land available for new construction in Chongqing has nearly been exhausted with rapid urbanization, land redevelopment has been adopted as a new strategy of urban development. Chongqing's industrial land has occupied prime urban location, however possessed increasing land-related problems such as inefficient land use, low output value and outdated urban functional structures. The transformation of the deteriorating industrial land has therefore become an essential part of land redevelopment in Chongqing. Yet it is worth noting that the process of redevelopment has brought about the demolition of old industrial buildings at an unprecedented scale.[2] This raises a fundamental question about the reasons driving the negative reality of industrial landscapes. For this reason, the Chongqing Steel Factory (CSF) redevelopment project provides the ideal opportunity to examine it as a case study in reference to the issue of power structures in industrial land redevelopment and their impacts on industrial heritage conservation. The research methods are semi-structured interviews, documental analysis and popular media review. This research follows a social city approach in that it addresses the concerns of the overwhelming power of the state-capital coalition for extracting economic values and the negligible voice of the grass-roots group for retaining heritage values in China's industrial land redevelopment projects.

For people outside China, Chongqing is an "invisible world-scale megalopolis."[3] The opening-up policy sets the coastal cities such as Shanghai, Guangzhou and Shenzhen as the primary bridges connecting China and the global market since 1978. On the contrary, the inland Chinese cities, including Chongqing, much less internationally-connected than the coastal counterparts, have lagged behind the Chinese leading cities in terms of economic development. Although Chongqing has contributed less to China's economic growth, this city has played a significant role in China's industrial development. As one of the earliest industrial cities in west China, Chongqing's industrial development history spans the treaty port period (1891-1936), the wartime period (1937-1949), the post-war period (1950-1962), the "Three Fronts" (*san xian*, in Chinese) regionalization period (1963-1977) and the reform period (1978-present).[4] Physically, Chongqing is a mountainous city located between mountains and rivers. This unique geographic defense advantage makes Chongqing a natural shelter in wartime. During the Second Sino-Japanese War (1937-1945) and the civil war (1946-1949) when the Nationalist government moved westward and made Chongqing the wartime capital of China, Chongqing quickly developed from a regional city in the southwest to a national political, economic and cultural center.

Following the establishment of the People's Republic of China in 1949, Chongqing's industry continued to develop according to socialist production policies aiming at transforming the consumption city into a production city. The city experienced a second industrial expansion between 1963 and 1977, under a policy of the "Three Fronts" regionalization – that is a regional scheme for the allocation of military-industrial resource from the eastern regions to the inland areas for the sake of national defense.[5] The central government moved the defense-related state-owned enterprises (SOEs) from the eastern regions to Chongqing and allocated 118 industrial projects and 243 enterprises to the city. Since the 1990s, a regional development strategy of opening up the West (*xi bu da kai fa*) was carried out in order to transfer the development focus from the coastal areas to inland regions.[6] Chongqing, as the forefront of this development strategy, was designated as the only municipality city in inland China in 1997, directly under the central government, possessing the same city status with the three other municipalities of Shanghai, Beijing and Tianjin. By seizing this development opportunity, Chongqing has been transformed into a growth pole in southwest China and an anchor to link the eastern region with western China.[7]

The following two decades saw the traditional industries in Chongqing's SOEs go into decline. Since the 2000s, due to the market-oriented SOE reform, most SOEs in Chongqing have been facing increasing problems such as inefficient production, outdated technology, and financial shortage, and then following a similar dilemma of bankruptcy, mergers, and reorganization (*guan ting bing zhuan*). The change in the land use system offered an opportunity for SOEs to capitalize on their fixed real estate assets in prime urban location by transforming the industrial land into a high-value land use, and then, transferring the land use rights to property developers.[8] This new redevelopment strategy has converted former urban industrial sites to residential, commercial, and new industrial spaces, but meanwhile, brought about the loss of industrial architectural character in urban Chongqing. With empirical evidence in the CSF case, this research argues unequal power relations between the state-capital coalition and the grass-roots heritage voice as the root cause for the disappearance of industrial heritage in Chongqing. This chapter consists of four sections. Following the introductory section, Section 2 outlines a theoretical approach by discussing the contribution of power relations to the production of space, and critiques existing literature on China's industrial land redevelopment. Section 3 investigates the power structure among the stakeholders by assessing the leading actors as well as their different roles and interests, reviews the planning process during 2008 and 2016, and reveals the reasons for the loss of industrial heritage in the

CSF case. Section 4 summarizes the study and discusses the implication for the practice arena.

Developing the theoretical approach of power relations

This section offers a sociological approach which looks at the contribution of power relations to the production of the space. David Harvey regards the ability to influence the production of space as an important means of social power and explains that power relations are always implicated in spatial and temporal practices.[9] The domination and control of space reflects how a wide range of powerful actors with different objectives and agendas interact. For Harvey, primary attention needs to be placed on the economic power of capital investors and the political power of state regulations. First, money could be equated with "the social power of private persons," which "confers the privilege to exercise power over others" as financial power has triggered the rise of "new but equally oppressive geographical systems for the containerization of power," embedding the private property rights of capital investors in urban space.[10] Second, space has been organized in a systematic way helped by the exercise of state regulations.[11] Political power and economic power are fused into "a genuine political economy of overwhelming power relations."[12] Against the view that power over urban space is just financial or political, Sharon Zukin highlights that urban space is also shaped by the cultural power of the public, especially that of consumers' taste. Consumers' tastes play a crucial role in guiding how capital investors shape and reshape urban space, which trigger the growth and even evolution of new urban spaces. Zukin argues that "all of these factors now shape the struggle to control the city's future."[13]

Concepts of the political power of local government, economic power of capital investors and cultural power of the public are seen as important in interpreting industrial landscape restructuring in post-reform China. Firstly, the value of entrepreneurialism was introduced into China's urban governance in the late 1970s when a series of reforms on the exercise of authority were carried out. The Chinese government is no longer just a resources distributor, but instead has become a land manager and finally a more entrepreneurial type of marker actor.[14] Recent studies concerning urban conservation point out that the entrepreneurial endeavor of local governments, chiefly aimed at raising land values in urban redevelopment, has resulted in the commodification of heritage precincts.[15] Specifically, the state-sponsored effort that emphasizes the construction of the cultural heritage precinct is simply to attract investment, which has, to a large extent, neglected the development of a local grassroots artistic network.[16]

Secondly, the capital investor has benefited from the national reforms and accumulated considerable private wealth in post-reform China.[17] This social group in China have "deep pockets" through networking their capital with the government, as well as possessing the lifestyle characteristics of the nouveau riche, and being eager to affirm their social status and material wealth by means of consumption.[18] Taking Shanghai for example, the pursuit of distinctiveness through selectively authentic conservation by local capital investors is not aimed at benefiting artists exclusively; instead, these efforts are geared towards building up high value office stocks together with retailing and entertainment space.[19] Similar viewpoint also argues that regenerating Shanghai's industrial landscape as creative space only attracted large companies with greater economic strength while excluded small creative industry companies or individuals.[20] Another body of studies focused on the cultural groups especially local grass roots artist communities who spontaneously transformed the vacant workshops and warehouses into art districts in the Chinese eastern cities.[21] One notable case is Beijing's 798 Art District, developed from an unknown art village to an international art destination.[22]

The existing literature on China's industrial land redevelopment has mostly focused on the leading cities in East China, while empirical studies on West China are scarce. Interpretations focusing on eastern regions, however, cannot be directly applied to the situations of West China, since the socio-cultural and political-economic situations of the eastern cities differ from the inland regions. Compared with the eastern leading cities, inland regions have less middle-class population and fewer political resources such as privileged policies delivered by the central state, and thereby are less economically and culturally developed.[23] It is still unclear whether main actors in industrial land redevelopment projects in western China can be divided into similar categories of the local government, the capital investor and the cultural group, and whether the demolition of historic industrial buildings is driven by these stakeholders and their power network. It is therefore necessary to conduct an investigation in inland China to throw light on the above issues. This study addresses the aim by posing these questions: who are the key actors in the implementation process of industrial land redevelopment in Chongqing? What are the roles and interests of the key actors? How do the actors shape the actual physical results of industrial heritage conservation efforts in Chongqing?

Case study: the Chongqing Steel Factory redevelopment

As one of the earliest and biggest steelworks in Chongqing, the CSF was selected as the case due to its essential advantages, in terms of urban waterfront location and industrial historical value. As opposed to Chongqing's other steelworks with similar historical value, the CSF covered a substantial land area of 466 hectares and was located along the western bank of Yangtze River, as shown in figure 5.1. Formerly named as the Hanyang Iron Plant in Wuhan, it was established as the earliest government-funded steelworks by Zhang Zhidong, the governor of the Huguang Area in the late Qing Dynasty in the 1890s. The factory was relocated to Chongqing by the Chinese Nationalist Party in the Second Sino-Japanese War (1937-1945), renamed as the No. 29 Arsenal in 1940, and was changed to the Chongqing Steel Factory after 1949. In the following half century, under the socialist construction (*she hui zhu yi jian she*) policy and Chongqing's heavy-industry development orientation, the factory has experienced industrial growth and then has become Chongqing's largest steelworks. In 2006, the government authorities launched the CSF relocation and regeneration plan to make way for developing tertiary industry in the prime urban location that the factory previously occupied. The factory was moved from the Dadukou District to a new site in the Changshou District on the outskirts of Chongqing. Considering that the CSF had a cluster of industrial heritage from the 1890s to 2000s, the original industrial site was planned as a heritage precinct to showcase Chongqing's industrial development history. As the project proceeded, the CSF project gradually became dominated by high-value property development, and most industrial heritage was demolished for new redevelopment as a result.

Figure 5.1 The location of the Chongqing Steel Factory in urban Chongqing.
Image Credit: Authors ©

The investigation of the CSF project collected data from semi-structured interviews, popular press reviews and documentary analysis. Semi-structured interviews were conducted with 41 interviewees, including government officials from the Chongqing Municipal Government (CMG) and its planning department, the Chongqing Urban Planning Bureau (CUPB); the original factory owner, the Chongqing Steel Corporation (CSC); the government-established investment company and state-owned land banking agency, Chongqing Yufu Assets Management Corporation (Yufu); the property developer, Chongqing Industrial Museum Co., Ltd (CIMC); the participating design consultants, including Chongqing Urban Planning and Design Institute, Chongqing La Cime Corporation Canada Ekistics, Chongqing Planning Research Centre, CMCU Engineering Corporation, HMA Architects & Designers; as well as local artists and experts. The interviewees were coded as G for the government officials, D for the land banking agency and the property developer, F for the factory people, C for the design consultants, E for the experts and A for the artists. In addition, the planning and design proposals of the CSF project, as well as local media outlets, were accessed to obtain supplementary information.

Power forms of the key actors in the CSF redevelopment project

Based on an analysis of interview and supplementary data, the power relations among the key actor in the CSF case can be divided into the political power of local government, economic power of the capital investor and cultural power of the heritage group. Firstly, local government is one of the most significant actors in industrial land redevelopment. The major interests of the CMG were tackling the factory pollution problems, solving the factory relocation cost and helping the factory to restructure. Given the pollution problems of the inner-city factories and the continuation of the manufacturing function on the outskirts of Chongqing, the CMG announced a policy of suppressing secondary industry and developing tertiary industry (*tui er jin san*) and launched programs of environmental relocation (*huanbao banqian*) for 207 factories in urban Chongqing.[24] Characterized as "three heavies" - namely, "heavy industrial base, heavy chemical industry and heavy pollution," - the CSF was regarded as the major pollution source in urban Chongqing.[25] The cost of relocating the CSF and tackling the social problem of compensating the laid-off workers was up to 40 billion RMB. To deal with the CSF relocation task, the CMG has played a complex role - "in the game of land redevelopment, the Chongqing government is like a referee but also an athlete." [26] As the referee, the CMG encouraged the partnership between Yufu and CSC to solve the factory relocation, empowered CUPB to be the project supervisor and mediator, and formulated the planning guidelines and land index, such as development intensity, plot ratio, building density and greening rate, as the game rules for other actors. As the athlete, the CMG made Yufu and CUPB as its representatives, and let them directly participate in the decision-making process. With this dual identity, the CMG has actually maintained its political power on how the industrial land would be redeveloped in future.

Secondly, the capital investor, Yufu, with its funding power, was a direct actor in determining the future of the industrial sites in urban Chongqing. Yufu, as the land banking agency established by the CMG in 2004, has two goals released by the CMG: relocating the decaying factories and redeveloping the original industrial sites in Chongqing. Since the CMG did not interfere much with Yufu on specific strategies on industrial land redevelopment, Yufu had retained control on land reservation and improvement, investment, planning and designing, as well as land use rights transferring in the CSF redevelopment project. Together with the bank loans and self-raised funds, Yufu initially financed 7.5 billion RMB and further invested over 10 billion RMB to get the land use rights of the CSF from the CSC group. Such economic expenditure was expected to be covered by the land-related interests in transforming the old industrial land into a high-value residential and commercial use. Some parcels of industrial land in the CSF had been heavily polluted, which unsurprisingly, had increased the economic burden on Yufu. For Yufu, in face of the reality of the high costs resulting from the CSF relocation, the remediation of land contamination, and other costs in transferring land, obtaining a better economic return through transferring land to property developers in short time had to be prioritized.

Thirdly, people who supported heritage conservation in the CSF case include the Yufu Chairman, the Deputy Bureau Director in CUPB, as well as design consultants and local experts. Concern for industrial heritage conservation arose because of the personal interest and effort of the Yufu Chairman. CUPB also contributed to the familiarization with the concepts and principles of industrial heritage conservation. The design consultants regarded industrial heritage reuse as beneficial for promoting the CSC brand and creating its industrial culture; but surprisingly, the CSC was not interested in heritage conservation. Given the problems of inefficiency and shortage of capital for production, the factory could not compete with the productivity of other steelworks. The production of the factory only contributed three million tons per year while other steelworks accounted for more than ten million tons per year. In response of high relocation cost and urgent business problems, the CSC therefore prioritized the tasks of quickly clearing the factory property, recycling the old steel from the factory buildings into new uses which could save several million RMB, upgrading technology and increasing annual production to compete with other steelworks.

The process of the loss of industrial heritage in the CSF redevelopment project

The industrial heritage value in the CSF case was eroded through four stages, as reviewed from the CSF planning process during 2008 and 2016. In 2008, the Deputy Bureau Director in CUPB commissioned local experts to conduct the Chongqing Industrial Heritage Conservation Master Plan. Based on the criteria of culture, society, science and technology, local experts assessed each industrial building, grouped the industrial buildings and sites into three categories; and then provided suggestions on the three categories of heritage items. The CSF was classified in the first category as one of the most important industrial heritage sites, with suggestions that over fourteen industrial buildings and facilities be retained. Due to time limitations, the heritage conservation proposal was more like a general concept, which listed a broad range of industrial heritage items but lacked specific assessment and reuse strategies for different industrial sites.

The intention to retain historic industrial buildings in the former CSF site was officially presented by the then Yufu Chairman. The idea was not approved initially by Yufu. As the Chairman and his colleagues stated, most directors in Yufu thought that adaptive reuse of industrial heritage was not Yufu's mission.[27] Instead, the priority needed to be placed on paying back the debt through property development. Nonetheless, the Chairman persuaded Yufu to proceed with industrial heritage conservation by citing the successful case of Shanghai's Xintiandi, arguing that creating a high-quality heritage landscape would help promote property values. In 2008, Yufu launched an international bidding of the CSF urban design, with two goals included. The first was to promote land values to remedy the industrial decline brought about by the factory relocation, and the second, to adaptively reuse industrial heritage as a cultural precinct. Four joint design consultants participated in the bidding with Canada Ekistics Town Planning Inc and Chongqing La Cime Urban Landscape Design Corporation winning the bidding.

Since the urban design proposal lacked the force of law to form a legal document, a land use version was prepared based on the urban design guidelines in 2010. Commissioned and supervised by CUPB, the Chongqing Planning Research Centre was responsible for the land use proposal. There were two different versions regarding industrial heritage conservation in the land use proposal. Both proposals are analyzed about the extent to which historic structure and components have been retained. The version encouraged by CUPB was to retain the whole industrial layout which included the production line, the living quarters and the railway, and embraced twelve heritage items by following integrated heritage management. In contrast, Yufu preferred to reuse the Steel Milling Plant as the one key area, since the milling plant was spacious, suitable for conversion into an exhibition space, with various industrial facilities and included the municipal level heritage protection item No. 29 Arsenal. At the end of 2009, when CUPB and Yufu were still arguing for their own versions of heritage conservation, the CSC suspended its steel production and proceeded to relocate the factory. The Jiangong Group was hired by the CSC to clear the CSF site quickly, and most industrial buildings were demolished in a short time. The Yufu Chairman personally tried to retain some heritage items by discussing the issue with the CSC; as a result, only the Steel Milling Plant was retained and converted into a heritage precinct in the final land use plan.

During 2010 and 2016, Yufu's subordinate property development company CIMC proceeded to carry out the reuse of the steelworks. The company commissioned Avanti Architects, CMCU Engineering and HMA Architects & Designers, to undertake the master plan and the architectural design. Building upon the master plan by Avanti Architects in 2010, CMCU Engineering and HMA Architects & Designers took the project further by completing a detailed architectural design. The project was further affected by two suggestions from local government authorities. The first was to build a city cultural flagship as it could be used to showcase the government's achievement, while the second was more realistic, which was to control the scale of the heritage precinct and consider how to deal with the cost of long-term management and operation. Yufu and CIMC "made a compromise between the two key opinions." [28] The project function changed, therefore, from a public cultural precinct to a more mixed-use one that consisted of a public museum, a cultural industry cluster, a commercial complex and a tourist attraction, with a massive reduction of the scale of the public exhibition area from 26000 m^2 to 5000 m^2, and a decrease of the scale of the retained structure from eight structural bays to five.

Reasons for the loss of industrial heritage: unequal power relations in the decision-making process

The CSF development trajectory exemplifies the decision-making process of industrial land redevelopment in Chongqing. It reveals imbalanced power distribution between the state-capital coalition with interests in extracting economic value from industrial land redevelopment, and the grass-roots group with concerns on retaining cultural value from industrial heritage conservation. Decisions controlled by the state-capital coalition, that is formed by the political power of the local government (the CMG) and the economic power of the capital investor (Yufu), always favored profit-making uses. The first decision was to extract property values from waterfront industrial land redevelopment.

The CSF interfaces with 7.5 linear kilometers of the Yangtze River, yet most of the land had not been accessible to the public. For the CMG, improving the physical waterfront environment and recasting a new image for the former CSF site would help solve the problem of industry decline brought by the factory relocation, attract more investment and drive up the land price of the Dadukou District. A similar viewpoint was advanced in the interviews that branding with the theme of waterfront industrial heritage was a good selling point for Yufu. In this regard, Yufu's decision to reuse industrial heritage as a cultural precinct was just to contribute to potential property value. The staff member in Yufu stated:

> The job of Yufu is to sell land to the property developers. The Chongqing Steel Factory site is a wasteland with very poor public transport nearby, which is not beneficial for selling land. For us, it is better to have a theme we can use in selling land. Adaptive reuse of waterfront industrial heritage can be a good theme and would help promote the property's value.[29]

The second decision was to reduce the scale of industrial heritage conservation. For Yufu and the CMG, heritage conservation is a costly operation. First, the land parcels that the retained industrial heritage had taken up, could not be developed into high-rise blocks. Honoring the grid of the historical streetscape, to some degree, constrains the construction of new avenues and buildings. The layout of the surrounding land parcels would meld into the fabric of the industrial heritage items, and the new road system would follow the existing road network, thereby causing small, fragmented land parcels to emerge. These small parcels, however, would likely lose their desirability in the real estate market as new bulky apartment blocks and large commercial districts are not able to fit easily into small and fragmented parcels. In addition, new construction in the heritage area would be subject to design guidelines, requiring that the heritage items be honored and that new facades be visually compatible with the historical environment surrounding them. This requirement would apply to plot shapes, architecture styles, fire safety, building sizes and street width. Furthermore, the antiquated construction of industrial buildings made it difficult and costly to adapt them to current dwelling standards and contemporary fire regulations. Although the Yufu Chairman and the director in CUPB personally appreciate the value of industrial heritage, considering the potential high cost of industrial heritage reuse, it became inevitable that the many unique industrial heritage items were demolished to make way for successful property development in the CSF case.

The very limited cultural power of the grass-roots heritage interests in the CSF case was reflected by loose planning guidelines on heritage conservation, the missing public voices in decision making, as well as the absence of local precedents and a supportive creative class. Firstly, a heritage assessment body is of great importance in effectively implementing the idea of industrial heritage reuse. The assessment work should be done before the factory removal, so that "the most valuable industrial heritage could be outlined and retained with a protection order."[30] Local heritage specialists, nevertheless, were not invited to conduct an assessment of the industrial heritage items in the CSF project. Only local planning experts were involved in offering advice on industrial heritage conservation. These expert opinions differed, which could not serve to provide a strict compulsory protection standard. In addition, according to the interview, the participating design consultants stated that since their client, Yufu, insisted on prioritizing property development, they had to provide design service tipping towards financial considerations.[31] The urban designers admitted that they proposed to keep more heritage items than in initial plans. Acknowledging it would greatly influence the commercial property development potential, the design team compromised by retaining a small area of industrial heritage in order to win the bidding.

Secondly, the CSF case included no public voices in decision making, although most interviewees highlighted the importance of the role of ordinary people in promoting the public visibility of the retained industrial heritage and offering public support for heritage conservation. The government official stated that "if ordinary people cared about the value of industrial heritage, then conversely, it could encourage the government to pay more attention to industrial heritage."[32] Besides, Chongqing lacks successful precedents of industrial heritage conservation, such as creative industry clusters or state-sponsored cultural flagships, as well as a critical mass of local highly educated workers and knowledge-based professionals. One architect doubted that the design strategy to reuse the industrial heritage purely for cultural consumption could succeed. She explained that "the general cultural atmosphere in Chongqing is very weak and not supportive of cultural consumption. The demand for local cultural pursuits is actually very low."[33] This statement concerning Chongqing's relatively underdeveloped art culture, in terms of local art market, artist community and the government's support for art, was also highlighted in the interviews with local artists.[34] These missing cultural components further decreased the confidence of the CMG and Yufu for adaptively reusing industrial heritage.

Conclusion

The evident gap between the ideals and the reality of industrial heritage reuse in the CSF project reflects the influence of power structure in industrial land redevelopment. In the process of industrial landscape restructuring, tensions and contradictions have been generated among various interest groups including local government officials, the land banking agency, property developers, factory staff, planners, and designers, as well as experts. Due to unequal power relations between the state-capital coalition and the grass-roots heritage voice, the economic interests of the state-capital coalition were prioritized over the long-term cultural needs of the public. Industrial land redevelopment in Chongqing has adopted property-led approach rather than heritage-led approach, which has produced negative impacts on industrial heritage reuse. Specifically, in the CSF case, the power structure in the implementation stage heavily relied on the state-capital coalition consisting of the government, the land banking agency and its subordinate property developer. With limited community engagement and a lack of genuine social elements, as well as loose and flexible planning guidelines on heritage conservation in the decision-making process, the project outcome guided by the main stakeholder inevitably yielded to the property development agenda.

The CSF case argues that the negative reality of industrial heritage conservation efforts in Chongqing is not just simply attributable to the pursuit of the state-capital coalition for land values, but also shaped by the missing cultural power of local grass-roots heritage voice in demanding to retain the historic industrial buildings. The reduction of the range of industrial heritage retained in Chongqing was not unique. Instead, this is a quite commonly experienced phenomenon in inland China. In drawing from Chongqing's experience, this chapter explores the relationship between the planning process and its final outcome in industrial heritage projects. It reveals that a project outcome is not just shaped by the original concept of influential individuals, but instead is largely influenced by a dominant power structure. The sociological approach of power relations will serve as an essential reference for policy makers and practitioners in the second-tier cities in inland China which still retain numerous industrial sites and have a potential to be reclaimed.

Acknowledgements

This research was financially supported by the National Natural Science Foundation of China (Grant No. 52008300) and Shanghai Pujiang Program (Grant No. 19PJC108).

Bibliography

Chen, Jie, and Bruce Judd. "Relationality and Territoriality: Rethinking Policy Circulation of Industrial Heritage Reuse in Chongqing, China." *International Journal of Heritage Studies* 27, no. 1 (2021): 16-38. https://doi.org/10.1080/13 527258.2020.1765188

Chen, Jie, Bruce Judd, and Scott Hawken. "Adaptive Reuse of Industrial Heritage for Cultural Purposes in Beijing, Shanghai and Chongqing." *Structural Survey* 34, no. 4/5 (August 2016): 331-350. https://doi.org/10.1108/SS-11-2015-0052

Chou, Tsu-Lung. "Creative Space, Cultural Industry Clusters, and Participation of the State in Beijing." *Eurasian Geography and Economics* 53, no. 2 (2012): 197-215. https://doi.org/10.2747/1539-7216.53.2.197

Currier, Jennifer. "Art and Power in the New China: An Exploration of Beijing's 798 District and Its Implications for Contemporary Urbanism." *Town Planning Review* 79, no. 2/3 (2008): 237-65.

Goodman, David S. G. "The Campaign to "Open Up the West": National, Provincial-level and Local Perspectives." *The China Quarterly* 178 (2004): 317-34.

Han, Sun Sheng, and Yong Wang. "Chongqing." *Cities* 18 (2001): 115-125.

Harvey, David. *The Condition of Postmodernity: An Enquiry into the Origins of Cultural Change*. Oxford: Blackwell, 1990.

Harvey, David. *Seventeen Contradictions and the End of Capitalism*. New York: Oxford University Press, 2014.

National Bureau of Statistics of China. "*China Statistical Yearbook 2019*." Accessed May 17, 2021. http://www.stats.gov.cn/tjsj/ndsj/

Ren, Xuefei, and Meng Sun. "Artistic Urbanization: Creative Industries and Creative Control in Beijing." *International Journal of Urban and Regional Research* 36 (2012): 504-521.

Shen, Jie, and Fulong Wu. "Restless Urban Landscapes in China: A Case Study of Three Projects in Shanghai." *Journal of Urban Affairs* 34 (2012): 255-277.

Su, Xiaobo. "Urban Entrepreneurialism and the Commodification of Heritage in China." *Urban Studies* 52 (2015): 2874-2889.

Wang, Jing. "The Global Reach of a New Discourse: How Far can 'Creative Industries' Travel?" *International Journal of Cultural Studies* 7 (2004): 9-19.

Wang, Jun. "'Art in Capital': Shaping Distinctiveness in a Culture-led Urban Regeneration Project in Red Town, Shanghai." *Cities* 26 (2009): 318-330.

Wang, Yiming. *Pseudo-Public Spaces in Chinese Shopping Malls: Rise, Publicness and Consequences*. London: Routledge, 2019.

Xu, Jiang, Anthony Yeh, and Fulong Wu. "Land Commodification: New Land Development and Politics in China since the Late 1990s." *International Journal of Urban and Regional Research* 33 (2009): 890-913.

Zheng, Jie, and Rogar Chan. "The Impact of 'Creative Industry Clusters' on Cultural and Creative Industry Development in Shanghai." *City, Culture and Society* 5 (2014): 9-22.

Zhong, Sheng. "The Neo-liberal Turn: 'Culture'-led Urban Regeneration in Shanghai." In *The Routledge Companion to Urban Regeneration*, edited by Michael Leary and John McCarthy, 495-504. London: Routledge, 2013.

Zukin, Sharon. *Naked City: The Death and Life of Authentic Urban Places*. New York: Oxford University Press, 2010.

Part 2:
The Built City

Chapter 6

Developing a collage city methodology: a case study of Canberra

Viktoria K. Holmik

University of Canberra, Australia

Abstract

Utopian and urban planning traditions play a critical role in the development of the city, addressing several universal questions such as: how can architecture and design influence the behaviour within a space? In the contemporary city, however, it has been argued that planners have disassociated themselves from these questions, leading to the absence of a contemporary planning methodology which incorporates utopian thinking into urban planning. Colin Rowe and Fred Koetter's *Collage City* (1978) proposes an urban design theory which addresses the complex nature of the city through the technique of the vest-pocket utopia. This research focuses on how the vest-pocket fragment, as developed by *Collage City*, can be understood as a technique for use by the urban planner. Through the case study method and the application of *Collage City* theory, this chapter explores the question of how the vest-pocket fragment can be applied to the utopia of Canberra.

Keywords: Canberra, Collage City, fragment, utopia, urban planning, vest-pocket

***

Introduction

Canberra is situated in the south-east of Australia, within the Australian Capital Territory, which is located in the state of New South Wales. It occupies an area of 2358 km² and was surveyed, chosen, and legislated as an independent Federal Capital for the new Commonwealth of Australia. Following Australia's Federation of the six British colonies to form the Commonwealth of Australia in 1901, the need arose to establish an Australian capital city. The conditions listed under Section 125 of the Constitution stated that the land vested to the Commonwealth for use as the capital territory was to be within the State of New

South Wales and a minimum of one hundred miles from Sydney.[1] The 1901 Congress in Melbourne was held to determine the requirements for the Federal Capital, the new capital needed to have an open layout, with extensive parklands and plentiful sunlight and fresh air.[2] Furthermore, "the Federal Capital should be a beautiful city, occupying a commanding position, with extensive views," these criteria leading to a seven-year search for the optimal location.[3] The Yass-Canberra region won the parliamentary ballot in 1908 for its picturesque bush-capital setting and the diversity of the topography and natural flora.[4] Construction began in 1913 and the city was officially named and established as the capital on 12 March, 1913. As with the rest of the continent, the site chosen as the new capital has a much longer history than that of the settlement by the British Colonies. The name Canberra has its roots in the languages of the Ngunnawal/Ngambri people, the traditional custodians of the land.[5]

Utopian and urban planning traditions play a critical role in the development of Canberra, addressing several universal questions such as the ability of the environment to transform the social sphere, and the possibility of the manifestation of the perfect environment and society.[6] In the contemporary city, however, it has been argued that planners have "disassociated themselves from universal questions" leading to the absence of a contemporary planning methodology which incorporates utopian thinking into urban planning.[7] Furthermore, the city is complex, comprised of intersecting and intertwining layers of people, places, histories and meanings, and as such, any analysis or methodological framework for the city needs to allow for this. Within the framework of social and built approaches, this chapter explores questions from the position of the built city. It delves into the relationships formed between the natural elements of the landscape, within a top-down planning method. The city of Canberra is utilised as a case study, because of its history as a planned ideal city, it is placed in a unique position to explore questions relating to the complex and dynamic relationships of built forms within the urban fabric.

The new, planned, Federal Capital was intended to encapsulate the ideals and principles of the new Australian democracy, and as such, Canberra occupies a unique place in city planning as a synthesis of twentieth century planning theories and ideals, evident in its built form. The chapter will start by contextualizing utopian theory and twentieth century urban planning, followed by an overview of Canberra's history and an analysis of its planning. Collage City theory, which proposes the superimposition and juxtaposition of different urban forms will then be explored in more detail to understand how the vest-pocket fragment, meaning the small-scale urban fragment, can be applied to Canberra. This research focuses on how the vest-pocket fragment, as developed by *Collage*

City, can be understood as a technique for use by the urban planner in the contemporary city.[8] Colin Rowe and Fred Koetter's *Collage City* (1978) was written as part of the reaction to Modernist planning and its perceived disavowal of history and tradition.[9] The focus of the chapter addresses the complex nature of the city, the fragmentation and multiplicity of interpretation, through the technique of the vest-pocket utopia. These are essentially miniature utopias, which limit the traditional totalitarian planning method to a small-scale enclave, thereby negating the issues associated with utopian planning.[10]

Through the case study method and the application of Collage City theory, this chapter explores the question of how the vest-pocket fragment can be applied to the utopia of Canberra to foster a more nuanced scale of urbanization. The vest-pocket fragments within the city of Canberra are the small-scale urban fragments, the forms which create the connectivity and network of interactions within the city, while the term utopia here is used to denote the qualities associated with utopian plans as being the perfect, but non-existent, place and society. In deploying the technique of the vest-pocket fragment, urban plans are approached as a series of utopian fragments, making it an extremely valuable technique in generating an approach for the ideal city of Canberra. This paper will move between Garden City theory, Collage City theory and the case study of Canberra, because for the city of Canberra, they are integrated. Since the selection of the Griffin plan for Canberra, its history and development have been informed by various strands of utopian and urban planning theory that are woven into the fabric of the city.

Situating the research: utopian visions

Utopia has played a critical role in the development of the city; as architects and planners strive to create the conditions of the utopian vision, they drive the progress of the city.[11] The definition of utopia is multifaceted and layered due to both its etymology and the implications of translating the term between different languages. Etymologically it has been derived from two Greek words "eu-topos" meaning "good-place" and "ou-topos" meaning "no place."[12] The definition of utopia as a perfect place which does not yet exist was first introduced in Thomas More's *Utopia* (1516).[13] In this socio-political satire, More details his plans for a perfect society in which the "citizens could not fail to be happy because they could not choose but be good."[14] Alongside this definition, the most significant contribution of his book was the introduction of the two streams of the utopian tradition: the physical utopias and the social utopias. The physical utopia aims to create the perfect environment, whether this be built or natural, reflecting the idealized values of the physical realm in a microcosm of the real world.[15] The social utopia aims to create "basic social transformation," that is, the perfect society, emerging through the harmonization of the society and planned environment.[16] These two streams of the utopian tradition aim to answer the following universal questions, the first being, if individuals are placed in a specific setting, how will their behavior be transformed?[17] In contrast to the social approach, the second question focuses on the built environment and examines how can design "create a clean logic of social and biological relationships"?[18]

What is revealed is the relationship between utopia and the architecture and urban planning fields, they all aim to influence experience and behaviors within a particular environment and the influence of the physical utopian stream is evident in the various theories that informed the planning of Canberra.[19] Alongside utopia, urban planning has played a critical role in the development of the city as it is understood today, with two major influences on the urban planning fields in the twentieth century, *Collage City* and the Garden City Movement.[20] *Collage City* develops a framework through which utopia and utopian ideals can be applied to existing cities, while the Garden City Movement reflects the thinking of utopian planners of the time and offers insight into planning of Canberra as an ideal city.[21] *Collage City*, the Garden City Movement, and the literature surrounding them continue to play a crucial role in urban planning and utopian theory.[22] *Collage City* proposes a fragmented approach to utopia and urban planning whereby a series of dissimilar elements are combined into one composition.[23] In contrast to this, the Garden City Movement offered a unique way of combining existing urban planning proposals to create the ideal community.[24] An examination of their contributions within these fields demonstrates their relevance to the current planning context as approaches based in the synthesis of existing fragments and urban conditions.

Creating Canberra

Canberra is situated in the south-east of Australia, within the state of New South Wales. It occupies an area of 2358 km^2 and was surveyed, chosen, and legislated as an independent Federal Capital in 1908 for the new Commonwealth of Australia following Australia's Federation in 1901. In 1912, Walter Burley Griffin won the international design competition to create a Federal Capital City for the new Commonwealth of Australia. His wife and business partner, Marion Mahony Griffin, was the co-designer of what is known as The Griffin Plan.[25] Their plan for Canberra is premised on its design and planning as a city in the landscape, and this sensitivity in connection to the landscape echoes the philosophy of the Chicago based Prairie School that the Griffins were heavily involved in through their work with Frank Lloyd Wright around the turn of the twentieth century. Emerging in the 1890s, the Prairie School introduced the design ethos of a democratic spirit in architecture and the expression of contextual character in the architectural forms. The Griffins further developed this through the graphic representation of their designs, where the building and nature are represented as a cohesive and complementary unit.[26] This design ethos and language is an important influence in the development of their plans for the new Australian capital, alongside several other utopian and planning theories evolving at the time.

The garden city plan in Canberra

While there were several influences that reflect the Griffins' utopian aims for the plan, including the City Beautiful Movement and the Organic City, the Garden City Movement was the most predominant. Walter Burley Griffin stated, "I planned a city not like any other city in the world...an ideal city – a city that meets my ideal of the city of the future."[27] With this statement he reveals his utopian aspirations for Canberra and embeds this agenda into the city's plan. The physical framework of the city is determined by the existing topography of the site, a series of geometrical shapes are then imposed upon the landscape to create order within the plan. The Land Axis, running from Mount Ainslie to Kurrajong Hill (now Capital Hill) and through to Mount Bimberi, is crossed by the Water Axis, originating at Black Mountain, and crossing the Molonglo River and the flood plains. These perpendicular and bisecting axes form the backbone from which the rest of the geometry grows. The second organizing geometrical framework is the establishment of the National Triangle, its apex at Kurrajong Hill, and bisected by the Land Axis.[28] The triangle is located at the center of the "urban uses framework," connecting national and local functions.[29] The apex at Kurrajong Hill was the symbolic center of the city and the nation. With the focus on centralizing geometry, a triangulated layout, major axes, as well as the integration of the landscape into the design, the basic elements of the Garden City plan are easily recognizable. The Land Axis, Water Axis and the National Triangle form the overarching framework for Canberra's built environment and establish the relationships between the various elements of the plan. This framework was the focus of the Griffins' plans for the city and as such the appearance and design of the individual buildings at the fine-grain or fragment scale was not addressed as comprehensively, leaving scope for the future design and construction of the city.[30]

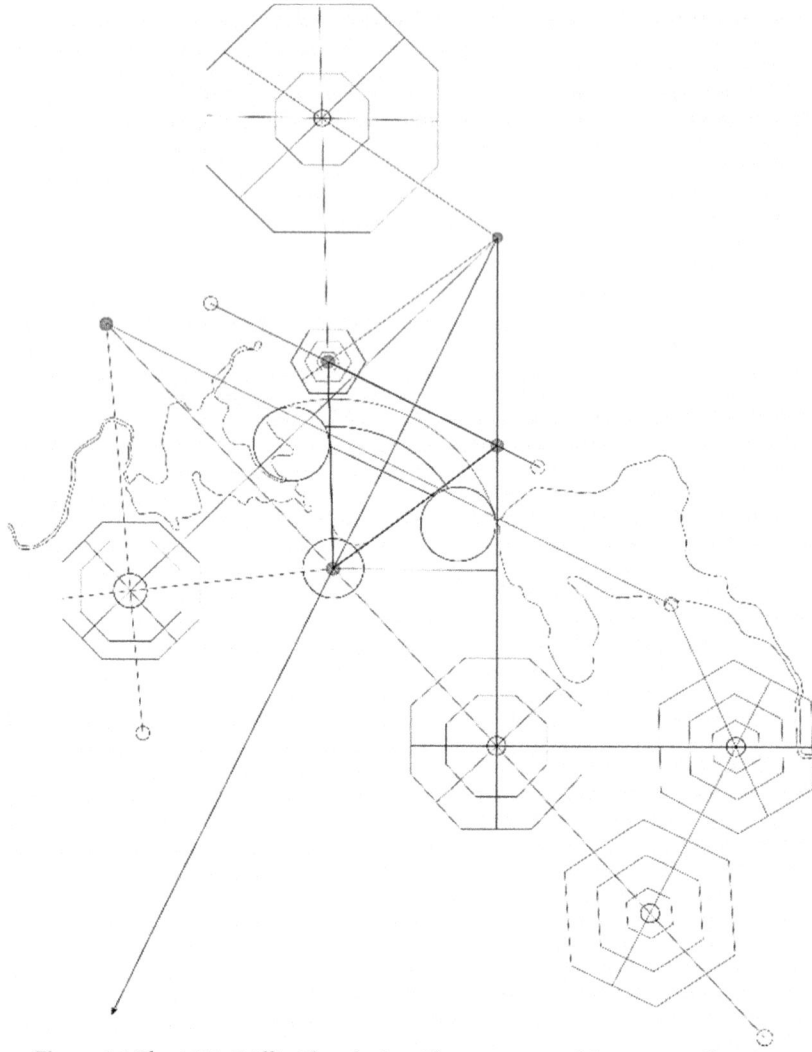

Figure 6.1 The 1911 Griffin Plan design. The geometry of the 1911 Griffin Plan
superimposed on the primary landscape formations. Image Credit: Author ©

While the "impression given is that modern Canberra is Griffin's City" with
minimal changes that have been implemented in line with Griffin's thinking,
the contemporary urban landscape is vastly different to the original plan.[31] The
1913 revisions to the plan were an attempt to reconcile the grandeur of the
initial site and the conditions of the Board.[32] The most significant change to the
design was the implementation of the Initial City to the south-east of Kurrajong
Hill and the National Triangle.[33] This opened the door to numerous changes to
occur in the following years, which all affected the order and legibility of the

plan, as well as the scales of interaction. The next critical stage in development was the National Capital Development Commission (NCDC) plan of 1959, based on the report developed by William Holford, introducing town planning for the motor car.[34] This changed the scale of the city, moving it from the pedestrian to the motorized vehicle, and the implementation of the road system had a profound effect on the planning of the entire city. The integrated intentions of the original Canberra began to fracture and further demarcated the move from the connectivity and nuance of the Griffin plan to the contemporary Canberra, a city that functions as a layering of planning ideas and eras.

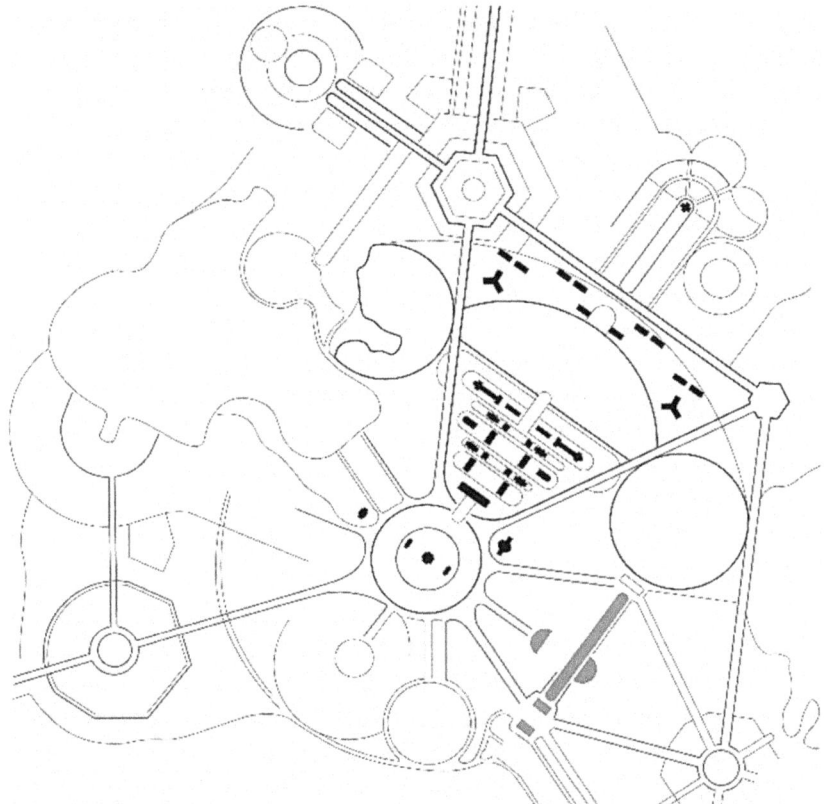

Figure 6.2 The 1913 Preliminary Plan by Griffin. Demarcation of national and cultural buildings and the introduction of the Initial City to the south-east. Image Credit: Author ©

The history of Canberra reflects the development of various urban design theories throughout the twentieth century, and the continual development of different sets of ideas. [35] While the centralizing geometry of the National Triangle and the Land and Water Axes have been maintained, there are many differences on the fragment scale.[36] The backbone of the plan remains embedded in the Griffins' ideal city; however, the Canberra of the present day is evidently in need of a planning strategy that incorporates the vest-pocket fragment scale of thinking as developed by Collage City theory. Consequently, it is the reformulation of Griffin's ideals and plans that will be crucial to the future urban development of Canberra, leading us once again to the question: How can the vest-pocket fragment as developed by Collage City theory be applied to the utopia of Canberra to foster a more nuanced scale of urbanization?

Building a methodology: collage city theory

Colin Rowe and Fred Koetter propose their Collage City theory as a design method to overcome the limitations of classical utopias and incorporate utopian thinking into contemporary urban planning. This is crucial in the current urban planning context, which has distanced itself from universal questions and in which the phenomenon of urban fragmentation is increasingly apparent.[37] It takes a central role in twentieth-century planning theory due to its innovative approach: shifting the focus from the scale of the urban form down to the fragments of the city.[38] What the authors identify is how utopia acts as an essential instrument in the development of the urban fabric and propose its use as a tool to bring order to the fragmented city.[39] Their text synthesizes several arguments, suggesting that a collage technique, as derived from art, may be the only way to overcome the problems created by utopia, as a way of seducing objects from their context, to superimpose them in different spaces to create new references and meanings.[40] It is important to note that the techniques proposed are not prescriptive, they are adaptable and dynamic, thus making them valuable to a city with a complex planning history and rapidly changing urban form.

The Collage City methodology is developed through the vest-pocket scale, which allows utopia and the city to be treated as fragments rather than "in toto."[41] It is the relationship between the vest-pocket fragments, which makes *Collage City* so innovative; the interactions created through the collage technique enable a dynamic compositional process, and as such, generate a dynamic, changing city. For Canberra, planned as an ideal city at the beginning of the twentieth century, the *Collage City* approach offers a way for the fragments to be reintegrated and collaged. This vest-pocket fragment scale has played a crucial role throughout the history of the Canberra plan. The Griffin plan provided both a framework for the city as a whole, but also offered small-scale opportunities for the creation of a network of enclaves or garden suburbs, which may act as those vest-pocket utopias.[42] The vest-pocket scale is closely linked with the encounter scale in Canberra, as the fragments create the connectivity and network of interactions within the city. As the individual experiences the interaction of the various fragments and the interaction of these within the urban fabric, they will create meaning based around their experience. It is the layering and superimposition of these fragments and experiences within the urban form that Rowe and Koetter have developed as the *Collage City*.

The process of encounter, interaction and collaging of meaning within Canberra through the technique of the vest-pocket fragment reflects the application of Collage City methodology to the city. What the fragments represent are the transitions within the city between the urban planning movements and theories of the twentieth century. They offer value due to their role in reflecting these twentieth century ideals as well as through their roles within the architectural and urban history of the city.[43] As such, this urban collage becomes a collection of set-pieces that reflect the values and ideals of twentieth century architecture and urban planning, the interaction of these creating the Canberra collage. These vest-pocket fragments possess the fine-grain value of the city and the following examples are a few of many; the three chosen based on their locations as key areas of focus within the Griffins' plans for Canberra: one from the developments of the Initial City, one from the Civic Centre and one from the National Triangle.

The first vest-pocket fragment identified within the plan reflects a core building type in the developments of the Initial City. Opened in 1927, the Capitol Theatre was the premier cinema of the new capital city and was an important building that reflected the early stages of development in Canberra, specifically the development of the Initial City. Its location on Canberra Avenue, facing Manuka Oval, meant that the theatre front acted as an arrival *porte cochere*, which connected the site to the wider plan, linking the theatre to the National Triangle through the arrival sequence. The theatre presented plays, state productions and films, and was designed in the Art Deco style prevalent in the era by the architect, Malcolm Moir, to the requirements of the theatre impresario, J. C. Williamson.[44] The building was demolished in the 1980s and as such is remembered as a lost fragment within the fabric of the city.[45] The theatre that has occupied the site, until its recent closure, relocated the Canberra Avenue entrance to the opposite side of the site, turning its back on the avenue scale and connectivity it offers to the wider plan.

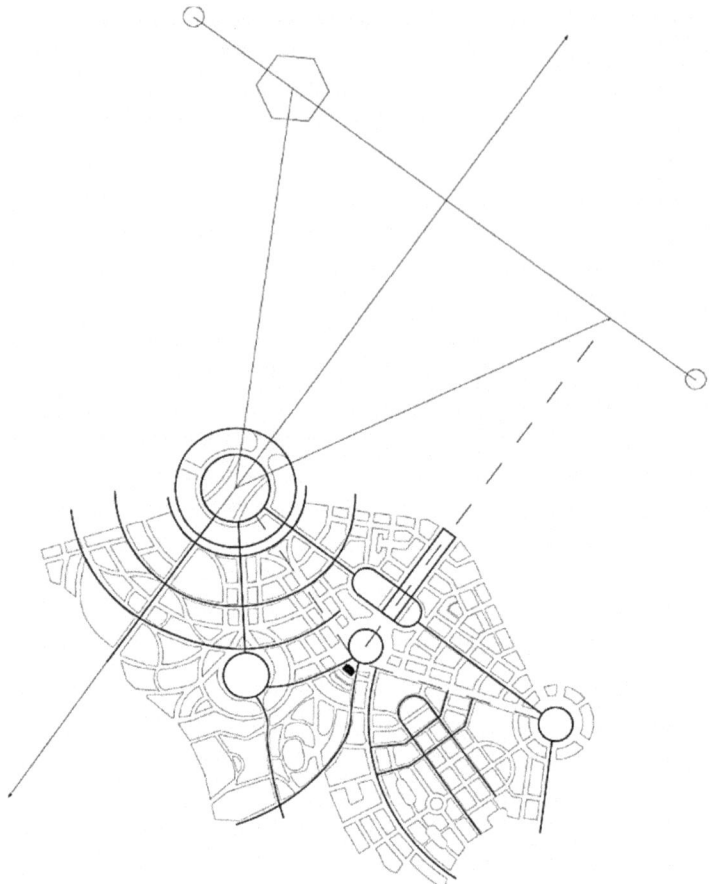

Figure 6.3 The Capitol Theatre as vest-pocket fragment design. The relationship of the Capitol Theatre to the geometry of the National Triangle, the Axes, and its immediate context. Image Credit: Author ©

The second vest-pocket fragment is connected to the Civic Centre and civic intentions of the original Griffin Plan. Designed by John Sulman and John Hunter Kirkpatrick, construction on the Sydney and Melbourne buildings began in 1926-7 when the tenancies were progressively sold.[46] They were placed along Northbourne Avenue as gateway buildings to the National Triangle, adjacent to the City Hill apex, offering a sense of arrival to the urban core.[47] The two buildings defined the city identity and civic experience of early Canberra and as such were key figures within the urban fabric. They remain integral fragments from the era as they offer the fine-grain scale within the plan, in contrast to the original development of large footprint blocks, which was focused on creating the "urban uses framework."[48] They offer the encounter scale due to the laneways located between the buildings and connect the city to the National Capital area. The arcades that characterize the design coherently unite and hold the buildings as civic urban artefacts with intrinsic value, and difference is enabled within separate tenancies. However, with lack of maintenance and the move of pedestrian retail foot traffic to the Canberra Mall the types of tenancies are not in keeping with the civic premise of the original intention and their positioning as gateways to the city.[49]

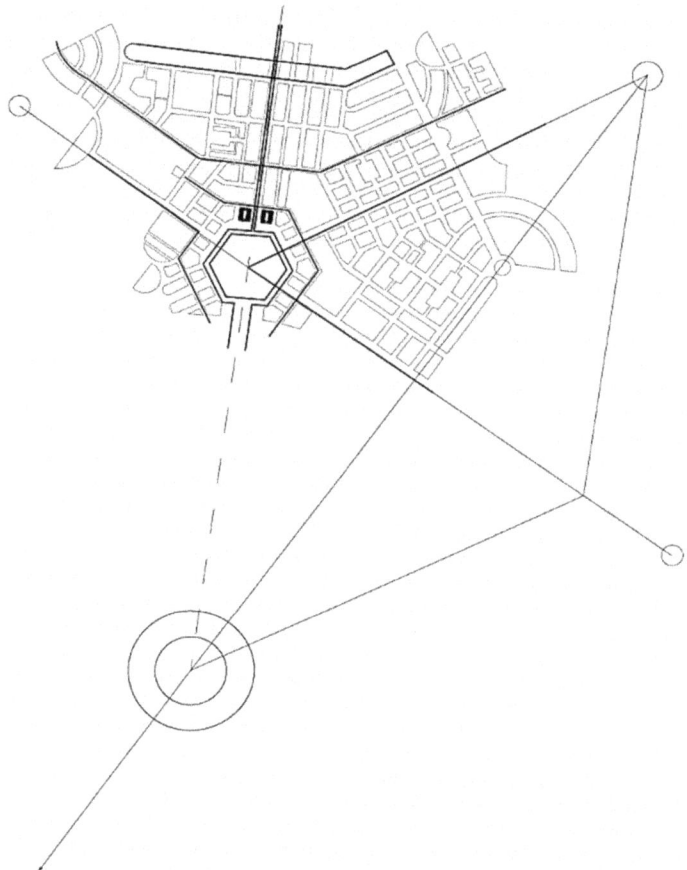

Figure 6.4 The Sydney and Melbourne Buildings as vest-pocket fragments design. The relationship of the Sydney and Melbourne buildings to the geometry of National Triangle, the Axes, and their immediate context. Image Credit: Author ©

The third vest-pocket fragment, located at the centre of the National Triangle creates strong connections to its context, reflecting key principles of Canberra's design. The current building housing the National Portrait Gallery collection was completed in 2008, though the collection was established before the building was even planned. It was housed in three rooms of Old Parliament House and managed by the National Library of Australia from 1993 until 2008.[50]

Designed by the architectural firm Johnson Pilton Walker Ltd, it is an award-winning project.[51] The external form of the building uses geometry to align itself with key vistas, the five gallery bays of the building are placed perpendicular to the Land Axis, linking the building to the framework of the Griffin Plan. The five gallery bays further reference the terracing and proportioning system of the National Triangle from the 1911 Griffin Plan. The whole building is governed by the human scale: the form is defined in proportion to the person, which allows for a more intimate and connected encounter with both the artworks and building itself.[52] These design principles make the National Portrait Gallery so significant to Canberra's built form; its function as a cultural institution is significant, but the manner in which it establishes connections to its immediate environment and the city itself make it particularly relevant to this case study.

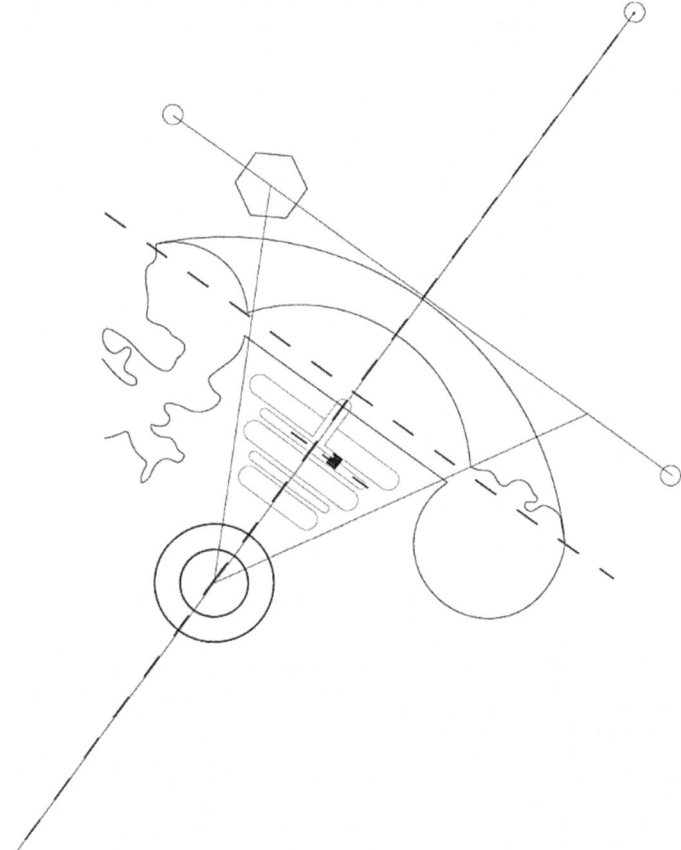

Figure 6.5 The National Portrait Gallery as vest-pocket fragment design. The relationship of the National Portrait Gallery to the geometry of the National Triangle, the Axes, and its immediate context. Image Credit: Author ©

Conclusion

For Canberra, planned as an ideal city at the beginning of the twentieth century, the city is premised on its design as a Garden City and a design set in the landscape, and as such, the fine-grain or fragment scale is still layering into the framework of the city.[53] Collage City as methodology is applied as a way to read the city in order to identify, reintegrate and collage the existing fragments. This fragment scale allows for local variable and individual characteristics within the urban fabric to take shape, for the pre-existing conditions to be layered and superimposed to create the new urban collage.[54] In this analysis of the vest-pocket fragment in relation to the ideal city of Canberra, Collage City theory has been utilized as a method which incorporates utopian thinking and addresses the universal questions which drive progress within the city. The reading of Canberra as a Collage City explores the complexity of the city and its built form, developing a multiplicity of reference and meaning for the vest-pocket fragments of the city. When these are layered within the overall composition, they create the connectivity and network of interactions within the city that foster a more nuanced scale of urbanization; and it is this way that *Collage City* may be used to inform the future urban development of Canberra.

Bibliography

Aalen, Frederick H. A. "English Origins." In *The Garden City: Past, Present and Future*, edited by Stephen V. Ward, 28-51. London: E&FN Spon, 1992.

ACT Government. "Sydney and Melbourne Buildings." Accessed January 11, 2021, https://www.act.gov.au/cityrenewal/places/city-hill/sydney-and-melbourne-building-precinct.

Australian Institute of Architects. "Register of Significant Twentieth Century Architecture - Sydney and Melbourne Buildings." Accessed June 9, 2020. https://www.architecture.com.au/wp-content/uploads/sydney-amp-melbourne-buildings.pdf.

Balbo, Marcello, and Francoise Naves-Bouchanine. "Urban Fragmentation as a Research Hypothesis: RabatSalé Case Study." *Habitat International* 19, no. 4 (1995): 571-82.

Bayón, Maria Cristina, Gonzalo A. Saravi, and Mariana Ortego Brena. "The Cultural Dimensions of Urban Fragmentation: Segregation, Sociability, and Inequality in Mexico City." *Latin America Perspectives* 40, no. 2 (2013): 35-52. Accessed April 13, 2020. https://www.jstor.org/stable/23466021.

Davis, J.C. *Utopia and the Ideal Society*. UK: Cambridge University Press, 1981.

Delmelle, Elizabeth. "The Increasing Sociospatial Fragmentation of Urban America." *Urban Science* 3, no. 1 (2019). https://doi.org/10.3390/urbansci3010009.

Department of Home Affairs Australia. "Information, conditions and particulars for guidance on the preparation of competitive designs for the Federal Capital City of the Commonwealth of Australia." Accessed April 13, 2020. https://nla.gov.au/nla.cat-vn921986.

Ellem, Christine. "No Little Plans." *Thesis Eleven* 123, no. 1 (2014): 106-22. https://doi.org/10.1177/0725513614543412.

Fishman, Robert. *Urban Utopias in the Twentieth Century: Ebenezer Howard, Frank Lloyd Wright and Le Corbusier.* Cambridge, Mass.: The MIT Press, 1982.

Green, Ernest. "The Social Functions of Utopian Architecture." *Utopias Studies* 4, no. 1 (1993): 1-13. Accessed January 22, 2021, http://www.jstor.org/stable/20719143.

Griffin, Walter Burley. "American Designs Splendid New Capital for Australia." *The New York Times* (New York), 2 June 1912. Accessed 11 January 2021. https://www.nytimes.com/1912/06/02/archives/city-twentyfive-miles-square-to-be-built-upon-what-is-now-a.html.

Griffin, Walter Burley. *Walter Burley Griffin - Letter dated January 1913 - Re His plan.* Letter. Canberra: National Archives of Australia, 1913. Accessed April 13, 2020. https://recordsearch.naa.gov.au/SearchNRetrieve/Interface/ViewImage.aspx?B=55919.

Hall, Peter, and Colin Ward. *Sociable Cities: The Legacy of Ebenezer Howard.* Chichester, West Sussex, England: J. Wiley, 1998.

Harrison, Peter, and Robert Freestone. *Walter Burley Griffin: Landscape Architect.* Canberra: National Library of Australia, 1995.

Harz, V. "Building a Better Place: Utopianism and the Revision of Community in Toni Morrison's *Paradise*." *Current Objectives of Postgraduate American Studies* 12 (2011). Accessed January 11, 2021. https://copas.uniregensburg.de/article/view/135/161.

Hatuka, Tali, and Alexander D'Hooghe. "After Postmodernism: Readdressing the Role of Utopia in Urban Design and Planning." *Places* 19, no. 2 (2007): 20-27.

Headon, David. *The Symbolic Role of the National Capital.* Canberra: National Capital Authority, 2003.

Howard, Ebenezer. *Garden Cities of to-Morrow.* Edited Frederick J. Osborn. Cambridge, Mass: M.I.T Press, 1965.

Hurtt, Steven. "Conjectures on Urban Form: The Cornell Urban Design Studio1963-1982." *The Cornell Journal of Architecture* 2 (Fall 1983): 54-78.

Johnson, Craig. "Utopia and the Dirty Secret of Architecture." *Colloquy: Text Theory Critique*, no. 14 (2007): 30-44.

Klanten, Robert, Lukas Feireiss, and Matthias Bottger. *Utopia Forever: Visions of Architecture and Urbanism.* Berlin: Gestalten, 2011.

Macarthur, John. "Appropriation." Chap. 5 In *The Picturesque Architecture, Disgust and Other Irregularities*, 215-24. Hoboken: Taylor and Francis, 2013.

McIntyre, Arthur. *Contemporary Australian Collage and Its Origins.* Australia: Craftsman House, 1990.

Meyerson, Martin. "Utopian Traditions and the Planning of Cities." *Daedalus* 90, no. 1 (1961): 180-93. Accessed January 22, 2021, http://www.jstor.org/stable/20026647.

More, Thomas. *Utopia.* Edited by P. Turner. London: Penguin, 2003.

Mozzato, Alioscia. "Colin Rowe and Aldo Rossi. Utopia as a Metaphor of a New City Analogous to the Existing One.", 2020. *sITA* 6 (2018): 142-58. Accessed April 13. https://sita.uauim.ro/6/a/72/.

Museum of Australian Democracy. "Constitution of the Commonwealth of Australia." Accessed April 13, 2020. https://www.foundingdocs.gov.au/scan-sid-91.html.

National Archives of Australia. "Suggested Names for Australia's New Capital." Accessed January 11, 2021. https://www.naa.gov.au/learn/learning-resources/learning-resource-themes/government-anddemocracy/federation/suggested-names-australias-new-capital.

National Archives of Australia and Museum of Australian Democracy. "Discovering Mildenhall's Canberra: Capitol Theatre, Manuka." Accessed June 9, 2020, https://mildenhall.moadoph.gov.au/photo/5000.

National Capital Authority. *The Griffin Legacy: Canberra, the Nation's Capital in the 21st Century.* Canberra: NCA, 2004.

National Film and Sound Archive. "Capitol Theatre, Manuka, Act." Accessed January 11, 2021, https://www.nfsa.gov.au/collection/curated/capitol-theatre-manuka-act.

National Portrait Gallery. "Architecture." Accessed January 11, 2021, https://www.portrait.gov.au/content/thebuilding/.

National Portrait Gallery. "History." Accessed January 11, 2021. https://www.portrait.gov.au/content/gallery-history/.

Ockman, Joan. "Form without Utopia: Contextualising Colin Rowe." *Journal of the Society of Architectural Historians* 57, no. 4 (1998): 448-56.

Pinder, David. "In Defence of Utopian Urbanism: Imagining Cities After the 'End of Utopia'." *Geografiska Annaler* 84, no. 3-4 (2001): 229-241.

Reid, Paul. *Canberra Following Griffin.* Canberra: National Archives of Australia, 2002.

Reps, John W., Graham Foundation for Advanced Studies in the Fine Arts, and National Capital Planning Authority. *Canberra 1912: Plans and Planners of the Australian Capital Competition.* Carlton South, VIC: Melbourne University Press, 1997.

Roe, Ken. "Capitol Theatre." *Cinema Treasures. Cinema Treasures LLC.* Accessed January 11, 2021. http://cinematreasures.org/theaters/35502.

Rowe, Colin, and Fred Koetter. "Collage City." *The Architectural Review* CLVIII, no. 942 (1975): 66-91.

Rowe, Colin, and Fred Koetter. *Collage City.* Cambridge, MA.: The MIT Press, 1978.

Sargent, Lyman Tower. "Utopia." In *The New Dictionary of the History of Ideas*, edited by Maryann Cline Horowitz, 2403-09. New York: Charles Scribner & Sons, 2004.

Shane, David Grahame. *Recombinant Urbanism: Conceptual Modeling in Architecture, Urban Design, and City Theory.* Chichester: John Wiley & Sons, 2005.

Sheaffe, Percy L. *Sheaffe Papers. Printed Material, 'Commonwealth of Australia, Department of Home Affairs. The Federal Capital. Report Explanatory of the Preliminary General Plan' by Walter Burley Griffin [3 Copies].* Canberra: National Archives of Australia, 1913. Accessed April 13, 2020. https://recordsearch.naa.gov.au/SearchNRetrieve/Interface/ViewImage.aspx?B=1873728.

Chapter 7

A case for a multi-dimensional development grid for Perth, Western Australia

Emil E. Jonescu

Hames Sharley, Australia

Abbey Wuu

Curtin University, Australia

Khoa Do

Hames Sharley, Australia

Abstract

Current municipal policies and development guidelines requirements have led to Perth city becoming segregated into mono-functional precincts that are impacting social, economic and environmental sustainability. Municipal data and ArcGIS further highlight mono-functionalism and disproportionate urban sprawl relative to population growth and sustainable development. This chapter focuses on development strategies that increase opportunities for urban social interactions, efficiency, linkages and overall liveability of the 'Built City,' supported by the critical discourse of Rem Koolhaas, Jan Gehl, Superstudio, and Archigram—international provocateurs from the field of architecture urban design. Moreover, through an iterative design process, the chapter explores Frei Otto-esque inspired techniques to propose an organic multi-dimensional grid layered over the existing case study precinct as a hypothetical—user-centred planning, placemaking and development medium. The chapter advocates for an inclusive, alternative, urban composition that supports city planning for community and inclusivity through collaging techniques presenting visual interpretations encouraging individualized interpretations for Perth.

Keywords: Perth, architecture, urban design, placemaking, building, mono-functional, behaviour, inclusivity, sustainability, density

***

Introduction

Perth is located between the Indian Ocean and the Darling Scarp, on the banks of the Swan River in Western Australia. The settlement was founded in 1829 and evolved into a strategic administrative post for the Swan River Colony. The waterway connection with nearby Fremantle Port allowed for the transportation of goods. Offset from the edge of the Swan River, this strategic alignment led to Perth's grid layout.[1] The earliest commercial route by land was St Georges Terrace which is now the hub of the central business district (CBD). Perth grew exponentially in a northerly direction through draining the freshwater swamps which saw the development of Northbridge. The formative city railway networks commenced in the 1880s gold rush boom, and spurred migration. During World War I, it became a hub for mainly European immigration, which continued in the following decades and indelibly changed the culture of the city. Northbridge was part of the Perth CBD until it was officially appointed an inner-city suburb in 1982. The real change to the urban and social environment happened with the urban renewal and redevelopment project the Perth City Link. Funding and delivery of the project was supported by partnerships between the WA State Government, the City of Perth, other agencies and private investors.

The Perth City Link programme, completed in 2013, involved sinking part of the suburban Fremantle railway line, which effectively divided the city into two parts — the CBD and the entertainment precinct.[2] The outdated municipal planning and development policies along with increased pressure to densify has led to the detriment of cultural and community sustainability. The impact has seen Perth's social complexion being segregated by physical and implied boundaries in the form of mono-functional precincts that preclude civic diversity. This case study provides an investigation into these practices, through examining the top-down political planning processes and the social issues that have ensued. To do so it addresses issues arising over reduced opportunities concerning urban social interactions, efficiency, linkages and overall liveability of the built which is inherently impacted by separatist sector-based precinct partitioning. Understanding the consequences of this kind of segregation requires the examination of the existing precincts, within the CBD, and their primary urban functions. In its re-evaluation of the built city, it advocates for an alternative holistic urban plan and considers the question — what are the potential implications for implementing a more organic, three-dimensional and user-centred urban development strategy?

To undertake this investigation, the methodology incorporates site analysis and mapping in conjunction with a literature review that draws on urban studies and architectural and critical discourse. The driving provocateurs are from within the field of architecture and include Rem Koolhaas, Jan Gehl, Superstudio, Archigram. Building on the research methodology municipal data and the geographic information system ArcGIS highlights the mono-functional community segregation and disproportionate urban sprawl relative to population growth and sustainable development. This chapter advocates for an alternative, user-focused and layered urban composition. In doing so it advocates for architecture and infrastructure that supports city planning for cultural diversity, community awareness and inclusivity. To this end, this research undertakes an iterative design process which involves a progressive sequence of refinement through prototyping and peer review. As an urban design proposition to the built-city it deploys Frei Otto-esque inspired soap film modelling techniques to develop a proposed organic multi-dimensional grid (MdG). The MdG is layered over the existing precinct as a hypothetical user-centred planning, building, and development. Collaging techniques are employed to present visual interpretations. The images presented are not representative of what a building or precinct *should* look like but are perceptions and interpretations of what the city can be.

Early growth and development history

Railway construction facilitated the convergence and transiency of gold-prospecting workers into Perth city and was followed by a mass exodus to Northbridge.[3] On this basis historical transiency was and continues to be a community norm in Northbridge which started as a residential settlement that catered for prospectors travelling to and from Perth from the Kalgoorlie and Coolgardie mine sites. Short-term accommodation, retail and hardware with goods and services are still evident in the writing, motifs, façade, style, character, and heritage of the existing buildings and the physical layout of modern-day Northbridge continues to draw reference to a former time. In the 1990s, Northbridge gentrified, resulting in significant reduction in tenancy, increased vacancy and loss of confidence in commercial asset values.[4] From this point, new incremental improvements began to stem from a diversification of activities around an evolving cultural precinct, the establishment of large organisations, government offices and the vocational education and training provider, TAFE. The expansion of the TAFE campus footprint creates improved symbiosis between its existing and new buildings to other infrastructure in the Cultural Centre such as the Blue Room Theatre, Perth Institute of Contemporary Arts (PICA), Art Gallery of WA, State Library of WA, and WA Museum. General upgrades that improved daily life, comfort, security and safety, diverse provision of activities promoting wider demographics and occupancy intensified through residential occupancy and frequency of on-street activation in the urban civic realm also contributed.[5]

Perth is undeniably a multicultural city. One third of residents were born overseas.[6] The community comprises of a rich, ethnic mix, whose diverse foods, culture and lifestyle opportunities could be further celebrated to benefit local, national and international visitors and local economy. Perth's economy is significantly impacted by mining activity and strength—both positively and negatively. The city's GDP considerably outpaced the Australian average from 2000-01 to 2013-14, while the declining mining boom has been equally challenging on Perth's economy. In the 1990s Perth's economy accounted for 6.0 per cent of growth, 11.5 per cent in the 2000s and 9.6 per cent in the 2010s. Regional Western Australia burgeoned, from 4.2 per cent in the 1990s to 7.4 per cent in the 2000s, and 8.8 per cent in the 2010s.[7] Perth is not a model of a liveable city. Persistent (sub) urban sprawl and inadequate public transportation has negatively impacted equitable access to services, the city and increased motor vehicular dependence. "Planners speak of 'healthy growth' when a city grows at 2.3% each year, without mentioning that this would mean doubling every 30 years."[8]

Perth's urban structure, density, scale, infrastructure and proximities provide an ideal and manageable case study to understand big city problems by international standards in a relatively small and manageable footprint. Ideal cities do not exist, particularly in light of the global diversity of perspectives and perceptions among their residents, commentators in the area of the built environment and the infinite number of design challenges and variables that must be met with solutions. The Oxford Dictionary defines 'ideal' as something that exists only in the imagination, in one's conception, and something desirable, but unlikely ever to be realised.[9] In architecture, with urban design and city planning, just as in everyday life, there is no ideal, but different expectations and outcomes based on specific solutions, archetypes and layouts. Western Australia's population density is lower than the Australian— collective average density with 1.0 and 3.0 persons per square kilometre respectively. Contentiously debated, it has been suggested that the Indigenous population in Australia was unlikely, at any time, to surpass one million people.[10]

> In 1788, new colonists arrived, at first as a trickle, but then in very rapidly increasing numbers. By 1900 the national population was around 3.8 million, by 1950 it was 8.3 million and just 50 years later it was 19.3 million…by October 2013 the population exceeded 23 million. Projections made by the Population Division of the United Nations indicate that Australia can expect its population to continue to increase in most scenarios, perhaps achieving 41.5 million under 'medium variant' assumption by 2100.[11]

Perth's population density is approximately 317 people per square kilometre and is "one of the least populated *developed* cities in the World."[12] Despite the low density, the city hosts a wide ranging multi-ethnic, multi-racial, and multi-faith population.[13] Geographically, Perth can be described as a 20 square kilometre CBD surrounded by sprawling suburban development extending up to 70km to the north and south, 50km to the east (limited by the Darling Scarp), and 10km to the west (limited by the Indian Ocean). The CBD itself is composed of 15 segmented mono-functional precincts including the Business precinct itself, located between King Street, Forrest Chase, the Perth City Link and Mounts Bay Road.[14] While a limited number of these precincts are close to the study area, it is evident from figure 7.1 that typological and/or functional clustering has proliferated. Consumerism and Business precincts provide sufficient parameters to adequately highlight critical concerns and offer visual interpretations that question the legitimacy of mono-functionalism within the greater context. Thus, the resultant urban development pattern is symptomatic of economic and political city-shaping policy. The CBD is also home to Central Park, the tallest building in Perth situated at 152-158 St George's Terrace Perth. Since its completion in the early 1990s it has re-defined Perth's skyline, serves as a popular reference-point and provides a generous green space at its extended private—public interface, making it a significant building. This well-regarded and popular building and precinct, however, segregates various user-groups based upon time place and circumstance, activity, and sub-culture.

Segregation by design

The preponderance of first-world economies reflects an urban layout set out as a grid, denoting economic efficiency, order and an ability to methodically and predictably develop and expand despite natural formations or other inhibiting parameters. Montreal, Barcelona, New York, Vancouver, Melbourne are but a sample. Inherently, gridded urban environments suggest ordered thought, civility, technology and intellect to apply these measures to achieve prosperous, commodious and competent cities that sustain opportunity and growth, and support healthy community interactions and inclusivity. Well-intended, municipal planning policies themselves can also lead to some less-desirable outcomes. For example, gridded planning and development typically manifest into monofunctional zones or precincts that segregate are, less convivial and limit opportunities for functional congruence.[15] Segregation reduces community opportunities to share in diverse activities. Limited, specialised or mono-function, however, leads to predictable and programmed events that dissuade inquiry, discovery, playfulness or interpretation. This leads to reduced diversity of urban experiences through limited scope and richness. Superstudio asserts that "if design is merely an inducement to consume, then we must reject design," and must continue to reject "until all design activities are aimed towards meeting primary needs."[16]

What the evidence suggests is that it is fundamental to the social needs of the community to nurture diversity as something to be embraced, celebrated, and used as a platform to promote cultural identity. This is in stark contrast to policies for development in Perth that continue to encourage mono-functional precincts. Singular functions, such as government and corporate business sectors when clustered together, (spanning an entire CBD, as it does along Perth's St Georges Terrace), and predominantly retail sectors in the surrounding vicinity, lead to extensive sections of Perth being disused beyond working hours. This population exodus or 'hollowing out' of the city centre in favour of Perth's expansive sprawling suburban corridor, has been coined the "Doughnut Effect."[17] This results in underutilised central capital assets and infrastructure, and reduced physical inhabitation in the city centre. This condition escalates the propensity for crime arising out of insufficient natural surveillance born of collective spatial occupation and activity.[18] City Planning Scheme 2 divides the city into unique precincts (figure 7.1). The development of such precinct plans allows Perth to set a vision for each specific area. These plans identify the opportunities and constraints in each precinct and are used to inform the determination of planning applications.[19]

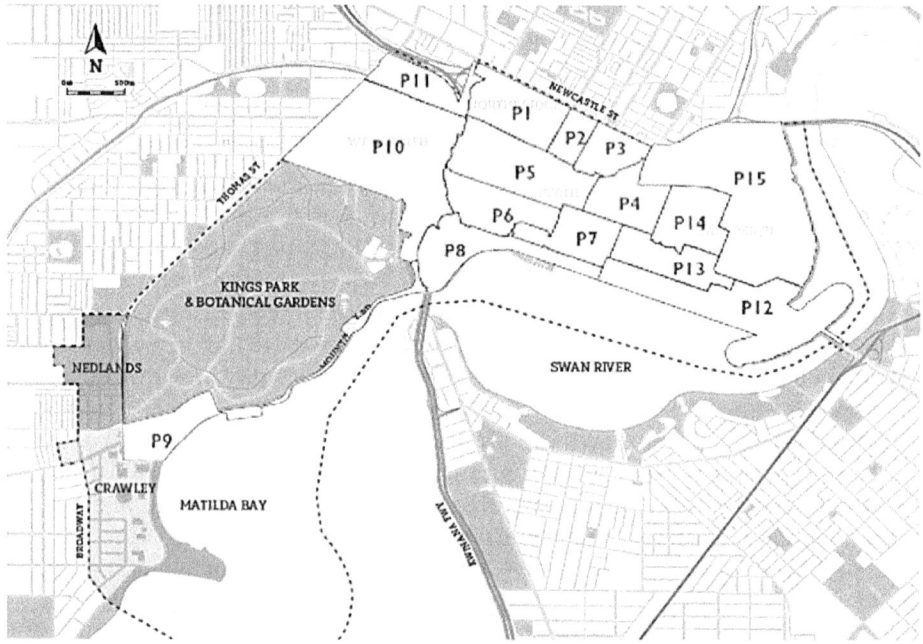

Figure 7.1 Mono-functional precincts with limited diversity of activities: open spaces within mono-functional spaces are typically under-utilised and monocultural. City of Perth Mapping, image modified by Jonescu 2018. Image Credit: ArcGIS Resource Centre ©

Precinct code/name	P1 Northbridge	P2 Cultural	P3 Stirling
P4 Victoria	P5 Citiplace	P6 St Georges	P7 Civic
P8 Foreshore	P9 Matilda Bay	P10 West Perth	P11 Hamilton
P12 Langley	P13 Adelaide	P14 Goderich	P15 East Perth

A shift in living arrangement options

Over the last ten years, there has been a significant increase in mixed-use medium-rise residential development in Perth typically coupled with a mixed-use lower plaza. Economic wealth and confidence on the back of Western Australia's mining industry have resulted in rapid increases in skilled migration and a need to provide sufficient living arrangement options and housing supply. Given this, it is questionable if all necessary amenities, including adequate and complimentary transport infrastructure, have been provided to support higher density nodes around well-considered blended land use. A latent insufficiency in this regard has the potential to lead to a false sentiment of failure. Positively shifting long-held community sentiments towards living densely, in Perth has been met with resistance due to gaps in symbiotic alignment. Correlations are required between density, provision, accessibility, inclusivity, transportation, safety, and many other factors beyond the simplistic notion of providing higher density living conditions. Outer-suburb sprawl in the Perth context has led to high-level replication of services requiring ever-increasing and sustained infrastructure networks, making them unsustainable. Influenced by cultural norms, feasibility and a paucity of exposure to other modes of living, Perth's sprawl suggests enduring societal attitudes favouring suburban lifestyle as an ideal. Moreover, sprawled living conditions—and by the very nature of suburbia, a lack of pedestrian traffic and passive surveillance—increases pressures on law enforcement efforts to manage crime across a vast metropolitan area.

Perth's metropolitan area is predominantly low-density development extending 140km from Yanchep in the north, to Mandurah in the south and 50km to the east from the CBD. Perth, like many cities, has developed beyond its economic, migratory and population growth capacity. Rapid increases in development initiation and planning phases have seen many larger projects commence, and due to the programmed length, have only recently been completed. However, the only aspect that has outperformed construction timelines has been a rapid economic downturn and a significant reduction in demand for West Australian (WA) minerals and their price.[20] With this, economic prosperity, skilled mass migration and population increases have declined, which "at its peak, the state's population growth was 3.7 per cent in the year to September 2012. Three years later, the rate was 1.3 per cent, with net overseas migration to WA falling from 57,000 people per year to 14,000."[21] Cook suggests that the City of Perth refers to culture as 'policy' for financial gain and is considered as inherently linked to the arts.[22] Within the context of city building, to which municipal strategic planning relates, this paper refutes this definition. It requires recognition of the significance of urban and architectural space which shapes behaviours, that over time becomes collective culture, and culture shapes ideology. This interpretation of policy limits overview of diversity and cultural creativity of diverse communities which place-making requires.[23]

Layers of government

Australia comprises of three levels of government, federal, state, and local. Branching from these, at each level are a number of bodies that are further involved in governing development for the purpose of infrastructure, architecture, and construction. Arguably it is the governance of local government that at this operational level has resulted in mono functional precincts and a number of structural issues in Perth. Infrastructure Australia is an independent statutory body with a mandate to prioritise and progress nationally significant infrastructure. IA development involves State and Federal public sectors (and to some degree Local Government). Within this body, all levels of government provide a number of guidelines that must be adhered to such that forthcoming projects are likely to be approved. Federal government procedures and State guidelines relate to the WA government's Strategic Asset Management Framework. Additionally, the regulatory requirements must adhere to the planning and development guidelines of permit authorities. There are three permit authorities: (1) Local Government, (2) Special Permit Authority by Ministerial approval and (3) State Permit Authorities by Ministerial approval. Permit authorities as identified in the relevant State Building Act are charged with issuing permits, retaining records and are responsible for ensuring that buildings in its district comply with minimum building standards.

For any development to proceed to construction, there are two separate and significant approvals processes required by all local Governments; (1) Development Approval (DA) and (2) submission for Building Permit. Firstly, Development Approval (DA) is an assessment process conducted by the local authority to ensure matters such as densities; zoning; site setbacks; height of building; overshadowing of adjoining properties; parking and other common and contentious items are addressed in the design proposal submission. Local government's role in development planning continues to become increasingly complex. It is a facilitator and collaborator in integrating its own numerous sub-disciplines and stakeholders, that must also consider the strategic goals of State and Federal Government. Furthermore, local government must also consider negotiating with developers, various consultants, and the community. Secondly, submission for a Building Permit is processed predominantly as a performance-based assessment in which the development is constructed and evaluated against the Australian National Construction Code (NCC). Obtaining a Building Permit deals with matters relating to the technical detail and physical construction of the development, such as, but not limited to—structural design, fire safety, accessibility and egress for occupants, toilet facilities.

To undertake these initiatives requires that local governments understand and identify community needs, and apply evidence-based arguments from data, research and observation. The Western Australian State Government has introduced measures to deal with larger initiatives through the Development Assessment Panel (DAP). The DAP is a system implemented to deal with major (multi-million dollar) projects and is situated outside of the Local Government, intended to remove local politics and potential conflicts of interest that can impact on Local Government decisions. Throughout these processes, where a Local Authority and/or DAP makes a discretionary decision in refusing conditional approval of an application, for example where a submission does not comply with the local planning scheme, applicants have the right to appeal that decision to the State's Administrative Tribunal.

A holistic solution

The urbanist and architect, Steven Holl, explains that a city cannot be completely appreciated from one perspective due to varying scales of complexity.[24] Furthermore, much like a collage (see figure 7.2), cities are experienced as segmented components that together form a cohesive picture, but due to their physical and geographical scale can never be considered or experienced as such. Prominent architects—Daniel Libeskind and Rem Koolhaas, further this notion, adding that collage is a critical methodology for design and research.[25] To decode or decipher the Urban Genetic Code of a place, it must be appreciated that the physical manifestation of a city is not its current condition, but is a product of its inherent historical attributes that is a compilation of evolved components and city-forming layers. As the illustrated equation in figure 7.2 indicates the Urban Genetic Code is a product of a bottom-up approach coupled with people-centre knowledge. Fundamentally, collaging as a methodology derives critical meaning through the techniques of peeling, overlapping, re-imagining and re-configuring which support the illustrative urban code.

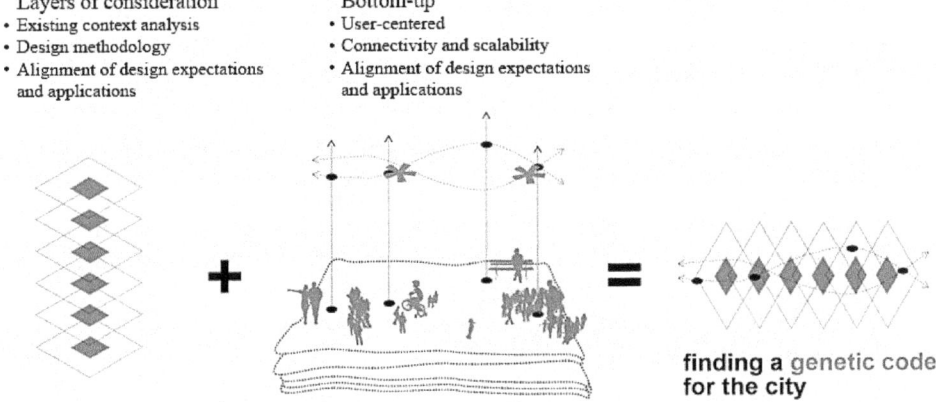

Layers of consideration
• Existing context analysis
• Design methodology
• Alignment of design expectations and applications

Bottom-up
• User-centered
• Connectivity and scalability
• Alignment of design expectations and applications

finding a genetic code for the city

Figure 7.2 Urban Genetic Code (UGC): designing the city by understanding its UGC, 2020. Image Credit: Do and Jonescu ©

This research utilises Collage as a qualitative research and critical explorative tool. Moreover, we apply this as a graphical communication technique to present ideas of layering and blending of social, cultural, economic, and functional diversity. Collage allows for imagining of a city comprised of a mélange of networks, typologies and organic needs-based development. This proposition more closely resembles a series of micro-ecosystems supporting a higher organism. Research through design, utilising collage as a primary technique in this proposal intends to be evocative, relying on individual perception, experiences and understanding to facilitate and 'imagining' rather than a prescriptive outcome. Lisa Given asserts that collage is a powerful research method primarily applied in the arts.[26] It allows for juxtaposition, imagination and experimentation, as supported in Paula Gerstenblatt's work on collage portraiture. Collage gave voice to "marginalized" elements that would not otherwise be considered.[27] Lynne Butler-Kisber & Tiiu Poldma (2010) suggest that it allows the researcher to communicate concepts and experiences to audiences where it is difficult to express in text.[28] The authors suggest that the method has attracted the acclaim of many disciplines for documentation, analysis, and as a means of communication.

This research applies the same juxtaposition technique to a series of seemingly disassociated themes, images, objects, texts, and materials. The method aims to encourage the participant—the reader—to imagine an entirely speculative and less conventional urban landscape, how it is created, what it may require, how it might form and feel, and what it would need to be nurtured and to thrive. To this end, Rio's and Brazil's favelas are layered with complexity and are a rich tapestry of diverse communities, developing more organically out of need and support. Organic development principles are further discussed through Frei Otto's 'bubble' attraction experiments and methods, later in this paper. At first glance, conventional thinking might consider this development as arbitrary; however, the eclectic development is a highly organised logical collective with a unique culture. This is highlighted through the observations of architects and urban planners who have taken up favela residence to study local life, rules, codes, culture, construction methodology, and urban development in the area. Comments and findings by Veysseyre (2014) include:

> While there are no official rules of construction, there is a law of mutual respect...everyone knows and talks to everyone else, and so they must come to peaceful agreements among themselves...At first glance, the favelas—to me—were an impressive, chaotic mass: waves of houses that invaded every free space.[29]

Findings and discussion: Rem Koolhaas' social condenser and Frei Otto's attractive occupation propositions

This research design framework considers Koolhaas' social condenser as an essential criterion.[30] The main thrust of the condenser is to promote a layering of sympathetic urban events and processes. This is aimed towards developing blended spatial relationships within what would otherwise be a largely predictable and programmed order currently embedded in Perth's gridded urban environment. The layered order offers exemption from typical 'programmed' activities and favours affordance. Over time this develops into customs and behavioural norms (or culture) further informing future design. Affordance (relating to environmental affordance) as a theory, according to Gibson's proposition (1979) is what the "environment offers the animal."[31] This generic definition refers more to what something could be used for rather than its intended purpose. A milk crate, for example, holds milk, yet it could be adapted for use as seating, a table, set of steps, shelving, storage, multi-functional, and so forth. Objects can be perceived to have considerable inherent affordances, limited only by individual factors such as education, skill, vocational training, ingenuity and need. Through the application of affordance principles and Frei Otto's methodologies, this research postulates a series of hypothetical developmental patterns that are fundamental, intuitive and primal.

The resultant configurations differ from development arrangements arising from compliance with imposed local planning schemes. Otto asserts: "[sic] Cities, estates and routing systems develop, change, and fundamentally cannot be planned."[32] Claims to ownership, land and building regulations, planning decisions and political interventions make it difficult for settlement structures to adapt to constantly changing requirements to such an extent that meaningful and totally ecological use of the surface of the earth is becoming increasingly difficult, although new techniques and flexible planning models mean that a connection could be found with the self-de-signing processes of urban-development history. Similarly to how the favela supports its own unique legitimate culture and social interactions, this method was tested (see figure 7.3a and 7.3b) to support an alternative perspective through which to consider development. While not conventional, application of this method achieves a biological order and logic that offers relevance to user-orientated design strategies. This organic layering ameliorates the doughnut effect, through overlapping function and activities. Moreover, the research adapts additional city-building components considered critical by key commentators in the field.

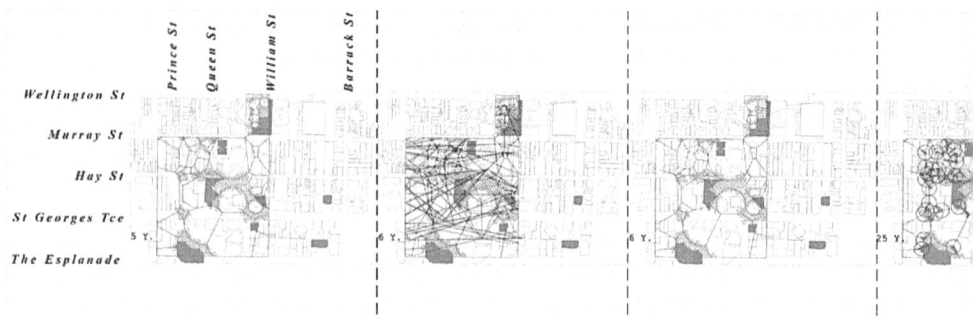

Figure 7.3a Study diagrams–Frei Otto's methodology, Wuu 2014, modified Jonescu 2019.
Image Credit: Wuu and Jonescu ©

In Mutations: Rem Koolhaas, Harvard Project on the City, Stefano Boeri, Multiplicity, Sanford Kwinter, Nadia Tazi, Hans Ulrich Obrist, suggests that—critical city making components include: Monuments, Planning, Buildings, Infrastructure and Trades and Services.[33] As these components are imperative aspects of this study, this research expands on their significance.

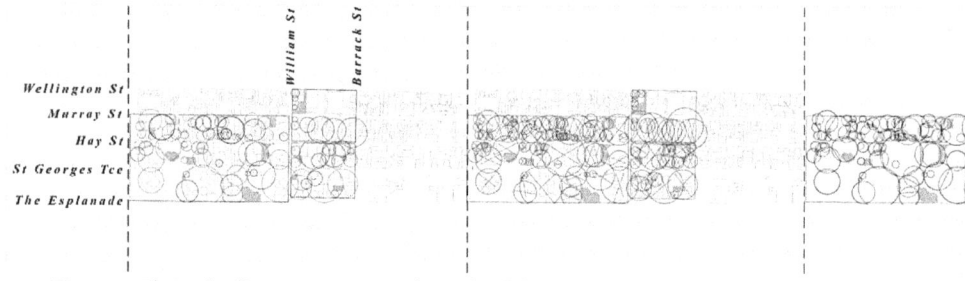

Figure 7.3b Study diagrams–Frei Otto's methodology, Wuu 2014, modified Jonescu 2019.
Image Credit: Wuu and Jonescu ©

City-making components

According to Koolhaas, a *Monument* is a prominent landmark that has the physical or perceived capacity to leverage and activate symbiotic relationships with its immediate environment.[34] Within this context a Monument is likened to a natural relationship with inherent benefits between host and parasite in the natural world. Within the parameters of this definition, a critical monument is an influencing structure or building with gravitas to its surroundings, (nearby buildings, industries, activities), and it is upon this notion that we evaluated and determined the critical monument within the CBD precinct study site to be the Central Park Tower. The evaluation matrix considered criteria such as building elevation above finished floor level, typology, delegated function, and adjunct development. Once determined, the monument provided opportunities to apply Otto's attractive occupation methodology to study occupant behaviours within the vicinity of the monument. The evaluation process proposes the monument to be the 249m high Central Park Tower (the tallest building in Perth). Moreover, the study determined that the Monument incorporated the landscaped forecourt and mezzanine area as significant aspects of the building that extend between St Georges Terrace and Hay Street, bound by William Street.

Koolhaas refers to *Planning*, the second critical building-block, as an urban spatial strategy that considers relationships between delineation and function.[35] According to the 2018 Planning Institute of Australia, "Planning is the act of researching, analysing, anticipating and influencing change in our society. In urban areas, planners guide and manage the way suburbs and regions develop, making sure that they are good places in which to live, work and play."[36] This research proposes an alternative planning paradigm that aligns with Otto's theory of Attractive Occupation and is applied through Plateau's Law of soap film formation. Soap film formation is based upon set principles of physics of attraction.[37] What is created are geometrical formations that closely resembled organic development and "movement in nature."[38] Within the urban context, typology and function delineate territory, as would the skin of the bubble. This methodology, when applied, highlights alternative critical pathways and nodes that form naturally and efficiently, an alternative to a prescribed formation. This has resulted in a form and functional MdG that more closely resembles a series of well-connected micro-nodes, and an organic grid similar to medieval city layouts and favelas, which rely more on community relationships and proximity linkage. Accordingly, this research proposes the resultant design of city planning as a product of an interactive intersect between physical aspects of the existing urban grid and a theoretical organic MdG overlay that could be sculpted and re-purposed as desired, through community interaction, integration and negotiation (see figure 7.4a-7.4e). The ideal desires/needs of the community, as well as its associated activities, determine the need for functional physical urban form, and critical infrastructure such as exits, pathways, nodes, intersections and divisions, rather than through a prescribed by policy approach. This theoretical proposition highlights how community interactions where need and desire might determine alternative and appropriate methodologies to inform city planning and urban space.

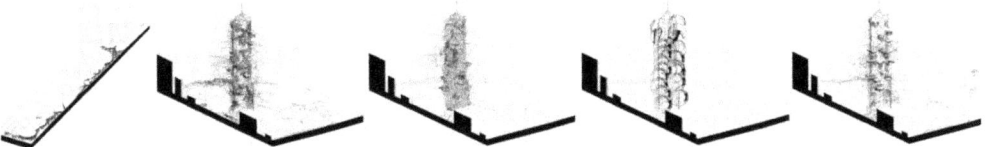

Figure 7.4a-7.4e (left to right): Process Design of Perth Central Park Building morphed with techniques of peeling, overlapping, and re-configuring and applying Frei Otto's attractive occupation methodology, Wuu 2014, modified Jonescu 2019.
Image Credit: Wuu and Jonescu ©

The City of Perth's Municipal guidelines determine which developments are in-keeping with the City's policies and priorities. Such policies are also the antecedent of mono-functionalism and the precursor of the doughnut effect. To counter this, as with Planning above, this research suggests that the building's components follow a similar process applied to the skin (see figure 7.5a-b: 7.5c-d) and armature of the structure, in particular at its interface at ground level. As a theoretical proposition, not limited by statutory requirements of construction, this paper suggests that there is an essential need for a critical understanding at the outset of the behaviours, relationships and community interactions that develop between life and infrastructure, architectural realisation, and the need to reconsider how this should inform future planning policy.

Figure 7.5a-b Collage, design of Perth Central Park Building with techniques of peeling, overlapping, and re-configuring the skin of the Monument building and its public interface, Wuu 2014, modified Jonescu 2019. Image Credit: Wuu and Jonescu ©

Figure 7.5c-d Collage, design of Perth Central Park Building with techniques of peeling, overlapping, and re-configuring the skin of the Monument building and its public interface, Wuu 2014, modified Jonescu 2019. Image Credit: Wuu and Jonescu ©

Pathway mapping follows a logical path of least resistance planning, highlighting Otto's method of space and movement. These thresholds are developed to work with the rationale of human thought.[39] This research suggests an alternative to gridded perimeter-based pathway infrastructure. Dr Nobuhiro Hagura, a leading researcher at the Center for Information and Neural Networks, University College London, attests that it is human nature to take the path of least resistance.[40] This proposal therefore, promotes a perceived simplified network with pathway connections and distances minimised to their most efficient route, working concurrently with the formation of relationships between building and opening thresholds.[41] Public squares and communal open spaces form integral components for interaction and community participation in events and everyday life. This research suggests an alternative methodology for considering a more user-focused and organic development strategy that encourages opportunities for growth and morphology within the Planning and Building grid, as required.

Conclusion

The research redefines the cause and effect of functional and spatial boundaries through the interrogation of existing precinct values and activation strategies in Perth, WA. The study argues that inclusive convivial spaces that are activated for longer periods throughout the day are likely able to be achieved through more organic and less rigid planning policies. This approach requires bottom-up thinking from a human scale perspective. This paper proposes increasingly—user-focused methodologies, in conjunction with Frei Otto's relative biological and organic growth and decay theories, to develop a theoretical multi-dimensional development grid (MdG) overlay informing future development policies for city planning. Moreover, this provides a means by which to integrate existing city design with future infrastructure. The purpose is to better integrate people with community activity and to dissuade population exodus from the CBD after working hours—the doughnut effect. Accordingly, the MdG highlights alternative approaches to considering planning and development guidelines that incorporate organic city-shaping opportunities beyond rigid precincts models. We suggest that through design thinking and elements of active occupation that account for the needs and desires of the community to be met, rather than economic clustering and cultural disassociation, cities stand to become more engaged at the human scale. What is proposed is to provide for improved bilateral relationships and influence between significant buildings and their surroundings.

The research presents imagery that is not limited by structural, political, economic constraints or existing development policies, but of a coalescent blending of spatial relationships. Collage has been used throughout this paper with the intent that it allows the reader to imagine the possibilities in layering, growth and decay of city thresholds, pathways and openings, which consider real-world realities of cities that are in constant flux. The theoretical MdG overlay, therefore, provides a tool through which to highlight community interaction and desire in the formation of spatial relationships. This thesis has provided what are likely unconventional development strategies and approaches to community and development morphology. While noting typical initial resistance to change, policies, community behavior, and organic simulation could offer additional aspects for design research to better understand nodes, relationships and opportunities of blended function and typologies.

Bibliography

Andraos, Amale, Rami El-Samahy, Patricia Heyda, Jennifer Lee, Christina Long, Allyson Mendenhall, Fransisco Menza, Hunter Tura, and Peter Zellner, "How to Build a City: The Roman Operating System." In *Mutations: Rem Koolhaas, Harvard Project on the City*, edited by Stefano Boeri, Stanford Kwinter, Nadia Tazi, Hans Obrist, and Armelle Lavalou, 10-19. Barcelona: ACTAR, 2000.

Appleyard, Reginald. "Western Australia: Economic and Demographic Growth, 1850-1914." In *A New History of Western Australia*, Charles Thomas Stannage, ed., 211-236. Nedlands: University of Western Australia Press, 1981.

Australian Bureau of Statistics [ABS]. "2016 Census QuickStats: Northbridge (WA) Code SSC51149 (SSC)." Canberra: *Australian Bureau of Statistics* (2016). Accessed January 20, 2017.

ArcGIS Resource Centre. 2019. ArcGIS Online. http://help.arcgis.com/en/arcgisdesktop/10.0/help/index.html

Australian Bureau of Statistics [ABS]. "2016 Census QuickStats: Perth (WA)." Australian Bureau of Statistics [ABS], 2016. https://quickstats.censusdata.abs.gov.au/census_services/getproduct/census/2016/quickstat/SSC51218.

Ball, Philip. *Shapes. Nature's Patterns: A Tapestry in Three Parts*. Oxford: Oxford University Press, 2009.

Ballow, Tom. *The New Science of Flight and Movement*. Victoria, British Columbia: Trafford Publishing, 2005.

Butler-Kisber, L, and T Poldma. "The Power of Visual Approaches in Qualitative Inquiry: The Use of Collage Making and Concept Mapping in Experiential Research." *Journal of Research Practice* 6, no. 2 (2011), 18.

City of Perth. *Modern Visions of the City of Perth*. Perth: City of Perth. Accessed February 22, 2020. https://engage.perth.wa.gov.au/3513/documents/6650.

City of Perth, "City of Perth SafeCity Community Safety and Crime Prevention Plan 2010-2013," Perth: City of Perth. Accessed August 15, 2018. https://catalogue.nla.gov.au/Record/5785558.

City of Perth, "City Planning Scheme No.2 (Part 2)," Perth: City of Perth. Accessed August 17, 2018. https://www.perth.wa.gov.au/develop/planning-framework/planning-schemes.

Development WA. "Perth City Link – Overview, Development WA - Shaping Our State's Future." Perth: Development WA. Accessed October 17, 2020. https://developmentwa.com.au/projects/redevelopment/perth-city-link/overview.

Dickman, Chris R. "Whither Wildlife in an Overpopulated World?" in *Sustainable Futures: Linking Population, Resources and the Environment*, edited by Jenny Goldie and Katharine Betts, 13-23. Victoria: CSIRO Publishing, 2014. https://doi.org/10.1002/psp.1965.

Cook, Patrick. "The Cultural City: The Role of Culture in Perth City Planning Policy." Bachelor's Dissertation, 2010.

Forster, Clive. *Australian Cities: Continuity and Change.* New York: Oxford University Press, 2004.

Gehl, Jan. *Cities for People.* Washington, Dc: Island Press, 2010.

Gerstenblatt, Paula. "Collage Portraits as a Method of Analysis in Qualitative Research." *International Journal of Qualitative Methods* 12, no. 1 (2013): 294-309. https://doi.org/10.1177/160940691301200114.

Gibson, James. *The Ecological Approach to Visual Perception.* New York: Psychology Press, 2015.

Given, Lisa. *The SAGE Encyclopedia of Qualitative Research Methods. The SAGE Encyclopedia of Qualitative Research Methods.* Vol. 2. SAGE Publications, Inc, (2008). https://doi.org/10.4135/9781412963909.n52.

Holl, Steven, Juhani Pallasmaa, and Alberto Gómez. *Questions of Perception: Phenomenology of Architecture.* San Francisco: William Stout, 2007.

Melet, Ed, and Eric Vreedenburgh. *Rooftop Architecture: Building on an Elevated Surface.* Rotterdam: Nai Publishers, 2005.

Miles, Steven. *Youth Lifestyles in a Changing World.* Buckingham England; Philadelphia: Open University Press, 2000.

O'Connor, Andrew. "WA state budget deficit to surge to almost $4b." *ABC News,* May 12, 2016. Accessed March 21, 2021. https://www.abc.net.au/news/2016-05-12/wa-state-budget-deficit-up-to-$4b/7409334.

O'Connor, Mark, and William Lines. *Overloading Australia: How Governments and Media Dither and Deny on Population.* Canterbury, N.S.W.: Envirobook. ISBN: 9780858812246, 2010.

O.M.A, Remment Koolhaas, and Bruce Mau. *S, M, L, Xl.* New York: Monacelli Press, 1995.

Otto, Frei. *Occupying and Connecting Thoughts on Territories and Spheres of Influence with Particular Reference to Human Settlement.* Edited by Berthold Burkhardt. London: Axel Menges, 2011.

Oxford Dictionaries. s.v. "Ideal." Accessed April 8, 2021, https://www.oxford dictionaries.com/definition/english/ideal

Perth Population. "Perth Population 2019." Accessed January 5, 2021. http://www.population.net.au/perth-population/

Piesse, Emily, and Laura Gartry. "Apartment Glut Looms in Perth Market." *ABC News,* April 7, 2016. Accessed March 21, 2021. https://www.abc.net.au/news/2016-04-07/perth-apartment-oversupply-fears-market-slows/7308280.

Planning Institute of Australia. "Planning Fact Sheet 01: What Is Planning." Accessed March 21, 2021. https://www.planning.org.au/wa.

Remment Koolhaas and Brendan McGetrick. Content: Triumph of Realization. Köln: Taschen, 2004.

SGS Economics and Planning, "Economic Performance of Australia's Cities and Regions," Canberra: *SGS Economics and Planning.* (2018): 11-34. https://www.sgsep.com.au/assets/main/SGS-Economics-and-Planning-Economic-performance-fo-asutralias-cities-and-regions-report.pdf

Shields, Jennifer. *Collage and Architecture.* New York: Routledge, 2014.

Sisson, Alistair and Paul Maginn. "Reclaiming Northbridge: Urban (Dis)Order and Territorial Stigmatisation in Perth's Night Time Economy Precinct."

Urban Policy and Research 36, no 2 (2018): 123-137. http://doi.org/10.1080/0
8111146.2018.1460266.

University College London. "Humans Are Hard-Wired to Follow the Path of
Least Resistance." Accessed August 13, 2017. https://www.sciencedaily.com/
releases/2017/02/170221101016.htm.

Veysseyre, Solène. "Case Study: The Unspoken Rules of Favela Construction."
Edited by Vanessa Quirk. *ArchDaily*, 2014. http://www.archdaily.com/531253
/case-study-the-unspoken-rules-of-favela-construction. Accessed November 17,
2014.

Weisstein, Eric. "Plateau's Laws." Wolfram Research, Inc., 2016. http://math
world.wolfram.com/PlateausLaws.html. Accessed August 22, 2014.

Chapter 8

The unsmart city:
pitfalls of predictability — Copenhagen

Jens Christian Pasgaard

Aarhus School of Architecture, Denmark

Karen Olesen

Aarhus School of Architecture, Denmark

Tom Nielsen

Aarhus School of Architecture, Denmark

Morten Daugaard

Aarhus School of Architecture, Denmark

Abstract

This chapter explores how smart city technologies affect the experience of the built city. The Danish capital, Copenhagen, is used as a case study as the city that has a progressive approach to implementing smart city solutions and because Denmark is among the most digitalized countries in the world. The smart city concept is discussed in relation to the qualities of urban unpredictability, and three aspects of smart cities are identified: a) densification and layering, b) intelligent surfaces, and c) digital surveillance. The aspects are approached through theoretical insights drawn from the social sciences, architecture, and urbanism, and the dilemmas associated with the optimization of urban spaces are exemplified by contemporary cases. The chapter concludes that the lesson from Copenhagen is that changes imposed by smart city technologies happen almost imperceptibly, and stresses the importance of being aware of the interests at stake when decisions concerning digital solutions are made.

Keywords: Copenhagen, smart cities, unsmart, urban unpredictability, densification, layering

***

Introduction

With its rich urban development, Copenhagen provides an exemplary case study concerning the consequences of making cities smarter. From being historically an administrative and merchant city at the center of the small Danish empire, it developed into an industrial city in the nineteenth century and, in the latter part of the twentieth century, into a sprawling urban region of around two million inhabitants.[1] This was followed by a period of deindustrialization and inner-city decline, and then suburbanization during the 1980-1990s. After this phase, Copenhagen underwent economic growth, urban renewal and its own "urban turn."[2] Within the new network-oriented post-industrial economy, Copenhagen developed into a strong hub for services, education and research.[3] Due to the fact that Copenhagen offers a high level of sustainability and energy efficiency it is often in the top ten of lists of the most liveable cities in the world. A key factor to this liveability is its densely built historical center, the informal character of its urban spaces and its urban life which is also attractive to tourists.[4] What makes Copenhagen an interesting case study is the set of dilemmas which exist between these urban qualities and smart city thinking; between complex and ambiguous urban spaces such as Bispeengbuen and the frictionless predictability provided by information technologies.

Smart City is a concept that refers to a current situation where more and more cities seek to optimize themselves on several fronts. Information technology is applied in order to enable cities to become more efficient, more resilient, and less resource-consuming. By managing traffic flows, regulating the consumption of water and electricity, and monitoring other services dependent on the activities of the city's inhabitants, authorities see the implementation of smart city technologies as a means to protect the environment as well as saving money. As a broad spectrum of smart solutions has emerged, smart city thinking is applied to an increasing number of components of the city that infiltrate several levels of scale. The consequences of this development on the built city and on the experience of the physical urban environment are in many cases almost imperceptible. On this basis, this chapter explores the consequences of these trends and focuses on three aspects of smart city development, which in isolation can seem unproblematic, but when brought together, call for scrutiny concerning the transformation of existing cities. These aspects are a) densification and layering, b) intelligent surfaces and c) digital surveillance and anonymity of individuals. The subject is approached through theory and propositions drawn from the social sciences, architecture and urbanism as well as from observation. The aim is to explore new insights concerning the benefits and drawbacks of smarter cities.

A contested concept

In recent years, the concept of smart cities has been widely debated. A large number of urban planners, educational institutions, and technology-oriented entrepreneurs and industries have celebrated the implementation of smart city solutions. These proponents highlight smart cities as more sustainable, self-sufficient, resilient, productive, innovative, and inclusive through e-democracy/e-governance, etc.[5] On the other hand, it has been argued that the concept makes no sense at all, as it is impossible to find cities not trying to act intelligently. Who wants to make a stupid city?[6] Rem Koolhaas also addresses the smart city movement and rhetorically asks, "Are Smart Cities Condemned to Be Stupid?", thereby drawing attention to the dangers of using smart city solutions for all forms of urban challenges and apocalyptic scenarios.[7] Another line of inquiry is concerned with the potential negative consequences of surveillance and exploitation of big data in urban contexts. Recently, the American social psychologist and philosopher Shoshana Zuboff describes how surveillance data, data interpretation, and predictions about future behaviors are now bought and sold at an unprecedented pace. What Zuboff portrays is a radical and all-embracing digital revolution that induces fundamental changes in human existence.[8]

While the debates concerning smart cities continue, it is evident that smart city thinking is making its way across many different scale levels with an unprecedented influence and pace. Urban data is continuously collected and analyzed, leading to more and more advanced responses. Smart city experts speak of different generations of smart cities (version 2.0, 3.0, etc.) and discuss the implementation of AI technologies, including machine learning. The development trend is, to a great extent, irreversible.[9] When observing recent urban development projects, it is easy to see how these smart solutions significantly impact on the urban form at the district level and affect the individual urban building typologies. Tools like the cloud-based AI software, Spacemaker, provide highly efficient ways to make data-driven decisions in the sketching process.[10] The different spatial scenarios can in a few minutes be tested to optimize the number of apartments with a view, the microclimatic conditions, and many more parameters. In particular, the tools make it possible to test different spatial configurations and plot-ratios extremely fast, letting the developer calculate the financial consequences of given spatial densities.

Contextualizing unpredictability – smart city Copenhagen

This chapter questions the value of the predictable and thereby proposes the benefits of *the unpredictable*. The unpredictable is here addressed as a desirable quality of our urban environments; however, in many urban contexts, predictability is exactly what inhabitants desire. This is, of course, the case in less privileged societies than the Danish, where social insecurity prevails. In this sense, it is important to make a distinction between predictability as a social concept and predictability as an aspect of the built city. When addressing the built city, the idea of the unpredictable links back to a number of architectural theorists who each have argued for the qualities found in seemingly dis-ordered or unanticipated spatial situations. This includes Alison and Peter Smithson's notion of Random Aesthetics and Conglomerate Ordering which differed from a rigid modernist aesthetics.[11] Similarly, Robert Venturi's *Complexity and Contradiction* (1966), praised the multiplicities of spatial and compositional arrangements found in pre-modern architecture and urbanism.[12] What is also worth mentioning is Thomas Sieverts' proposition about Spontaneous Architecture in suggesting a set of aesthetics which let you perceive the emotional aspects of reality beyond its instrumental and functional features.[13] Another example is sociologist Richard Sennett's seminal *The Uses of Disorder* (1970), in which he argues that the ideal of a planned and ordered city is flawed.[14] Sennett has recently revisited this idea together with Pablo Sendra in *Designing Disorder—Experiments and Disruptions in the City* (2020).[15]

Denmark is one of the most digitalized countries in the world and, at the same time, a privileged Scandinavian welfare society with a high degree of trust, not only among citizens but also between citizens and government authorities.[16] In 1968, Denmark became the first country to roll out an extensive Civil Registration System (CPR). The CPR supported the universalist welfare state policies that focused on the individual and their freedom from being formally tied to family, employer, birthplace or other traditional ways of registering citizens. Now, the individual is, from birth, in direct relation to the state and could receive the kind of benefits that were available for their specific situation. This new relationship between freedom and registration was a development in a strong and long tradition of building registers in Denmark, and the large amount of data from the Danish population is frequently used in research on everything from health and social science to criminology. Danes are used to being registered without experiencing limitations of their individual freedom or the risk of the information falling into the wrong hands and used against their will or interests.

A low degree of corruption and the high level of trust and social capital within the population makes Denmark and Copenhagen an interesting case when understanding the implications of new technologies and the exploitation of data.[17] Danes have adapted to the information technology revolution in an almost unquestioning way, for example tech companies are granted access to an abundance of personal data through social media platforms. With the swift rolling out of Internet connections followed by fiber-optic broadband networks, and later mobile phones and smartphones, Denmark has been a willing recipient and wide open to the new surveillance capitalism that Zuboff described. Taking this into account three aspects of smart city technologies and current urban development are discussed: A) Densification and layering; B) Intelligent Surfaces and C) Digital surveillance and anonymity of individuals.

A) Densification and layering

Since the turn of the millennium, there has been an increasing focus on the densification of existing urban structures. Generally, the dense and compact city is less resource-intensive than the scattered city, because each section of infrastructure and each meter of the supply network can serve more people. If dense is combined with smart, the result can be a dramatic optimization of the urban fabric. The aim is to make the most effective use of space which manifests itself in the way building stock and urban spaces are treated. Many architects no longer see a contradiction between a dense city and a green city and often succeed in raising the plot ratio and, at the same time, make space available for more trees, more biodiversity, and more recreational areas. The architects' approaches and solutions are a product of a more three-dimensional and sophisticated understanding of the city, with more layers and merged functions. One example of this is the P-House Lüders from 2016, designed by JAJA Architects (figure 8.1 and 8.2). The structure contains 485 parking spaces on seven floors, a supermarket and a 2,400 square meter-large activity roof with play and exercise equipment. A sculptural stairway on the south side of the building functions as a running track to the roof, which is accessible to the public from 07:00-22:00.

Figure 8.1 The Parking House Lüders, aerial photograph, 2019.
Image Credit: The Danish Agency for Data Supply and Efficiency ©

Figure 8.2 The Rooftop in use, 2019. Image Credit: Catherine Alexandra Zaia ©

Additionally, the facades are equipped with numerous boxes for plants, that supposedly contribute to the overall biodiversity of the district. The building is situated in the new built North Harbor of Copenhagen, which has received the highest certification of sustainable urban districts.[18] A research laboratory uses the entire district as a large-scale test-ground for smart tech solutions and several buildings in the district are equipped with technology that, besides optimizing the energy consumption, can return data to the laboratory.[19] The collected data is hereafter analyzed, and the results will inform the next generation of sustainable districts and the construction of future apartment complexes. Architects who are often supported by a wide range of technical specialists have become skilled at turning the challenging sustainability requirements into new positive design solutions.[20] In general, urban spaces have many more functions than were previously expected from them. Besides delivering recreational spaces for the young and old, they frequently include habitats for animals and plants, parking facilities for cars and bicycles, local drainage of rainwater solutions, etc. In addition, roof terraces and balconies are increasingly being adapted to local food production which contributes to increasing the city's biomass, storing CO_2, cleaning the air, and improving the microclimate. It is all about creating a more sustainable society and meeting the UN's 17 Sustainable Development Goals.[21]

B) Intelligent surfaces

As the layered city becomes smarter, so does the building stock itself. Gradually, over the past decades, the building regulations have tightened the insulation requirements, and today several new building structures contribute positively to the city's overall energy account.[22] The buildings are increasingly designed as spatial configurations of smart prefabricated building components. Roofs and facades can easily be equipped with energy-producing and intelligent surfaces holding technologies that continuously measure and analyze the citizens' energy consumption. A prominent example of this new generation of intelligent buildings is the Copenhagen International School, designed by C. F. Møller Architects. The building is situated in the North Harbor of Copenhagen and was completed in 2017. It is wrapped in more than 6,000 square meters of solar panels, and the façades work as "one of the largest building-integrated solar power plants in Denmark."[23]

The smart building initiatives are by default positive; however, they also demonstrate an imperceptible shift in our relationship with the city, its buildings, and its spaces. The urban surfaces no longer act as a discrete background to the life that unfolds in the city but are increasingly programmed, utilized, and managed from above. The result is a fundamental change in public space where new conflicts may arise between those who own the buildings and what is produced by them and those who manoeuvre around, on, and between them. It is not only the surfaces of buildings but also their programming that is getting smarter. One example is the Airbnb service which has turned an online service for vacation rentals into a hyper-efficient industry, where homes are in use all the time and function as money-making instruments. The Airbnb initiative and the accompanying cash flow foster experience-oriented places and makes tourism-related functions grow exponentially, while other everyday functions become less visible and eventually disappear. Paradoxically, this can make cities less well-functioning. When entire city districts are inhabited by short-term visitors with no interest in the social and economic life of the neighborhood, these districts can ultimately lose their attractiveness as housing areas.

C) Digital surveillance and anonymity of individuals

Although smart technologies are gaining ground everywhere and notably in cities of all sizes, it is primarily in large cities with many inhabitants and high resource consumption that they can make a difference. Large cities produce a large amount of data and it is here that the big data technology providers have a serious interest in being present. In this context, we encounter another dilemma of the smart city and yet another conflict between our traditional view of the city and contemporary urban developments. Since the process of urbanization accelerated in the latter half of the nineteenth century, the big city has been associated with the anonymity of the individual. Georg Simmel's "The big cities and the spiritual life" (1903), describes how modern life in the big city leads to fragmentation, individualization and impersonal relations between people.[24] Simmel pointed out the problems of urban life, but added that the individualization of the metropolis contains a potential for liberation as it offers its residents an anonymity that is not found in smaller communities. In the big city, it is possible to move among strangers without feeling watched. Walking aimlessly in a foreign city provides a sense of freedom and a feeling of being part of the city's collective life and, at the same time, of being almost invisible. However, the freedom and anonymity of the city can quickly turn into an illusion with the ubiquitous dominance of smart technologies. When every citizen has a smartphone that records their movements, consumption, and physical form, the question is whether the anonymity and freedom of the big city is real or just something we imagine.

Alex Pentland of the Media Lab, MIT researches how social networks influence human interactions, and proposes that in a digitally mediated society, citizens align with one another creating social patterns that can be manipulated. "For individuals, the attraction is the possibility of a world where everything is arranged for your convenience—your health checkup is magically scheduled just as you begin to get sick, the bus comes just as you get to the bus stop, and there is never a line of waiting people at city hall."[25] Pentland points out how these new capacities could eventually lead to a quantitative and predictive science of society. Such a reality is of course not a law of nature, but something human-made that should be critically evaluated.

Urban predictability

Since industrialization, the city has attracted people as a place to earn a living and at the same time offering a high density of experiences and sensory impressions. The city provides positive obstructions and friction in the sense that a walk through the city usually includes unplanned encounters. The unpredictability of the city is not only a product of its accumulation of people and activities but also of its history. All cities have strange holes and voids: these can be scars and remains from demolished structures of the past; clashes between different spatial ideologies; structural linkages between a modern grid and an older, more organic street pattern, etc. Cities have, therefore, backsides, shady sides, and pockets that are leftovers from previous incarnations of the city that can appear enigmatic and may trigger the imagination.

It is possible to explore and even get lost in the strange, abandoned spaces of the city because their shape and location do not immediately make sense and because they appear aimless, without obvious function. As the philosopher and cultural critic, Walter Benjamin, recalls when describing his childhood in Berlin, there is a joyous fear of getting lost in the city, in suddenly being in places where you have no idea where you are.[26] The unpredictable most often contrasts efficiency and abandoned spaces fit poorly in a hyper-efficient, smart city. As the mapping of cities becomes more and more refined in the search for unused, non-functional places that can somehow be put into play, important cultural environments can be lost and there is a risk that the city will become unenchanted, more predictable, and less intriguing.[27] In a discussion of social media as a scam, British writer Adam Curtis argues: "What I'm saying is that human beings have been reduced to a very simplified version of themselves, which they've accepted, in order to fit into this machine model both of society and the internet. But we are extraordinary and we can do extraordinary things. We are so much more, than what they are forcing us to accept."[28] Perhaps there is a limit to how effective a city can be if it is to retain its fascination and aesthetic diversity?

Bispeengbuen—Below the Arc

A specific example of the dilemmas associated with the persistent desire to optimize urban spaces in Copenhagen is the ongoing debate on how to deal with Bispeengbuen. The six-lane elevated expressway was constructed in the early 1970s to avoid traffic jams at a vital approach road to the city center. Despite intense protests at the time of planning and construction, the massive concrete structure was harshly erected as a curved road very close to existing housing blocks. However, the insensitive construction also created an informal space situated beneath the columns of the highway bridge, colloquially known as Below the Arc. This space, arisen as an unintended consequence of the large-scale traffic intervention, has for years been used for parking lots but has also, and increasingly, been used for a number of more or less official activities.[29] As such, the un-programmed surface has become a rare and highly valuable space that can accommodate different cultural encounters and events. Some days, the space is empty and appears as a strange shadowy leftover in the city center (figure 8.3). On other days, it is loaded with people (figure 8.4).

Figure 8.3 Bispeengbuen without activities, 2019. Image Credit: Catherine Alexandra Zaia ©

Figure 8.4 The music event "Bas under Buen" (Bass under the arc) taking place at "Bispeengbuen." Image Credit: Flemming Bo Jensen ©

Despite accommodating popular subcultural events, Bispeengbuen is also a controversial site. The bridge constitutes a physical and psychological barrier between the districts of Nørrebro and Frederiksberg and creates massive noise pollution to the nearby housing blocks. The space under the bridge has been criticized for its general ugliness, and there is a fear that the dark and disorganized space will attract illegal activities.[30] Consequently, and despite the programmatic possibilities of this shady side of the city, there is also a very strong desire to change the concrete structure into an urban asset. Throughout the last decade, there has been a persistent discussion about whether the two involved municipalities and the state should finance a major new infrastructural investment. The question that is being considered is whether it is possible to build a new six-lane tunnel that makes it possible to tear the concrete bridge down and turn the space of Bispeengbuen into a new recreational green corridor linking the area to the city center. One positive outcome would be that the small river Ladegårdsåen, which today is running in pipes below the asphalt could then be opened up and exposed.

The architectural office, TREDJE NATUR (Third Nature), along with the consultant group, COWI, have presented a feasibility study (2015-2016) for the City of Copenhagen "highlighting the possibilities and consequences of establishing a traffic tunnel below Åboulevarden, with new climate-oriented urban spaces on top."[31] As a consequence, Bispeengbuen would most likely be facing radical changes. The multi-purpose solutions project would optimize the traffic flow through Copenhagen and would create a significant recreational space on top. The blue canal space would be a critical component in the city's overall cloud burst strategy. Furthermore, the scenario makes space for a number of new attractive housing blocks with direct access to sunny plazas and the green and blue corridor. This would be a space where cars are replaced by bikes and pedestrians (figure 8.5).

Figure 8.5 Bispeengbuen. Transformation of the Åboulevard (visualization),
Feasibility study by TREDJE NATUR and COWI (conducted 2015-2016).
Image Credit: TREDJE NATUR and COWI ©

Recently the project "Urban 13" has invested new energy into the subcultural activities and a spatial and financial compromise has been presented.[32] In this scenario only three lanes of the expressway are converted into park space.[33]

The removal of motorized traffic would be welcomed by many Copenhageners and could even make the site a new tourist attraction in the city. However, such a radical transformation would also remove one of the few unprogrammed, uncertain spaces that is left in the inner-city fabric and put an end to the spontaneous cultural events. The aim of this discussion is not to advocate for any of these solutions, but rather to highlight the inherent dilemmas and trade-offs arising from large-scale smart city projects.

Conclusion – unintended effects

It is essential that cities respond in innovative and holistic ways in order to address various challenges such as urban energy consumption, population growth, climate change, traffic congestion, parking, massive pollution, safety threats and waste separation. Taking this into account, the steady increase of networks and technological sophistication will result in faster and much more efficient handling of all sorts of urban flows.[34] The possibility of making real-time responses to changing situations means that the smart city increasingly works as an organism adapting to shifting weather conditions and fluctuating patterns of activity and consumption. The technologies have the capacity to reduce the negative impacts from all sorts of peak load situations and reduce the feeling that the city is stressed. In many contexts and situations, it would be unwise not to take advantage of the emerging smart city technologies, which can be crucial to improve the basic conditions of life and prevent technical breakdowns in the urban environment.

Supported by everyday needs as well as strong economic forces, the sum of smart and well-intentioned initiatives paints a picture of future cities where more or less nothing happens by coincidence. Eventually, this will become a problem. The plethora of smart initiatives create an understanding of the city as primarily functional with a focus on effectiveness without friction. The lesson from an efficient and privileged society like the Danish is that the loss of friction seems to happen almost imperceptibly. If friction is considered to be a precondition for citizen engagement with both the social and the political urban space, then the smart and smooth technologies may lead to a reduced version of the city and its architecture. The discussion about the city's space and form is increasingly influenced by analyses and calculations. Facing the challenges of climate change, cities are forced to act, and it seems that only rational solutions are gaining momentum. Linking to current debates on securitization and resilient cities, the arguments for cities being constantly alert further justify unreflective smart city solutions. These are promoted by a large number of advisors from different disciplines who have become indispensable in many ways but who have also turned their specialist knowledge into a business. Despite the fact that both architects and politicians usually focus on the qualitative parameters, it is often the quantitative arguments that win. The problem remains that it is difficult to argue against numbers, especially when they support sustainability and economic growth.

In the complex debate on the future of urban technological development it is important that qualitative arguments concerning good urban spaces and good urban architecture is not overlooked. Returning to Koolhaas' critique, he states that "With safety and security as selling points, the city has become vastly less adventurous and more predictable."[35] Copenhagen is used as the focal point of this article because Copenhagen Municipality has a progressive approach to implementing smart city solutions. Today, Copenhagen exports these solutions. The Copenhagen Solutions Lab, founded by the municipality, received the so-called World Smart Cities Award in 2014 for the initiative Copenhagen Connecting. Linking to the aforementioned issue of trust, it is interesting that the jury for this award celebrated data-trust specifically, stating: "Copenhagen has the best plan in the world for collecting and using data to create a greener city, a higher quality of life for its citizens and a better business climate."[36] In the last years, the span of smart projects fueled by the Copenhagen Solutions Lab has become very wide.[37] Faced with the magnitude of urban smartness, we should not forget that the power of digitalization and social media are disputable. It is necessary to discuss what we lose by subscribing to this limiting approach and what financial interests are at stake when making decisions. Do we need to cultivate and cherish the unsmart city?

Bibliography

Benjamin, Walter. Berliner Kindheit um neuzehnhundert. Berlin: Suhrkamp, 2012.

Bennike, Christian. "Den næste Amager Fælled-sag: Red Bispeengbuen!" Information, October 21, 2017. https://www.information.dk/moti/2017/10/naeste-amager-faelled-sag-red-bispeengbuen.

Berrone, Pascual. "From Smart Cities to Smart Governance." Presentation at the conference "Business Improvement Districts – En ny samarbejdsmodel for vækst og udvikling i byområder," VIA University College, Aarhus, Denmark, November 29, 2017.

Brandt, Kasper Bruun Vindum." "Politikere giver grønt lys til at rive halvdelen af Bispeengbuen ned." TV2/Lorry, January 13, 2021. https://www.tv2lorry.dk/koebenhavn/politikere-giver-groent-lys-til-at-rive-halvdelen-af-bispeengbuen-ned.

By & Havn. "Bæredygtig byudvikling i Nordhavn."Accessed February 25, 2021. https://byoghavn.dk/nordhavn/baeredygtig-byudvikling/.

Bygningsreglementet.dk/Indenrigs- og Boligministeriet. "Energiforbrug (§ 250–§ 298)." Accessed February 25, 2021. https://bygningsreglementet.dk/Tekniske-bestemmelser/11/Krav.

Castells, Manuel. *The Rise of the Network Society*. Malden, Mass: Blackwell Publishers, 1996.

CF Møller Architects. "Copenhagen International School – Nordhavn." Accessed February 25, 2021. https://www.cfmoller.com/p/Copenhagen-International-School-Nordhavn-i2956.html#.

Cohen, Boyd. "The 3 Generations of Smart Cities." Fast Company, October 8, 2015. Accessed February 24, 2021. https://www.fastcompany.com/3047795/the-3-generations-of-smart-cities.

Copenhagen Capacity. "Denmark is fourth most digital country in the world." June 18, 2020, accessed February 24, 2021. https://www.copcap.com/news/denmark-is-fourth-most-digital-country-in-the-world.

Copenhagen Solutions Lab. "Projects." Accessed February 25, 2021. https://cph solutionslab.dk/en/projekter.

Energylab Nordhavn. "A Smart City Energy Lab." Accessed February 25, 2021. http://www.energylabnordhavn.com/.

European Commission. "The Digital Economy and Society Index (DESI)." Accessed February 24, 2021. https://ec.europa.eu/digital-single-market/en/digital-economy-and-society-index-desi.

Hodgkinson, Tom. "Adam Curtis: Social Media is a Scam." Idler Magazine February 3, 2021. https://www.idler.co.uk/article/adam-curtis-social-media-is-a-scam/.

Jensen, Mette Frisk, and Svendsen, Gert Tinggaard. "Corruption and Bureaucratic Reforms 'Getting to Denmark?'" In *The Oxford Handbook of Danish Politics*, edited by Peter Munk Christiansen, Jørgen Elklit, and Peter Nedergaard, 177-192. Oxford University Press, 2020.

Koolhaas, Rem. "Rem Koolhaas Asks: Are Smart Cities Condemned to Be Stupid?" ArchDaily, December 10, 2014. Accessed February 23, 2021. https://www.archdaily.com/576480/rem-koolhaas-asks-are-smart-cities-condemned-to-be-stupid, ISSN 0719-8884.

Lindberg, Kristian. "De elsker Københavns største betonklods: »Det ville være en katastrofe at fjerne Bispeengbuen. Jeg forstår slet ikke, at man kan få den tanke!«" Berlingske, October 21, 2018. https://www.berlingske.dk/kultur/de-elsker-koebenhavns-stoerste-betonklods-det-ville-vaere-en-katastrofe-at.

Nielsen, Tom. "The Making of Democratic Urban Public Space in Denmark." In *Public Space Design and Social Cohesion: An International Comparison*, edited by Patricia Aelbrecht and Quentin Stevens, 37-57. Routledge, 2019.

Nielsen, Tom. "The Return of the Excessive: Superfluous Landscapes." *Space and Culture* 5, no. 1 (2002): 53-62.

Pentland, Alex Paul. "Society's Nervous System: Building Effective Government, Energy and Public Health Systems." MIT Open Access Articles, October 2011.

Sennett, Richard and Sendra, Pablo. *Designing Disorder: Experiments and Disruptions in the City*. London, New York: Verso, 2020.

Sennett, Richard. *The Uses of Disorder: Personal Identity & City Life*. New York: Knopf, 1970.

Sieverts, Thomas. Zwischenstadt: zwischen Ort und Welt Raum und Zeit Stadt und Land. Wiesbaden: Vieweg+Teubner Verlag, 1997.

Sieverts, Thomas, Koch, Michael, Stein, Ursula, and Steinbusch, Michael, eds. *Zwischenstadt – Inzwischenstadt? Entdecken, Begreifen ,Verändern*. Wuppertal: Verlag Müller + Busmann, 2005.

Simmel, Georg. "Die Großstadt. Vorträge und Aufsätze zur Städteausstellung." In Jahrbuch der Gehe-Stiftung Dresden, 185-206. Dresden: Th. Peterman, 1903.

Simpson, Deane. "Copenhagen under the Metric Regimes of the Competitive and Attractive City." In *Atlas of the Copenhagens*, edited by Deane Simpson, Kathrin Susanna Gimmel, Anders Lonka, Marc Jay, and Joost Grootens, 17-53. Berlin: Ruby Press, 2018.

Simpson, Deane, Gimmel, Kathrin Susanna, Lonka, Anders, Jay, Marc, and Grootens, Joost, eds. *Atlas of the Copenhagens*. Berlin: Ruby Press, 2018.

Smithson, Alison and Smithson, Peter. *Ordinariness and Light*. London: Faber & Faber Ltd., 1970.

Spacemaker. "Early stage planning. Re-imagined." Accessed February 24, 2021, https://www.spacemakerai.com/.

State of Green. "'Connecting Copenhagen' is the World's Best Smart City Project." Accessed February 25, 2021. https://stateofgreen.com/en/partners/city-of-copenhagen/news/connecting-copenhagen-is-the-worlds-best-smart-city-project/.

TREDJE NATUR. "Enghaveparken—Climate Park." Accessed February 25, 2021, https://www.tredjenatur.dk/en/portfolio/enghaveparken-climate-park/.

TREDJE NATUR. "Transformation of The Boulevard." Accessed February 25, 2021. https://www.tredjenatur.dk/en/portfolio/transformation-of-the-boulevard/.

Urban 13. "Urban 13." Accessed February 25, 2021. https://www.urban13.dk/.

Venturi, Robert. *Complexity and Contradiction in Architecture*. New York: The Museum of Modern Art, 1966.

Webster, Helena, ed. *Modernism Without Rhetoric—Essays on the work of Alison and Peter Smithson*. London: Academy Editions, 1997.

Zigurat Global Institute of Technology. "Global Smart City Management." Accessed February 23, 2021. https://www.e-zigurat.com/en/smart-cities-masters-program/.

Zigurat Global Institute of Technology. "Smart City Series: The Barcelona Experience." Accessed February 23, 2021.

Zuboff, Shoshana. *The Age of Surveillance Capitalism*. London: Profile Books Ltd., 2019.

ØsterGro. "Welcome to ØsterGro." Accessed February 25, 2021. https://www.oestergro.dk/in-english.

Chapter 9

Bankside, SE1 — A central London concerted waterfront regeneration strategy?

Caroline Donnellan

Boston University Study Abroad London, UK

Abstract

The former run-down, inner-city historic area of Bankside on the south bank of the River Thames underwent a sustained period of major redevelopment since the late 1990s. With its newly revitalized industrial and contemporary buildings, old and new places and spaces, and improved transport hubs and amenities, Bankside emerged as a concerted waterfront regeneration strategy. Except there was no concerted waterfront regeneration strategy. The *Southwark Unitary Development Plan* (1995) and the *London Plan* (2004) identified London Bridge as a site for a new waterfront strategy but did not include Bankside. What changed was that a confluence of public and private initiatives, stakeholders, and other actors recognized Bankside's potential as a dynamic index of change. This chapter examines Bankside through the lens of the built city concerning its planning and lack thereof by focusing on the developments along and close to the waterfront. It discusses how public and private partnerships, and other initiatives generated a mix of commercial and green strategies which impacted the urban environment, the public realm, and the bigger vision for London.

Keywords: London, Southwark, Bankside, public, private, waterfront, regeneration

***

Introduction

The post-industrial area of Bankside on the south bank of the River Thames underwent a sustained period of major redevelopment from the mid-1990s. With Bankside's eclectic mix of contemporary and readapted industrial buildings, reclaimed and regreened spaces, improved transport networks, and amenities, it emerged as an "exciting and varied environment."[1] Bankside had been recast as a central London concerted strategy — except there was no central London concerted strategy. Prior to Bankside's transformation into a chic central London SE1 postcode, it was viewed very differently by the official planning authorities. Southwark Council did, however, recognize Bankside's potential and identified it as a regeneration area and added that "investment will be welcomed and public/private sector partnerships encouraged."[2] There was no major funding stream, nor master plan, forthcoming, nor was there the desire to support one. The office of the Mayor of London, created in 2000, published the *London Plan: Spatial Development Strategy for Greater London* (2004), which identified London Bridge as one of its redevelopment sites due to "the area's heritage and environmental character."[3] The other designated London South Central "Opportunity Areas" including Nine Elms, Battersea, and Elephant and Castle, could not compete with London Bridge for transport but were nonetheless included in the *London Plan*.[4] Why it is surprising that Bankside was overlooked is because Tate Modern opened in 2000 and was at the vanguard of other cultural organizations, creative industries, as well as businesses relocating to the area.

Bankside's attraction was its location, waterfront, and industrial heritage, as James Douet identifies: "architects and builders have great opportunities to adapt and re-use old industrial buildings [...] for their quantity as well as versatility. Their embodied energy helps environmentalists to deliver sustainable development goals. Adapting and repurposing them are now mainstream strategies for urban planners."[5] Despite this being the case, the London Mayor failed to recognize Bankside's potential until the *London Plan* was revised in 2008 when it was categorized as both an opportunity, and as a strategic cultural area.[6] The Government also failed to recognize Bankside's potential, having earlier diverted public funds to Canary Wharf. The conundrum emerged after the development was sold to the private sector and was then resold back to the Government through a rescue package in 1993, before being sold again to the private sector. The later Conservative governments shifted direction by selling off public assets at undervalued land prices. In view of this — should development remain the preserve of top-down planning when there are alternative, bottom-up and more robust ways to plan a city? As the Bankside model suggests, when independent, forward-thinking organizations are allowed greater autonomy they can effectively work together which Gert de Roo and Camilla Perone identify as "the rise of self-governance and the awareness of self-organizing processes that take place in the everyday environment."[7] With this in mind, this chapter examines how Bankside was able to reinvent itself as part of "the *genius loci*, the heart of London" after a period of fragmentation from the rest of the city.[8] It does so by drawing on planning and policy, regeneration analysis, and urban history to assess how Bankside created its own concerted waterfront regeneration strategy. It begins by mapping Bankside's development as a strategic part of Southwark to assess its formative relationship with the City of London, and how this shaped its urban identity.

Changing geographies: Bankside, Southwark, and the City of London

The establishment of the Roman military supply base on the north bank of the River Thames in 47 AD led to the creation of the first London Bridge (50 AD) and Londinium, which lies within the present boundary of the City of London. Over a short period of time Londinium developed into a thriving hub of an "imperial bureaucracy" which had at its physical core the Forum (71-85 AD).[9] With its complex of political and civic buildings, it had two central courtyards, which functioned as public meeting places, "ceremonial parade grounds," and a marketplace.[10] The designated area for official entertainment was the amphitheatre (70-80 AD).[11] Encircling the network of public and private buildings was the massive masonry defensive city wall (c. 200 AD).[12] What was created within the city wall was an enduring sense of Londinium as being a place of trade and administration. Across London Bridge on the other side of the river, Southwark (the name later evolved from the Old English *sūþ* - south and *weorc* - work) developed to serve Londinium as a thoroughfare from the southeast of England. Archaeological evidence suggests that Southwark first emerged as a military route and "continuation of Watling Street, from the Kent coast, and Stane Street, from the Sussex coast."[13] The Watling Street axis ran through Londinium which was a destination in itself and a hub for other routes. What was outlawed within Londinium was facilitated in Southwark which included manual trades, unofficial entertainments, and other religions. Many of these activities were clustered around the bank of the river (Bankside) which were in stark contrast to those of its venerable neighbor across the water.

While Southwark emerged as a large suburb that increasingly attracted the less well-off, by the later Saxon period it became part of the county of Surrey, which strengthened its commercial links with the south-east, and notably with Kent through the hop trade. The opening of London Bridge Rail Station in 1836 saw the hops being transported to Southwark by rail. The Hop Exchange in Southwark Street was built in 1866 to facilitate a large single market space for the hop dealers.[14] The Bankside location was on account of the local brewing industry and its proximity to the water. In 1889 Southwark became part of the county of London which re-aligned its geographic area back to London. A new industry, electricity, arrived at Bankside, which also required the resources of the river when the first power station opened in 1891. The power station joined the rest of the factories, warehouses, workers' homes, and slums in this degraded urban environment. As Paul Knox identifies: "By the end of the nineteenth century, the ugly industrial character of the townscape along the south bank of the Thames had become a problem: An unfitting vista for the heart of an imperial capital."[15] Within thirty years the imperial capital was on a downward spiral. Southwark however, maintained its position longer than other urban areas, due to its "diverse industrial activity, with the manufacture of products ranging from leather to glass, beer and gas."[16]

Following World War II, a bombed-out capital and a working river that was no longer working saw Southwark lose its connection with central London. While many of Southwark's industries disappeared, electricity continued to be produced at Bankside. A new larger building designed by Sir Giles Gilbert Scott was constructed on the site in 1947 to provide electricity for the London grid. The building became a landmark for Bankside with its monumentally stark design and "stunning scale of the bare walls of immaculate brick work."[17] With the 1973 oil crisis, Bankside Power Station was no longer economically viable to run. The Bankside waterfront also ceased its working operations because of "the eastward shift of trade in the Port of London."[18] The impact of containerization saw the demise of the London Docks which were unable to accommodate the new larger sea vessels which affected other areas along the Thames including Bankside. The onset of urban decay at Bankside was reflected across British inner-city areas. The response by the Conservative Secretary of State for the Environment, Michael Heseltine, was to launch thirteen Urban Development Corporations to stimulate the private sector through partnership incentives. The London Docklands Development Corporation (LDDC) was created in 1981. The West India Docks on the Isle of Dogs in the London Borough of Tower Hamlets was assigned as an Enterprise Zone in 1982. This enabled "freedom from planning restrictions, exemption from rates and 100 per cent tax relief on capital expenditure for the next 10 years."[19] What it meant was that developers had *carte blanche* to bulldoze the historic site and to create a new blueprint for the area.

The Government's focus was on reimagining British cities from obsolete, post-industrial sites to money making service orientated ventures. "In the later 1980s and 1990s a new vision for cities gradually emerged, which emphasized concepts of economic competitiveness and social cohesion. Slowly, governments and businesses began to see cities less as a problem and more as an asset."[20] The re-imagining of British cities came at the cost to those who lost their employment when their former industries were closed. Regardless of the social impact, Margaret Thatcher's Government ploughed ahead with its programme of deregulation in town and country planning.[21] A further directive that impacted on planning was the Local Government Act (1985) which resulted in the abolition of the Greater London Council (GLC) in 1986. The closure of the GLC's city planning unit saw the launch of the London Planning Advisory Committee (LPAC). LPAC was somewhat nebulous in providing strategic planning but for guidance only to the London borough councils and the City of London Corporation. LPAC also advised the Government on major development proposals. Under its new leader Nicky Gavron in 1994, LPAC's strategy was revised into a "Four-Fold Vision For London" which advocated for "a strong economy," "a good quality of life," "a sustainable future" and "opportunities for all."[22] While well intentioned, it was somewhat vague as without any clear implementation of these aims, the onus fell on London borough councils to develop their own planning initiatives.

An urban and creative renaissance

The General Election in 1997 saw a shift in Government thinking about cities and the nation. The new Prime Minister Tony Blair oversaw his party rebranded as New Labour. For New Labour to be effective required a shift in the nation's ideological identity. "Taking a centrist approach, New Labour hailed a new vision of Britain with the invention of Cool Britannia."[23] Supporting this directive, New Labour replaced the Department for National Heritage in 1997 with the Department for Culture, Media and Sport (DCMS). This was renamed the Department for Digital, Culture, Media and Sport, 3 July 2019 and retains the same DCMS acronym. The initial core DCMS initiative was the Creative Industries Task Force (CITF) which linked economic performance with creativity. The newly assigned creative industries were identified as architecture, music, arts, and antique markets, performing arts, crafts, publishing, design software and computer services, designer fashion, television and radio, and film and video. Museums, galleries, and libraries continued as part of the cultural sector but were later added to the creative industries. In boosting cities' marketability, Neil Lee identifies the creative industries as "a key sector for regenerating inner cities and stimulating flagging urban economies."[24] A further city's initiative was through the Department of Environment, Transport and Regions Urban Task Force (UTF) created in 1998. Richard Rogers was appointed the UTF's chair, and outlined its aims were to address urban and social decay, and to provide guidance for revising the planning system.

> We need a vision that will drive the urban renaissance. We believe that cities should be well designed, be more compact and connected, and support a range of diverse uses—allowing people to live, work and enjoy themselves at close quarters—within a sustainable urban environment which is well integrated with public transport and adaptable to change.[25]

The UTF's intentions were not met and left its members questioning the Government, as Peter Hall later claimed: "As too often over the last four years, government policy on land and development has consisted of bombastic rhetoric empty of real substance."[26] With a lack of real government guidance, individual organizations were already developing their own strategies for Bankside. Before the performing arts were subsumed into the creative industries, Shakespeare's Globe had embarked on its own development programme which as an independent charity had to generate its own funding model. From the onset

Shakespeare's Globe was envisioned as being more than a theatre by its founder and then Executive Director Sam Wanamaker, who outlined that the project was about creating "an international working monument to the world's greatest play-wright."[27] Wanamaker's memorial to William Shakespeare was realized through his reconstruction of the Elizabethan Globe Theatre. The original Globe building of 1599 was established by William Shakespeare's playing company, the Lord Chamberlain's Men, it however burned down in a fire in 1613. The later 1614 Stuart building was pulled down in 1644 when the Puritans closed the theatres. For the 1990s Elizabethan reconstruction, elements from the later Stuart building were also incorporated into the design developed by Wanamaker with Theo Crosby from Pentagram design consultancy.

Shakespeare's Globe opened in 1997 on its new Bankside site located approximately 750 ft. from the original building, which enabled it to engage with the "physical elements of the existing local culture heritage" including the waterfront.[28] Wanamaker's vision was focused on an older Elizabethan heritage and not a later industrial one. For this reason, when the Tate announced it was buying Bankside Power Station and would be converting it, Wanamaker opposed the scheme. The paradox was and remains that Shakespeare's Globe is rooted in the twentieth century. While the building has the appearance of an Elizabethan playhouse with its white wattle and daub timber exterior, it "sits, however, on a great concrete shaft, elevated above the river and clearly visible from the north bank."[29] Shakespeare's Globe is a twentieth-century building and so is Tate Modern. Bankside Power Station into Tate Modern was made possible through funding from the National Lottery. The original aim was to open a new exhibition space for the national collection's international modern and contemporary art works. The National Lottery's Millennium Commission award saw Tate revising its role to urban developer. For this reason, as much consideration went on thinking about the outside of the building as it had done on the inside. "The surrounding area was envisaged as an important new public space. The gallery was to be set within a local landscaped park and its wider urban context."[30] Beyond Tate Modern, the neighbouring area of Bankside was intended to become a diverse and lively mixed-use quarter. Tate Modern was therefore as much about place-making as it was about creating a new museum, which demonstrates how "culture can be employed as a driver for urban economic growth."[31]

Prior to Tate Modern's development, the organization petitioned Southwark Council to create a pedestrian footbridge crossing over the River Thames to the City of London, which was realized through an architecture competition. The London Millennium Footbridge, commonly known as the Millennium Bridge, was designed by Arup (engineers), Foster + Partners (architects) and Sir Anthony Caro (sculptor). The steel footbridge opened new sections on the north and south banks of the Thames which had previously been "blighted by poor access."[32] In creating a new corridor, the Millennium Bridge was more than about re-configuring the north south axis; it was about turning Bankside into a central London location. This was formalized when Queen Elizabeth II officially opened Tate Modern, 11 May 2000 and the Millennium Bridge, 10 June 2000. When the Millennium Bridge opened to the public there was an immediate issue caused by the accumulative pedestrian walking movements. This resulted in induced lateral vibration, through the noticeable movement of the bridge. The Millennium Bridge was closed on 12 June 2000 while re-adjustments were made until it re-opened on 27 February 2002. Despite the Millennium Bridge's closure, visitors came to view it, and to photograph it, and turned it into a landmark attraction. The Millennium Bridge has since featured in major films including *Harry Potter and the Half-Blood Prince* (2009) and *Spectre* (2015), which has further raised Bankside's profile.

A public and private housing conundrum

The increasing visibility of Bankside as a primary London location attracted investors including Native Land, who bought from the Tate a two-acre land plot that was originally part of Bankside Power Station's grounds. The architects Rogers Stirk Harbour + Partners designed NEO Bankside (2006-2012) as a mixed-use housing and commercial development. The complex consisting of four hexagonal pavilions ranging from 12 to 24 storeys contains 217 apartments, and ground level retail units of 11,200 sq. ft. NEO Bankside became part of the vanguard of high-end residential developments which have significantly increased the local property prices. Matthew Gandy identifies the detrimental impact of gentrification that has arisen: "The character of London is changing and projects such as NEO Bankside are connected to the wider transformation of the city into an increasingly segregated and polarised metropolis."[33] A further issue outlined by Oliver Wainwright is that "it has set a very dangerous precedent in the way it exploits local policies and undermines the principle of creating mixed communities. [...] the original planning application, made in 2006, used its viability assessment to prove that the borough's 40% affordable housing target was simply not achievable – and that only 27.5% affordable housing could be provided instead."[34] Further high-end luxury developments have appeared on the Bankside skyline including the arty sounding Triptych Bankside at 185 Park Street. The £400 million development designed by Squire & Partners consists of three towers of 169 residences, an office building, and retail, wellness, and cultural spaces. At the time of writing, a 3-bedroom flat with a floor area of 1,410 sq. ft. has a guide price of £2,755,000 which is approximately £1,953 per sq. ft.

While the upper end of the housing market is catered for at Bankside, more affordable and intermediate homes are an ongoing issue for Southwark Council. The lack of social housing began when the Conservative Government pushed through the Housing Act (1980) which enabled council tenants the *Right to Buy* their homes from their local authorities in England and Wales. Half of the proceeds were paid to the local authorities, who were instructed by the Government to pay their debts rather than reinvesting the money into building new public housing stock. The impact saw a significant amount of council properties being sold-off to the private sector without them being replenished, as has been the case with Falcon Point at 31-42 Hopton Street by Tate Modern. The public housing development built in the 1970s contains 110 flats and includes the Founder's Arms pub and the Bankside Gallery. More than 50% of the flats have been purchased, with some of them let out, which has seen a surge in their private rental values compared to the public council rents of similar properties within the same block. Falcon Point's freehold was sold in 2015 as part of a £308 million purchase deal.[35] The ground lease of Falcon Point is still owned by Southwark Council and expires in 2077. The other properties in the sale included Sampson House at 64 Hopton Street, and Ludgate House at 245 Blackfriars Road.

Despite objections being made by the Twentieth-Century Society the brutalist building of Sampson House (built 1976-1979) and the glass structure of Ludgate House (built 1989) were demolished in 2019. The sites are being used for Bankside Yards, which is a new one billion-pound, mixed-use, 5.5-acre waterfront development. Within this commercial venture, 3.3 acres of land have been allocated for the public realm. The developers, consisting of Native Land (UK), the Singaporean Temasek and Hotel Properties, and the Malaysian Amcorp Properties, outline that this will be the "UK's first fossil-fuel free major mixed-use development."[36] The main feature of Bankside Yards are the fourteen Victorian railway arches which had previously been obscured from public view. With the focus on the site's industrial heritage, there will be an additional nine new buildings, ranging from five to forty-eight storeys for retail, office, cultural and residential use. Along with the six hundred planned new private homes, the developers are making a £65 million to £100 million donation to Southwark Council to fund public housing albeit in another part of the borough. Beyond Bankside Yards there are other new developments that fuse readapted industrial sites and contemporary buildings.

There are other developments that fuse even the idea of the industrial with the contemporary. On Southwark Bridge Road was the former site of St Christopher's House which was a massive office block built from 1959 to 1961. It was demolished in 2003 to make way for a new development. On behalf of Land Securities Properties, the architectural practice Allies and Morrison designed three new sustainable buildings with low carbon emissions. The aim was to incorporate the industrial character of the area into the new development. "The simple forms and detailing of the buildings evoke the industrial character of Bankside whilst providing flexible and efficient floorplates capable of accommodating a wide range and combination of future tenants."[37] The buildings formerly known as Bankside 123 were envisioned as a group whereby each one was "given a distinct identity by the use of a wide palette of materials – metal and glass, terracotta, and precast concrete. In contrast to the monolithic uniformity of St. Christopher's House, the new blocks are carefully amassed in response to their context."[38] Bankside 1 was rebranded the Blue Fin Building which completed in 2008 and provides 500,000 sq. ft. of working space and a 7,500 sq. ft. terrace with panoramic views of the London skyline. With the building's glazed skin, it has a further outer skin of 2,000 blue vertical fins "to provide solar shading for the offices within."[39]

While the distinctive blue fins signal a shift to a more contemporary image of Bankside, the ground floor Refinery Bar on the corner of Southwark Street and Canvey Street does not. With its exposed brickwork, oak floorboards, and steel detailing, it represents a link with the industrial past, and industrial style developments in the local area. An example of this is the readapted post-industrial luxury apartment hotel of Native Bankside at 1-2 Bear Gardens, which is set within an old tea warehouse on a cobbled street. Redesigned by SPPARC Studio the building retains its original utilitarian facade with its arched factory windows, and perfunctory brickwork. In this regard, the building references the industrial past, and echoes aspects of the surrounding urban environment, while working alongside the contemporary developments, infrastructure, and the public facilities. These include the parks, gardens, recreation grounds, open spaces, and amenities. They are administered by Southwark Council with the aim to improve the quality of the area for public enjoyment and to have a carbon neutral footprint through reducing emissions by 2030.[40]

One of the core environmentally friendly partnership initiatives is Better Bankside. The partners include the Architecture Foundation, Tate Modern, Southwark Council, Cross River Partnership, Transport for London, Native Land, Land Securities, Living Bankside, Bankside Open Spaces Trust, Borough Market, and the Mayor of London. The not-for-profit organization was established in 2005 to work within the designated Business Improvement District to promote economic, environmental, and social action in the area. At the core of Better Bankside's work is its placemaking strategy which is Bankside Urban Forest. The Urban Forest refers to the brick and iron networks of "extensive viaducts that cut across the area [which] conceal a quarter of a million square feet of vaulted spaces."[41] In opening up this dense grey urban environment, the aim has been to combat air and noise pollution. Since its launch in 2007, it "has delivered over 25 projects, planted over 250 trees, increased green cover in the neighbourhood by more than 1000m2 and improved over 10,000m2 public space across the area."[42] The aim of the regreening strategy is to support people and wildlife. The objective of this new urban eco system is to create connections between residents, businesses, workshops, and their environment. An impact of improving the network of streets and spaces and the reduction of traffic speeds has resulted in more pedestrian and cycling strategies being implemented.

The Low Line and walkability

A further public and private partnership initiative is the Low Line (coined by a local Southwark resident David Stephens) which began as a walking route linking Bankside to Waterloo. The Low Line references the High Line in Manhattan, New York, a 1.45-mile-long park on the west side of Manhattan that has been created out of a disused, southern viaduct section of the New York Central Railroad's West Side. While the High Line is high and linear, the Low Line is low and meandering. What they share is re-purposed railway architecture, a green strategy, and the aim to improve the public realm. Unlike the High Line, the Low Line is a developing route which follows the Victorian rail viaducts that span Bankside, London Bridge and Bermondsey. The Low Line has become "a new walking destination for London."[43] Coordinated by Better Bankside the vision is to re-define this area by having greater walkability of density, mix, and access. Jane Jacobs outlines this need for walkability around the city streets, and states: "In dense, diversified city areas, people still walk, an activity that is impractical in suburbs and in most gray areas. The more intensely various and close-grained the diversity in an area, the more walking."[44] Jacobs makes the point that cities are about walking. What has changed since her time is that grey spaces have become, at least at Bankside, walkable areas, that can also provide pedestrian strategies including that of the Low Line. In creating walkable routes, the Low Line connects people, places, spaces, and neighbourhoods through a collaborative commercial and regreening strategy. Similarly, to Bankside Urban Forest, some of the Low Line destinations are about reclaiming spaces around and near the rail viaducts. Francesca Froy and Howard Davies outline how: "Once marginal spaces are increasingly coming into commercial use in UK cities. This includes spaces under railway arches – which, despite being part of the country's Victorian heritage, have proved surprisingly adaptable to current business needs."[45]

These reclaimed spaces include Flat Iron Square on the junction of Southwark Bridge Road and Union Street that was launched in October 2016. Flat Iron Square was created from the former voids around the bases of seven railway arches which now provides 40,000 sq. ft. of new space. The landscape designers, Witherford Watson Mann Architects, have incorporated a regreening strategy that has restored the former degraded urban environment into a revitalized area. In line with the wider aims of regreening strategies, it is to be "restorative, life sustaining, and regenerative — for people as well as for landscapes."[46] Flat Iron Square's commercial aspect is realized through its restaurants, bars, food trucks, and added attraction of music events. A more visibly green Low Line destination is Red Cross Garden located south of the railway viaducts and Union Street which was originally designed by the social reformer and supporter of social housing, Octavia Hill. It opened in 1888 for the poor with the aim to have "a nice park to be created in one of the worst slum areas in London."[47] During World War II, it became underused and lost. The environmental charity Bankside Open Spaces Trust secured Heritage Lottery and Southwark Council funding to revitalize the garden. With Red Cross Garden reclaimed as a public space, it was officially opened by the Princess Royal (Princess Anne) 1 June 2006. A different type of Low Line destination is the historic Borough Market at 8 Southwark Street. The food market plays a vital role in the life of the city and has become a popular destination for Londoners, locals, and visitors, who are reminded of the area's urban environment when the overhead rail tracks shudder with the trains going in and out of London Bridge Rail Station.

A more contemporary (and taller) nearby development is Renzo Piano's landmark, The Shard which opened in 2013. The 1,004 ft. high, mixed-use, skyscraper is physically connected to the concourse of the revamped London Bridge Rail Station beneath it, which completed in 2018. The work was overseen by Grimshaw Architects and was funded by a £1 billion Government-sponsored Thameslink investment. The newly redeveloped London Bridge Rail Station and the Shard are the focal point of the London Bridge Quarter with its pedestrian hub, transport interchange, improved amenities, shops, cafes, bars, restaurants, and luxury hotel, the Shangri-La. In this way, the London Bridge Quarter responds to the *London Plan* (2004) directive: "London Bridge station and its environs are proposed together with improved public transport and interchange facilities and better pedestrian integration with the surrounding area. This is a good location for a tall, landmark mixed-use development. The planning framework should draw visitors eastward along the riverside."[48] The bigger vision was also, therefore, about creating stronger links from London Bridge eastwards to Canary Wharf rather than westwards to Bankside. Southwark Council also earlier proposed creating an "Urban Development Area" from London Bridge to the South Dock (Canary Wharf).[49] What this outlined was the ongoing support of Canary Wharf as well as for the regeneration of London Bridge.

Conclusion

Bankside was recast as a central London waterfront location due to a complex situation and conflicting circumstances. While Southwark Council recognized Bankside's potential as a regeneration area in the mid-1990s, it also proposed that it could take an ancillary role as a water transport facility to serve Canary Wharf. "It is important that provision is made for additional passenger jetties to enable

Southwark residents to take advantage of employment opportunities in the Docklands, to relieve congestion in areas such as Bankside, and to support local tourism."[50] With the initial focus on supporting Canary Wharf and jobs, the role of tourism at Bankside was underestimated, when it dramatically increased five years later. Following the opening of Tate Modern in 2000, 5.25 million visitors arrived in its first year, which impacted on businesses, and notably the hospitality sector, and played therefore a much wider role than solely attracting local interest. As Kenneth Powell asserts Tate Modern "has had a spectacular effect, confirming the rise of Bankside as a dynamic commercial and cultural quarter."[51] Shakespeare's Globe, and the other attractions, including the diverse social, urban, and green activities within this intriguing cityscape, have also contributed to attracting visitors to the area. The question is why did these organizations themselves relocate to Bankside when there was no visitor offer?

What began the chain of events was when the various Conservative governments from 1979 to 1997 took a *laissez faire* approach to planning outside of their own projects. The impact saw the planning system become near obsolete, as Hana Morel states: "By the early 1990s, the limitations of the single-tier model for London government (a result of the abolition of the GLC) was evident. Boroughs lacked broader strategic vision and could not coordinate their work on London-wide issues (e.g. transport, strategic planning or economic development)."[52] With the failure to implement a holistic plan for London, the Government also took a hands-off approach to funding. With the arrival of the National Lottery this created a new level of competitiveness for its award winners which included Tate Modern and the Millennium Bridge. Other Bankside projects including the Red Cross Garden also received Lottery funding. Blair's New Labour Government created a further level of competition through the commoditization of the creative and cultural sectors which saw organizations and businesses migrating over the river to Bankside in search of a new edgy urban identify. What cemented the deal was Southwark Council's willingness to support them, and to implement commercial, and urban initiatives which were largely supported by public and private partnerships. Andrew Jones claims: "Evidence also shows that it would be wise to ensure that future strategies concentrate upon public/private sector partnership, especially in securing the integration of land uses which are appropriate to waterfronts."[53]

Public and private partnerships are determined, however, by their stake holders, and their intentions. When the Conservative Government launched the LDDC it was a public and private partnership before it was sold in its entirety to the private sector in 1987. When Canary Wharf was hit by the 1990s recession and further financial difficulties in 1993, it was rescued with public money "only to have the original speculators buy it back and bounce into a booming second phase initiated in the mid '90's."[54] Ultimately, the beneficiary of the development was the private sector. The Canary Wharf Group plc is presently under the ownership of Brookfield Property Partners and Qatar Investment Authority. Conversely, Bankside is a very different development; it is significantly smaller, it has a variety of diverse uses, it was not overseen by the government, had not a single targeted major funding source or masterplan, and nor did it require a bailout. It is, however, similar to Canary Wharf in being a waterfront strategy, and there the similarity ends. Bankside created its own urban renaissance through an interconnecting set of self-organizing interventions, forces, and perspectives, and is why city planning should not be solely the preserve of top-down authorities. With more formal kinds of interventions, this had a tendency, notably from the 1980s, to be about big visions, big ideas, big city areas, and big money. Alternatively, city areas such as Bankside developed organically-delivered, more imaginative, and interesting designs. In doing so its developments provide a wide range of uses which facilitates high end as well as other kinds of ventures. In Bankside's ability to change, it should again be able to adapt to new urban, economic, and social climate.

Since the pandemic lockdowns, the working environment has seen a rise in remote working. According to McKinsey and Company, "Over time, some organizations could reduce their real-estate costs by 30 percent. Those that shift to a fully virtual model could almost eliminate them."[55] If the workspace environments at Bankside are not occupied, they can be re-adapted for new uses. What is important is that Bankside continues to embrace change and complexity in acting as a catalyst for different kinds of activities, including building developments and regreening strategies. At the same time, the Bankside paradigm reflects a wider national model that is emerging, as Steffan Lehman asserts: "All over the UK, a paradigm shift in urban thinking is now happening, where brownfield and waterfront sites are becoming urban laboratories, highlighting the need for participatory planning, social inclusion and new ways of 're-greening' spaces to transform our neighbourhoods, streets and public spaces."[56] What the Bankside example suggests is that it is possible to develop an alternative urban plan when independent, forward-thinking organizations have greater autonomy to self-organize themselves into a robust and concerted urban plan. This has the additional benefit of allowing for more scope to better reflect an area's own distinct sense of place, and for more nuanced kinds of spaces. At the same time, Bankside is far from an ideal urban model with its housing conundrum, which needs the same kind of effort and vision that is being poured into the private developments. Despite Bankside's flaws it nonetheless proposes an alternative approach to planning in redeveloping a degraded urban environment into a vibrant, and vital part of the city centre.

Bibliography

Allinson, Ken. *London's Contemporary Architecture: A Visitor's Guide*. Oxford and Burlington MA: Architectural Press, 2003.

Bankside Yards London "SE1. Arbor reaches milestone with topping out ceremony." Accessed May 8, 2022. https://banksideyards.com/press/bankside-yards-to-be-uks-first-fossil-fuel-free-major-mixed-use-development/

Beasley, John D. *Southwark: revisited*. London: Tempus, 2004.

Better Bankside. "Bankside Urban Forest." Accessed May 8, 2022. https://betterbankside.co.uk/what-we-do/bankside-urban-forest/

Boland, Brodie, Aaron De Smet, Rob Palter, and Aditya Sanghvi. "Reimagining the office and work life after COVID-19." *McKinsey and Company*, June 2020. https://www.mckinsey.com/business-functions/people-and-organizational-performance/our-insights/reimagining-the-office-and-work-life-after-covid-19

Bradley, Simon, and Nikolaus Pevsner. *London 1: City of London*, New Haven and London: Yale University Press, 1997.

Campkin, Ben. *Remaking London: Decline and Regeneration in Urban Culture*. London and New York: I. B. Tauris, 2013.

Cherry, Bridget, and Nikolaus Pevsner. *London 2: South*. New Haven and London: Yale University Press. 2002.

de Roo, Gert, and Camilla Perrone. "A multilevel rationality model for planning behaviour." In *Handbook on Planning and Complexity*. Edited by Gert de Roo, Claudia Yamu, Christian Zuidema, 35-62. Cheltenham: Edward Elgar Publishing Ltd, 2020.

Donnellan, Caroline. *Towards Tate Modern: Public Policy, Private Vision*. London and New York: Routledge, 2018.

Douet, James. Introduction to *Industrial Heritage Re-tooled: The TICCIH guide to Industrial Heritage Conservation*, edited by James Douet, 1-4. Lancaster: Carnegie Publishing Ltd., 2012.

Farrell, Terry. *Shaping London: The patterns and forms that make the metropolis*. Chichester: John Wiley and Sons Ltd., 2010.

Froy, Francesca, and Howard Davis. "Pragmatic urbanism: London's railway arches and small-scale enterprise." *European Planning Studies* 25, no. 11 (2017): 2076-2096. https://doi.org/10.1080/09654313.2017.1367141

Gandy, Mathew. "NEO Bankside." *Architectural Design* 82, no. 1 (2012): 50-53. https://doi.org/10.1002/ad.1348

Hall, Peter. "How much better than no bread?" *Town and Country Planning* 70, no.1 (2001): 1-4. https://archive.tcpa.org.uk/archive/journals/2000-2009/2001/january-march-84/1617349?q=peter%20hall

Home, Robert K. "Deregulating UK planning control in the 1980s." *Cities* 8, no. 4 (1991): 292-300. https://doi.org/10.1016/0264-2751(91)90046-T

Jacobs, Jane. *The Death and Life of Great American Cities*. New York: Vintage Books, 1961.

Jenner, Michael. *London Heritage: The Changing Style of a City*. London: Michael Joseph, 1988.

Jones, Andrew. "Issues in Waterfront Regeneration: More Sobering Thoughts-A UK Perspective." *Planning Practice & Research* 13, no. 4 (1998): 433-442. https://doi.org/10.1080/02697459815987

Knox, Paul. *London: Architecture Building and Social Change.* London: Merrell Publishers Limited, 2015.

Lee, Neil. "The Creative Industries and Urban Economic Growth in the UK." *Environment and Planning A: Economy and Space* 46, no. 1 (2014): 455-470. https://doi.org/10.1068/a4472.

Lehmann, Steffen. *Urban Regeneration: A Manifesto for transforming UK Cities in the Age of Climate Change.* Cham: Palgrave Macmillan, 2019.

London SE1 Community Website. "London SE1 Community Website."Accessed May 8, 2022. https://www.london-se1.co.uk/news/view/8308_Low_Line. "About." Accessed May 8, 2022. https://www.lowline.london/#about

LPAC. *1994: Advice on Strategic Planning Guidance for London.* London: HMSO, 1994.

Mayor of London. *The London Plan: Spatial Development Strategy for Greater London.* Greater London Authority, London, February 2004.

Mayor of London. *The London Plan: Spatial Development Strategy for Greater London: Consolidated with Alterations since 2004.* Greater London Authority, London February 2008.

Miles, Steven, and Ronan Paddison. "Introduction: The Rise and Rise of Culture-led Urban Regeneration." In *Culture-Led Urban Regeneration.* Edited by Ronan Paddison and Steven Miles, ix-xv. London and New York: Routledge, 2007.

Morel, Hana. "Policy and Practice of London's Historic Environment." *The Historic Environment: Policy & Practice* 10, no. 2 (2019): 152-177. https://doi.org/10.1080/17567505.2019.1574098.

Murray, Stephen. "The Evolution and Transformation of Bankside, London, 1947-2019." *Journal of Urban History* 47, no. 1 (2021): 68-84. https://doi.org/10.1177/0096144219864677.

Murphy, Michael D. *Landscape Architecture Theory: An Ecological Approach.* Washington DC, Covelo and London: Island Press, 2016.

Powell, Kenneth. *City Reborn: Architecture and Regeneration in London, from Bankside to Dulwich.* London and New York: Merrell, 2004.

RIBA. "Find an Architect: Bankside 123." Accessed May 8, 2022. https://www.architecture.com/find-an-architect/allies-and-morrison-llp/london/bankside-123

Rogers, Richard. "Bankside Urban Study: The Bankside Triangle." *Tate Press Release.* May 11, 2001. https://www.tate.org.uk/press/press-releases/bankside-urban-study-richard-rogerss-vision-bankside

Rogers, Richard. Introduction to *Towards an Urban Renaissance; Final Report of the Urban Task Force,* by Urban Task Force, 8. London: Taylor & Francis, 1999.

Sheldon, Harvey. "Roman Southwark." In *London Under Ground: The archaeology of a city.* Edited by Ian Haynes, Harvey Sheldon, and Lesley Hannigan, 121-150. Oxford: Oxbow Books, 2000.

Skyscrapernews.com. "The Blue Fin Building." Accessed May 8, 2022. www. sky scrapernews.com/buildings.php?id=1447

Southwark Council. "Climate Emergency: Our commitment to tackling the emergency." Accessed May 8, 2022. https://www.southwark.gov.uk/environment/climate-emergency?chapter=2

Southwark Council. "Southwark Unitary Development Plan (1995) Policy R.2.1." Report presented at the London Borough of Southwark Council, London 1995.

Teedon, Peter. "Designing a Place Called Bankside: On Defining an Unknown Space London." *European Planning Studies* 9, no. 4 (2001): 459-481. https://doi.org/10.1080/713666488.

Travers, Tony. *The Politics of London: Governing and Ungovernable City.* Hampshire: Palgrave Macmillan, 2004.

Wanamaker, Sam. "Shakespeare's Globe Reborn." *RSA Journal* 138, no. 5401 (1989): 25-34. https://www.jstor.org/stable/41375089

Williams, Stephanie. *Docklands.* London: Architecture Design and Technology Press, 1990.

Wainwright, Oliver. "New Bankside: how Richard Roger's new 'non-dom accom' cut out the poor." *The Guardian,* July 21, 2015. https://www.theguardian.com/artanddesign/architecture-design-blog/2015/jul/21/neo-bankside-how-richard-rogers-new-non-dom-accom-cut-out-the-poor

Witherford, Stephen. *Bankside Urban Forest: To lose oneself in a city - as one loses oneself in a forest.* Lausanne: LAPA Studio Publication, 2008.

Chapter 10

A comparative study of the barriers and opportunities for urban development in Wellington and Melbourne

Angela Foster

Victoria University of Wellington, New Zealand

Abstract

In providing a comparative urban analysis of Wellington and Melbourne, this chapter explores a number of questions around the future of city design. The questions include: What can be done to promote sustainable urban intensification that adopts design conditions which will create good living environments? How is change possible concerning the suitability of design proposals to engender positive urban growth? As public consultation becomes more important, how can all stakeholders become part of the process? A solution is through creating a digital feedback loop that functions as a tinder style app for urban design where everyone can be involved in what their city becomes. In this way and by reducing governmental decisions, a wider percentage of people will have a stake in how their city is designed. The question this chapter raises - is participation the future of urban design and a way for cities to keep in touch and respond to the needs of their citizens?

Keywords: urban design, urban politics, Melbourne, Wellington, public consultation, public participation

***

Introduction

Wellington is a harbor city, encapsulated by a series of ranges on the peninsula between Cook Strait and Wellington harbor in the southwest of the North Island, New Zealand. As the country's capital, Wellington houses New Zealand's Parliament, most Government departments, and has one of the busiest airports in the country. Alongside Government, tourism is Wellington's next biggest sector, but due to limited financial growth there has however been little urban development. Reduced infrastructure spending has resulted in a population increase on average of only 0.45% annually, on four hundred thousand residents. By contrast Melbourne, in southeast Australia, also a harbor city, occupies much of the Port Phillip Bay coastline and is home to a population of five million that has consistently increased by 2.3% annually. It is a competitive financial center in the Asia-Pacific region, along with a strong pharmaceutical and manufacturing base. An analysis of urban development in Wellington, compared with that of Melbourne, has revealed a disconnect between the perceived public consultation and actual public, creating barriers in the planning process. In New Zealand, the diffusion of power from Central Government to multiple agencies has created uncertainty in the planning process and culminated in a box-ticking practice. As a practitioner of urban design and through a professional interest in governmental processes this research examines political and social changes in the urban environment.

The aim of this research is to assess the barriers and opportunities affecting the planning approval process, and consequently the built form, through the case studies of Wellington and Melbourne. City environments are a result of a social and political climates and, while these two centers are culturally similar, they have a vastly different urban fabric. Through a comparative process the impact policy can have on the micro and macro can be analyzed. Both Melbourne and Wellington have consistently been voted in the top five world's most livable cities.[1] Gabriela Quintana Vigiola asserts what is important to research is a sense of place, as it enhances the knowledge of practitioners, which generates high-quality urban proposals and solutions.[2] This research begins by using autoethnographic and qualitative research methods to explore the topic. An analysis of planning governance papers, semi-structured interviews, and my own experience as a practitioner, has created an understanding of current influences on the built environment. The qualitative research uses analysis and insights gained through the interview process. Interviewees were intentionally selected to explore their unique perspectives on current governance structures in New Zealand, and abroad.

For the research process what is essential, as Brent Flyvbjerg asserts, is to allow practice to inform and direct the contextual analysis.[3] Relating to this the literature review includes Central Government documents identifying deficiencies in current local Government procedures, one example being "the loopy rules report."[4] There were fewer deficiency focused papers on Melbourne policy, therefore strategy documents, information tools and public consultation methods, were also used to establish the Melbourne context. These publications provide much of the background for the questions posed to interviewees to instigate the discussion. The interview questions focused on the comparative experience of the participants alongside Melbourne processes. The participant information was categorized into social, political, and urban form critiques to establish a common theme, while also aligning my own experience within the city of Wellington. A dominant thread in the conversations and literature review was the lack of public interaction and public understanding of the urban design process. It is difficult to understand the effects of urban design on the city's livability and built form when neither living in it, nor involved in its planning.

Design understanding

Planning and urban design management plays a fundamental role in producing good urban design. Michael Gunder describes the necessary interplay of design understanding within the discipline and how the lack of general knowledge affects urban outcomes.[5] The integration and cross pollination between the physical design and planning of cities enables core values to serve the public interest through social equity. Comparing the governance approaches in two cities and the effect on the built form provides a useful tool for evaluating and understanding how it influences urban design responses and place making. This case study finds emerging patterns within local government decision making which shapes urban design, and the social drivers behind it. To analyze the political platform in Wellington, and its influence on propagating urban livability and smart growth, it is necessary to review urban governance and how it is a steppingstone to sustainable development. Peter Nijkamp suggests looking at sustainable development from a perspective of quality of life in "XXQuality," where good urban governance is about the principles of inclusiveness, citizenship, accountability, and effect process.[6] If planning policies focus on ensuring that growth is managed, then it affects all decision making in the city, and is reflected in the built form. Creating better places, while balancing the private and public objectives for social gains, engenders growth. Cities are challenged by urbanization. The aim is to strive to avoid the negative societal impacts. If unmanaged, local bodies suffer under the strain of reducing funding as infrastructure cost increases without the financial basis to continue as a population declines or stagnates. On this basis as Adam Smith asserts "Government, first and foremost, must strive to create an environment that supports rising productivity."[7]

In Leanne Hodyl's "To investigate planning policies that deliver positive social outcomes in hyper-dense, high-rise residential environments" (2015) she identifies how in four of the world's densest cities, Hong Kong, Vancouver, New York, and Tokyo, managing height and bulk in a positive way can lead to community benefits.[8] A different approach is adopted by The Ministry of Environment. "Building competitive cities: Reform of the urban and infrastructure planning system - A technical working paper" (October 2010) describes how in New Zealand there is the tendency to take a rules-based approach, where a conservative process of avoidance involves remedying or mitigating adverse effects on the existing environment.[9] The report also identifies how multiple party involvement, with the council's reliance on external consultants, can lead to a lack of coordination and consistency between parties as a symptom of the increasingly complex urban planning decision-making process. There are currently eighty-five local authorities in New Zealand, each with their own district plan, where the structure and format are virtually unique to that Council. The absence of a common process makes consistency in decision making even harder, with no baseline for external professionals on both sides of the process.

Wellington, New Zealand

In the early 1990s there was a flurry of civic construction which upgraded the waterfront land, creating parks and new public architecture, and had a positive impact on the city. In recent years, however, following the Christchurch earthquake, Wellington's construction industry has struggled due to the cost of new structural design and strengthening requirements. This, combined with added bureaucracy, has slowed growth. There are few new developments underway and those proposals which are put forward are slow to obtain approval in the increasingly risk-averse planning environment. Twenty years ago, after the introduction of a new district plan that linked into the Resource Management Act 1991 (RMA), the responsibility for Wellington's cityscape shifted from a centralized bureaucracy to under-resourced local governments. The outcome was that city leaders were required to design, finance, and deliver multi sector economic development initiatives which were once seen as the responsibility of Central Government.

Heralded as a bold new way to simplify the process, the RMA was designed to manage the quality of the natural environment in urban areas. The lack of direct reference to the urban condition resulted in any new construction being seen as negative. The inevitable conclusion being the effect on consumption of resources, wind, sun, and existing spaces or places can only be considered adverse. The unanticipated consequence of the Act was that Council projects were also subjected to increased public objections, as public approval was now required on most Council developments. Councils faced the negative effects of their own policies, and their own planning approvals proved harder and harder to obtain. As any new project had an effect, development stalled, what ensued was a period of "austerity urbanism."[10] The phrase applies where governments are forced to adapt to the uncertain future and political economy by retrenching and spending less, which indirectly impacts on the maintenance of the urban fabric. When governments retrench on public development, this can negatively affect business confidence to a point where private developers disengage from the community. Ultimately, the system slowly ceases to function.

Melbourne, Australia

Melbourne has a central city population and land area similar in size to Wellington, but the urban development is not on the same level. In the 1980s Rob Adams, Director of City Design at the City of Melbourne, put in place an urban design strategy that increased investment in the built environment through civic development and public consultation. The business and finance sector grew, and the economy flourished. This difference in policy and advocacy ultimately helped Melbourne mature to becoming an economic center and opened the way for architecturally significant buildings and landscapes. The process of engagement with the community began with the city initiative "Future Melbourne 2026." [11] Two thousand residents were canvassed to generate a Citizen Jury Report. This report contained nine goals for the city, which are broken down into key measurable deliverables in the Council Plan 2017-2021. Melbourne was able to engage in this way as the environment effects of urban sites are managed by City of Melbourne planners.

If the Minister for Planning decides that an Environment Effects Statement (EES) is required due to the scale or potential adverse effects, only then is further engagement necessary. In Wellington, the RMA prescribes that all projects must address effects, and consequently the impacts of growth or change are categorized as negative, which must be mitigated in some way. Another example of Melbourne's engagement, utilizing easily accessible online platforms, is the Development Activity Model. Here the public can understand the future built environment and be involved in its evolution.[12] These tools, and the like, are the key differences between Wellington and Melbourne. Public transparency is about building trust, while adding value to the urban design process, and positively affecting the built form.

Good urban design

Urban withdrawal in the Wellington area is evident to the local residents and to the government.[13] During a relatively stable economic period in 2013, New Zealand, John Key, the Prime Minister, quipped "Wellington is dying" - was he right?[14] Cranes are a sign of a city's growth, however, there are currently few in Wellington's central business district.[15] The temporary solution undertaken by some developers is to construct compliant, low cost, minimum standard structures which can negatively impact on the urban fabric and character of the neighborhoods they are constructed in. As a result, the built and social environment suffers. By comparison, Melbourne has one hundred and forty-five cranes and a booming economy. Melbourne's skyline has changed considerably as it manages intensification. In a similar period, Wellington has changed little, prompting business to move to other urban centers.

What is needed for the vitality and development of cities and "places to dance."[16] Rebecca Kiddle uses this phrase as a metaphor for socializing, and where community physically occurs. Kiddle points to the importance of informal public space which can only be created by policy makers. Governance processes need to engender creative responses to the built form, and to include place making through design, to encourage the mixing of public and private spaces. As public consultation becomes more important in demonstrating livability in the built environment, how is it possible to include the relevant generations, not just those with money and time? One avenue of thought is the design of a digital feedback loop that functions as a Tinder style app for urban design. The thinking behind this comes from the need to establish a framework that reduces governmental and decision-making risk. While good urban design is integral to culture and society, as Donald Watson "Urban design and city building are surely among the most auspicious endeavors of this or any age, giving rise to a vision of life" (2003) asserts it is also an ethical endeavor.[17]

The issue is these important decisions are left in the hands of a small number of decision makers for the many Government agencies. What this means is that agencies can no longer act autonomously under the pressure of increased public scrutiny when residents are demanding accountability for developments in their neighborhood. As population density increases how can good urban design be delivered for the future? There are increasing demands on infrastructure, along with urban and suburban sustainable growth. An emerging question is how to ensure that those funding the projects are encouraged to contribute successfully to the cityscape, through a simple, nimble, and inclusive process. A solution has been through the opportunities for social media applications to lead the way. This has led to helping regulatory bodies to identify how more public participation, rather than less, can contribute to the decision-making process and further good urban design, and increase livability, in the built city.[18]

Participation processes in action

Alongside Melbourne there are several other cities including Vancouver and the Vancouver Plan, San Francisco's SPUR and UK's CABE that realize the benefits of engagement are involving the community to ensure regional contexts are promoted.[19] CABE is an example of a policy which was successful in its early years, but as it grew it became progressively unwieldy, until finally it was abandoned. It did, however, establish some key important principles of engagement which have been recognized and incorporated into other cities' approaches to planning processes. One city is Copenhagen which has been making real headway with its innovative and more socially aware design processes. Renowned for implementing the "putting people first" policy.[20] Where the goal was to strengthen the urban experience through good urban design and through participation in the democratic processes. Specific architectural initiatives were also incorporated into policies across several ministries to ensure people and place was integrated into all aspects of Danish life. How Copenhagen put this into practice was by facilitating public private partnerships and driving a philosophy of "integrated urbanism."[21] A strategy of linking the social, cultural, environmental, and economic aspects of urban space paved the way for increased livability and public satisfaction in the planning process.[22]

The urban design collaborative Arki_lab utilizes livability and public satisfaction in its planning approach. The practice established itself in 2012 in Denmark around a philosophy of developing spaces through socio-cultural exploration, empowering communities to participate and thereby generating good sustainable design. Golam Mathbor, a professor at the School of Social Work at Monmouth University, notes that the education of citizens is a prerequisite to their participation in urban design.[23] The value of public engagement is then an exploration into how public space is meaningful to those citizens. Mathbor identifies that when we engage with the people, we generate a collective who can then share a passion about place and look to understand their city better. They learn to engage in the participatory processes and the result is better for it. Arki_Lab took this bottom-up approach to the next level when they created CoCityApp to engage with their people.[24] It is a smartphone application which encourages passersby to engage in the ideas for the city. It works by taking a picture, allowing the author to create a collage by overlaying improvements to the scene. The new street scene is then uploaded to a single platform. The outcome is a collection of collages which are made accessible to all citizens and local ministries.

The CoCityApp is a tool that encourages citizen involvement to explore their city, enabling residents to share thoughts on the local urban environment. Importantly this type of technology can be a key facilitation tool for decision makers where real-time imagery of the city through the eyes of its citizens can be captured. This type of tool highlights how traditional methods of public participation in the government decision-making process are no longer valid. They do not achieve genuine citizen engagement, as involvement is often limited to those with time or money. Including a wider demographic can engender innovation, leading to improvements in urban planning practices that can facilitates growth while improving livability. The question is how to engage with the public effectively? What is needed is communities of practice, where urbanites share a passion about place and look to understand it better.

By working together, regulatory bodies and the public can progress place making through developing feedback loops. The impact is that it empowers communities, and fosters good design, where a sustainable methodology helps manage growth in a risk averse political environment.

Bottom-up principles

To improve ongoing civic participation, rather than just momentary engagement, we must utilize bottom-up principles. Denmark has pioneered user democracy with decentralized planning where the role of the state is limited to "facilitation, support and enabling citizens to lead self-determined fulfilled lives."[25] This policy is founded on the understanding that the right to land is not synonymous with the right to develop, and the planning process involves a public-private partnership. As a philosophy it generates good urban design in the built city and develops the Danish design culture. Similarly, to Melbourne, the inclusion of the public in the process has the benefit of increasing design awareness of the benefits of good architecture and good urban infrastructure. For three decades Melbourne has focused on the built urban environment, appointing a Government Architect, investing in capital works, and advocating for good design. It identified that the quality of design affects how spaces function, effectively addressing human needs through the built form. Developing and maintaining this design culture in the public arena is imperative to engendering good urban design. Professor Alan Pert, director of the Melbourne School of Design, notes that "the important thing about schools is they become laboratories for the city."[26]

Advancing an architectural culture is important and one way to do this is to put design into the public forum through media coverage. Exhibitions like "Melbourne Now 2023" provide space for art and architecture to be presented to reinforce Melbourne as a creative city.[27] "Sampling the City" showcases architecture that embraces good urban design principles in the built city, reinforcing the design message to the public.[28] It is easy to see how this engenders a highly professional planning process and effective policy that enables good design to be accepted, appreciated, and consequently proliferate. Across the ditch, Wellington is seen as the arts capital of New Zealand. Speak to any Wellingtonian and they will wax lyrical on recent events, markets and concerts occurring weekly. On the flip side, when urban design and planning improvements are publicly discussed the negative effects are the focus and the quality of design is never mentioned. There is a clear distrust of the Council's discussion making and a misunderstanding of the planning process. This negativity is evident in a recently consented project for Shelly Bay, a dilapidated army complex on the Miramar peninsula overlooking Wellington Harbor.[29] After considerable debate, three years after the initial proposal was issued for public submissions environmental and civil court hearings, the project has finally been approved.

Under the embattled RMA, Wellington's planning body is criticized for being slow and unresponsive by creating a slow developing and neglected city. An indication of a city that is not neglected is through its high-quality public and private spaces which are paramount to its distinctiveness, vitality, and livability. A city's culture is a function of a creative response to its architecture, urban design and landscape architecture stemming from an informed public. A design culture by its very nature embraces innovation and creativity that sees change, and the ambition to improve, as necessary for the public good. Guy Jukier identifies "design activism" as a desire to make "a better world."[30] As our cities grow it is ever more important that innovation be embraced, if not there is a risk of decline. The lack of a design culture and willingness to put design first has limited Wellington's ambitions and resulted in the stagnation of the city environment. By contrast Melbourne has embraced growth and engaged in urban revitalization since the early 1990s. Engaging communities through multi-media strategies can increase public interest, engendering trust and understanding the process, improves urban outcomes. By utilizing effective communication urban design can have a strong advocacy role to play in connecting communities.

The New Zealand Government policy paper "The Value of Urban Design," (2005) outlines how user participation in urban design activity can improve the fit between design and user needs.[31] What it speculates for is more effective use of resources, by providing an informed direction for decision making that offers time or cost savings, by encouraging increased user support for positive change; develop a greater sense of "user ownership" over changes, and legitimize user interests and enhance a sense of community and local democracy. When communities distrust the process, and projects are forced into litigation, the planning body tends to substitute design consideration for regulations as the safest course of action. The shaping of cities then becomes a crude assessment of rules: parking design, road widths and hierarchies, land use, density requirements, health and safety issues and volume standards, with little or no attention paid to context or relevance. The resulting built city is one of uninspired blandness. Once the practice of minimum requirements is established it quickly becomes the norm and development soon becomes the path of least resistance. The city's vibrancy is lost, and the design quality is lost. Wellington has fallen into this trap, sanctioning developments that strictly adhere to criteria rather than encouraging quality design and site-specific solutions that improve the quality of the built city but require subjective analysis against planning guidelines. The reliance on box ticking has the potential to dumb down design and provide sameness as the path of least resistance is encouraged. It has been suggested that fewer rules can create better design and better cities.

Urban Governance as a concept has changed over the thirty years, from one of a hierarchical authority where command and control was accepted, to one where governance is seen as a facilitator and coordinator of public and private interests. Trust in policy and process needs to be established for the city to embrace change. This is where digital communication technologies can create new avenues for empowering stakeholders to share information and generate dialogue. The capacity for diverse groups to scrutinize development proposals, advocate differing agendas and effect change can be escalated with the convenience of these new digital applications. Then, both public and private sectors can encourage and generate a climate of trust, facilitating new approaches to better negotiate citizen involvement. In Ajay Garde's research on citizen participation of an urban park, the notion of striving for design excellence, or innovative solutions, is achieved through providing good visual information to public participants.[32] It allows the public to understand and evaluate the visual at a more informed level, and Garde argues, they are more likely to be more actively involved. If urban citizens delegate power to representatives and those representatives proves to be a bottleneck, and do not utilize the feedback, the consequence is they are disempowered to make good decisions.

In New Zealand, the RMA dictates consultation, but does not encourage any real engagement. What is needed is real collaboration within a simplified and leaner decision-making process, to legitimize good outcomes. Social media applications have become commonplace and accessed by more generations than any other communication tool to date. It has the potential to support these opportunities and engage with those who would not normally have considered commenting on urban design. Involving the wider demographic in the assessment of government initiatives improves transparency and the collaborative process, and accessing emerging technologies is the next step.in reshaping the political realm. One proponent of these systems, and an augmented democracy, is César Haldigo.[33] He has a radical suggestion for fixing our broken political system: automate it! In a TED talk, he proposes a theory to use technology, namely artificial intelligence (AI), to bypass politicians. Using algorithms citizens create personalized AI representatives that participate directly in democratic decisions, on their behalf. Ultimately the avatar becomes the stakeholder in the political process.

Conclusion

Architects and urban designs hold a unique position to champion active citizens. The industry already utilizes technology in the design, marketing, and delivery of projects. The next step is to incorporate an interactive tool for all citizens, as there has never been a period with a more tech savvy public to work with.[34] Devon Maloney conducted a survey of around seventeen thousand participants globally and identified that over the past five years applications have proliferated and more than three-quarters of the workforce use this technology to improve the way they work and engage within their business.[35] The new digital era can be the next step in urban collaboration with the Tinder style app offering the option of swiping left or right to give feedback to the decision makers. Brian Head refers to a growing awareness of urban complexity and inter-connectedness of many community problems, and the need to share responsibility for resolving these complex social and environmental issues.[36] Head identifies that a participatory approach can remove uncertainty, and provide the vital feedback needed to help processes progress in a timely and cost-effective manner. Transparency in city life through technology can be the new tool to promote a society centered approach. In doing so it can encourage a sense of social responsibility through engagement, leading to quicker, more effective decision making. A process that Wellington so desperately needs to stimulate sustainable good urban design and improve the built city environment.

Bibliography

Adams, Rob. "Transforming Australian Cities for a More Financially Viable and Sustainable Future." Transforming Australian Cities. Victorian Department of Transport and the City of Melbourne, March 2010. http://www.transforming australiancities.com.au/wp content/uploads/Transforming-Australian-Cities-Report.pdf

Blicher, Sune. "New Danish Architecture Policy Is Putting People First." Danish Agency for Culture. Accessed April 5, 2021. https://news.cision.com/danish-agency-for-culture/quotes

Byczkowska-Owczarek, Dominika. "Researcher's personal experiences as a method of embodiment research." In *The Routledge Handbook of Planning Research Methods*. Edited by Elisabete A. Silva, Patsy Healey, Neil Harris, and Pieter Van den Broeck. Abingdon: Routledge, 2016.

Carmona, Matthew, Claudio de Magalhães, and Lucy Natarajan. *Design Governance: the CABE Experiment*. New York and London: Routledge, Taylor and Francis Group, 2017.

Carmona, Matthew. "The Tools of Design Governance (Formal and Informal)." *Journal of Urban Design*, no. 22 (2017): 38-74. https://doi.org/10.4324/97813 15748979-8

City of Melbourne, Victoria, Australia. "Creating the Plan." Accessed March 21, 2021. https://www.melbourne.vic.gov.au/about-melbourne/future-melbourne/creating-the plan/Pages/creating-the-plan.aspx.

City of Melbourne, Victoria, Australia. "Development Activity." Accessed March 21, 2021. https://www.developmentactivity.melbourne.vic.gov.au/

City of Melbourne, Victoria, Australia. "Melbourne Now 2023." Accessed March 21, 2021. https://www.onlymelbourne.com.au/melbourne-now-ngv#.YFfjeO gzaUk

City of Melbourne, Victoria, Australia. "Sampling the City." Accessed March 21, 2021. https://www.ngv.vic.gov.au/melbournenow/projects/528.html

City of Vancouver, British Columbia, Canada. "Vancouver Plan." Accessed March 21, 2021. https://vancouver.ca/home-property-development/vancouver-city-wide-plan.aspx

Cooper, Ian. "Inadequate Grounds for a Design-Led' Approach to Urban Renaissance?" *Building Research & Information* 28, no. 3 (2000): 212-19. https://doi.org/10.1080/096132100368975

Design Council UK. "The Councillor's guide to urban design." Accessed March 21, 2021. https://www.designcouncil.org.uk/resources/guide/councillors-guide-urban-design

Fabian, Louise, and Kristine Samson. "Claiming Participation – a Comparative Analysis of DIY Urbanism in Denmark." *Journal of Urbanism: International Research on Placemaking and Urban Sustainability* 9, no. 2 (2015): 166-84. https://doi.org/10.1080/17549175.2015.1056207

Edgar, Ray. "Architecture students envision a new-look Melbourne." *The Sydney Morning Herald,* December 18, 2020. https://www.smh.com.au/culture/art-and-design/architecture students-envision-a-new-look-melbourne-20201214 -p56n8d.html

Flyvbjerg, Bent, and Steven Sampson. *Making Social Science Matter: Why Social Inquiry Fails and How It Can Succeed Again.* Oxford, UK: Cambridge University Press, 2001.

Frisk, Rasmus, Thomas Aarup Due and Yalda Pilehchian. "Building cities with people." Paper presented at the 8th International Urban Design Conference Empowering Change: Transformative Innovations and Projects Brisbane QLD, 16-18 November 2015. https://www.arkilab.dk/wp-content/uploads/2016/06/1.pdf

Garde, Ajay. "Citizen Participation, Design Competition and the Product in Urban Design: Insights from the Orange County Great Park." *Journal of Urban Design* 19, no. 1 (2013): 89-118. https://doi.org/10.1080/13574809.2013.854697

Gunder, Michael. "Commentary: Is Urban Design Still Urban Planning? An Exploration and Response." *Journal of Planning Education and Research* 31, no. 2 (2011): 184-95. https://doi.org/10.1177/0739456x10393358.

Hallahan, Marine, Hamish Rutherford, and Kate Chapman. "Prime Minister Side-Steps 'Dying' Comment." *Stuff News.* May 7, 2013. https://www.stuff.co.nz/national/8639116/Prime-minister-side-steps-dying-comment

Head, Brian W. "Community Engagement: Participation on Whose Terms?" *Australian Journal of Political Science* 42, no. 3 (2007). https://doi.org/10.1080/10361140701513570

Hidalgo, Cesar. "A bold idea to replace politicians." Ted Talk. April 2018. https://www.ted.com/talks/cesar_hidalgo_a_bold_idea_to_replace_politicians? language=en

Hodyl, Leanne. "To Investigate Planning Policies That Deliver Positive Social Outcomes in Hyper-Dense, High-Rise Residential Environments." The Winston Churchill Memorial Trust of Australia, 2015. https://apo.org.au/node/52757

Joss, Simon. "Future Cities: Asserting Public Governance." *Palgrave Communications* 4, no. 1 (2018). https://doi.org/10.1057/s41599-018-0087-7

Julier, Guy. "Political Economies of Design Activism and the Public Sector." Te Putahi, n.d. https://teputahi.org.nz/wp-content/uploads/2015/10/Julier_Design_Activism.pdf

Kiddle, Rebecca. "Where Do We Dance? Planning Social Spaces in the Suburbs." *NZ Local Government Magazine*, no. 56 (June 2019): 10-13.

Maloney, Devon, and Lucas Puente. "The app era is here: Now to optimize for it." October 31, 2019. https://slack.com/intl/en-nz/blog/transformation/the-app-era-is-here

Martinez-Fernandez, Cristina, Ivonne Audirac, Sylvie Fol, and Emmanuele Cunningham Sabot. "Shrinking Cities: Urban Challenges of Globalization." *International Journal of Urban and Regional Research* 36, no. 2 (2012): 213-25. https://doi.org/10.1111/j.1468-2427.2011. 01092.x

Mathbor, Golam. "Enhancement of community preparedness for natural disasters: The role of social work in building social capital for sustainable disaster relief and management." *International Social Work* 50, no.3 (2009): 357-369. https://doi.org/10.1177/0020872807076049

Ministry for the Environment, New Zealand. "3 Key Urban Design Qualities - The Seven Cs." Accessed April 5, 2021. https://www.mfe.govt.nz/publications/towns-and-cities/new zealand-urban-design-protocol/3-key-urban-design-qualities-seven

Ministry for the Environment, New Zealand. "Building competitive cities: Reform of the urban and infrastructure planning system - A technical working paper." October 2010. https://www.mfe.govt.nz/publications/rma/building-competitive-cities-discussion-document

Ministry for the Environment, New Zealand. "The Value of Urban Design: The Economic, Environmental and Social Benefits of Urban Design." June 2005. http://www.mfe.govt.nz/publications/urban/value-urban-design-full-report-jun05/index.html

Ministry for the Environment, New Zealand. "3 Key urban design qualities – The seven Cs." March 2021. https://www.mfe.govt.nz/publications/towns-and-cities/new-zealand-urban-design-protocol/3-key-urban-design-qualities-seven

Nijkamp, P. "XXQ Factors for Sustainable Urban Development: A Systems Economics View." *Romanian Journal of Regional Science* 2, no. 1 (2008): 325–342.

Peck, Jamie. "Austerity Urbanism." *City* 16, no. 6 (2012): 626–55. https://doi.org/10.1080/13604813.2012.734071.

Pew Research Centre. "Social media fact sheet." June 12, 2019. https://www.pewresearch.org/internet/fact-sheet/social-media/

Porter, Michael E. "Clusters and the New Economy." *Harvard Business Review* 76, no. 6 (1998), 77-90. (Reprinted in Managing in the New Economy, HBSP, 1999; and in Systems of Innovation: Growth, Competitiveness and Employment, Edward Elgar, 2000).

Sherwin, Murray. "Towards better local regulation." Productivity Commission, New Zealand Government. May 2013. https://www.productivity.govt.nz/assets/Documents/f32eda4453/Final-report-Towards-better local-regulation.pdf

Shibley, Robert G., Donald Watson, and Alan J. Plattus. *Time-Saver Standards for Urban Design.* McGraw Hill, 2003.

Silva, Elisabete A., Patsy Healey, Neil Harris, and Pieter Van den Broeck. *The Routledge Handbook of Planning Research Methods.* New York: Routledge Taylor & Francis Group, 2016.

Smit, Malcolm. "Towards a Complex and Integrated Urbanism," UrbanNext, December 10, 2018. https://urbannext.net/towards-a-complex-and-integrated-urbanism/.https://urbannext.net/towards-a-complex-and-integrated-urbanism/

Watson, Donald. "Time Saver Standards for Urban Design." The McGraw-Hill Companies, Inc. 2003. https://www.accessengineeringlibrary.com/content/book/9780070685079

Wilson, Alexander, Mark Tewdwr-Jones, and Rob Comber. "Urban Planning, Public Participation and Digital Technology: App Development as a Method of Generating Citizen Involvement in Local Planning Processes." *Environment and Planning B: Urban Analytics and City Science* 46, no. 2 (2017): 286-302. https://doi.org/10.1177/2399808317712515

Wellington City Council, New Zealand. "Have your say – Shelly Bay Development." August 14, 2017. https://wellington.govt.nz/~/media/have-your-say/publicinput/files/consultations/2017/07/shelly-bay/shelly-bay-proposal.pdf?la=en.

Notes

Introduction

1 Sigmund Freud, *14. Art and Literature* (Harmondsworth: Penguin Books, 1990), 340-341. Freud discusses the "*heimlich*" (homely) as the familiar and domestic, which trauma subverts into the "*unheimlich*" (unhomely) as the uncanny, the strangely familiar.

2 Patrick Geddes, *Cities in Evolution: An Introduction to the Town Planning Movement and to the Study of Civics* (London: Williams & Norgate, 1915), 1.

3 Marshall Berman, *All that is solid melts into Air: The Experience of Modernity* (London and New York: Verso, 1983), 15.

4 Richard F. Weingroff, "The Man Who Changed America, Part 1," *Public Roads* 66 (2003): 24.

5 Scott G. Ortman et al. "Cities: Complexity, theory and history," PLoS ONE, 15, no. 12 (2020): 1-24, doi: https://doi.org/10.1371/journal.pone.0243621

6 Jane Jacobs, "Downtown is for people," (The Editors of Fortune), in *The Exploding Metropolis*, (New York: Doubleday Anchor Books, 1958), 140.

7 Ebeneezer Howard, *To-Morrow: A Peaceful Path to Real Reform*, (London: Swan Sonnenschein & Co., 1898), 13.

8 Ebeneezer Howard, *Garden Cities of Tomorrow*, (London: Swan Sonnenschein & Co., Ltd 1902), 162.

9 Jacobs, Downtown is for people, 140.

10 Jane Jacobs, *The Death and Life of Great American Cities* (New York: Vintage Books, 1961), 7.

11 Oliver Wainwright, "Street fighter: how Jane Jacobs saved New York from Bulldozer Bob," *The Guardian*, April 30, 2017, https://www.theguardian.com/artanddesign/2017/apr/30/citizen-jane-jacobs-the-woman-who-saved-manhattan-from-the-bulldozer-documentary.

12 Jacobs, *The Death and Life of Great American Cities*, 4.

13 Ricky Burdett. "Designing Urban Democracy: Mapping Scales of Urban Identity," Public Culture 25, no. 2 70 (2013): 349–367, doi:10.1215/08992363-2020638.

14 Stefano Moroni and Stefano Cozzolino. "Action and the city. Emergence, complexity, planning," Cities, 90, no. 1 (2019): 42-51, https://www.journals.elsevier.com/cities.

15 Roland Barthes, *The Death of the Author* (London: Fontana Press, 1977), 142.

16 Steven Feld and Keith H. Basso, *Senses of Place* (Santa Fe: School of American Research Press, 1996), 8.

17 Pierre Bourdieu, *Outline of a Theory of Practice* (Cambridge: Cambridge University Press, 1977), 125.

18 Bourdieu, 125.

19 Jane Jacobs, *The Economy of Cities* (New York: Vintage Books, 1970), 197.

20 Jacobs, *The Death and Life of Great American Cities*, 87.

[21] Robert Venturi, *Complexity and Contradiction in Architecture* (New York: The Museum of Modern Art, 1977 [1966]), 16.

[22] Benjamin Sitton Flowers, *Skyscraper: The Politics and Power of Building New York City in the Twentieth Century* (Pennsylvania: University of Pennsylvania Press, 2009), 75.

[23] Gert de Roo, "Spatial Planning and the Complexity of Turbulent, Open Environments - About purposeful interventions in a world of non-linear change" in *The Routledge Handbook of Planning Theory,* ed. M. Gunder et al. (London and New York: Routledge, 2019), 314.

[24] Gert de Roo, "Introduction to the Handbook on Planning and Complexity" in *Handbook on Planning and Complexity,* ed. Gert de Roo et al. (Cheltenham: Edward Elgar Publishing Limited, 2020), 7.

[25] "Historic Cairo," UNESCO, accessed April 14, 2022, https://whc.unesco.org/en/list/89/.

[26] Ahmed Sedky, *Living with Heritage in Cairo: Area Conservation in the Arab–Islamic City* (Cairo & New York: The American University in Cairo Press, 2009), xvii.

[27] Kristof Van Assche, Raoul Beunen and Martijn Duineveld, "Strategy in complexity: the shaping of communities and environments," in *Handbook on Planning and Complexity,* ed. Gert de Roo et al. (Cheltenham: Edward Elgar Publishing Limited, 2020), 151.

[28] Hebatalla Abouelfadl, Dalila ElKerdany and Christoph Wessling. "Introduction," in *Revitalizing City Districts: Transformation Partnership for Urban Design and Architecture in Historic City Districts,* ed. Hebatalla Abouelfadl et al. (Cham: Springer, 2017), vii.

[29] Mark Wenman, *Agonistic Democracy: Constituent Power in the Era of Globalisation* (Cambridge: Cambridge University Press, 2013), 28.

[30] Jacobs, The Death and Life of Great American Cities, 14.

[31] Peter Carnevale, "Creativity in the Outcomes of Conflict," in *The Handbook of conflict resolution,* ed. M. Deutsch et al. 2nd Edition (San Francisco: Jossey-Bass, 2006), 414.

[32] Lin Ye. "Urban regeneration in China: Policy, development, and issues," Local Economy 26, no. 5 (2011): 337-347, doi: 10.1177/0269094211409117.

[33] Sheng Zhong, "Artists and Shanghai's culture-led urban regeneration," Cities 171, no. 56 (2016): 165-171, https://doi.org/10.1016/j.cities.2015.09.002

[34] Harry den Hartog, "Shanghai's Regenerated Industrial Waterfronts: Urban Lab for Sustainability Transitions?" Urban Planning 6, no. 3 (2021): 181-196, https://doi.org/10.17645/up.v6i3.4194

[35] Jay Gitlin, Barbara Berglund, and Adam Arenson, "Introduction Local Crossroads, Global Networks, and Frontier Cities," in *Frontier Cities: Encounters at the Crossroads of Empire,* ed. Jay Gitlin et al. (Philadelphia: University of Pennsylvania Press, 2013), 4.

[36] Christian Zuidema, "Post-contingency - considering complexity," in *Handbook on Planning and Complexity,* ed. Gert de Roo et al. (Cheltenham: Edward Elgar Publishing Limited, 2020), 66.

[37] Benjamin Davy. "Polyrational property: rules for the many uses of land," International Journal of the Commons, 8, no. 2 (2014): 472-492, http://www.thecommonsjournal.org.

[38] Neil Smith, *The New Urban Frontier: Gentrification and the Revanchist City* (London & New York: Routledge, 1996), 41.

[39] Gerard Lemos, *The End of the Chinese Dream: Why Chinese people fear the future* (New Haven and London: Yale University Press, 2012), 16.

[40] Helen X. H. Bao et al. "City profile: Chongqing (1997-2017)," Cities 94, no. 1 (2019):161-171, doi: https://doi.org/10.1016/j.cities. Asia 2019.06.011

[41] Xuan Sun et al. "Land Cover Changes and Urban Expansion in Chongqing, China: A Study Based on Remote Sensing Images," Environment and Urbanization, 12, NO. 1S (2021): 39S-58S. doi: 10.1177/0975425321998035.

[42] Ling Huang, Junhang Luo, and Xiang Peng, "Three Stages of Urban Community Development and Regeneration Planning in Chongqing (2010-2020)," in *Chinese Urban Planning and Construction: From Historical Wisdom to Modern Miracles*, ed. Lanchun Bian,et al. (Cham: Springer, 2021), 133-155.

[43] OECD, Urban Renaissance: Canberra A Sustainable Future: A Sustainable Future (Paris: OECD Publications, 2002), https://read.oecd-ilibrary.org/urban-rural-and-regional-development/urban-renaissance-canberra_9789264196094-en#page1.

[44] Susa Eräranta, "Social complexities in collaborative planning processes," in *Handbook on Planning and Complexity*, ed. Gert de Roo et al. (Cheltenham: Edward Elgar Publishing Ltd, 2020), 182.

[45] Colin Rowe and Fred Koetter, *Collage City* (Cambridge, MA and London, England: MIT Press, 1978) 142.

[46] Kirrily Jordan and Jock Collins, "Symbols of Ethnicity in a Multi-ethnic Precinct: Marketing Perth's Northbridge for Cultural Consumption," in *Selling Ethnic Neighborhoods: The Rise of Neighborhoods as Places of Leisure and Consumption, ed* Volkan Aytar et al. (New York: Routledge, 2012), 121.

[47] Graeme Turner. "The cosmopolitan city and its Other: the ethnicizing of the Australian suburb," Inter-Asia Cultural Studies, 9, no. 4 (2008): 568-582, doi: 10.1080/14649370802386487.

[48] Stefano Moroni and Stefano Cozzolino, "Conditions of actions in complex social–spatial systems," in *Handbook on Planning and Complexity*, ed. Gert de Roo et al. (Cheltenham: Edward Elgar Publishing Ltd, 2020), 195.

[49] Hans Thor Andersen et al. "Crisis in the Resurgent City? The Rise of Copenhagen," International Journal of Urban and Regional Research, 34.3, no. 9 (2010) 693-700. doi: 10.1111/j.1468-2427.2010.00984.x

[50] Thomas Bjørner. "The advantages of and barriers to being smart in a smart city: The perceptions of project managers within a smart city cluster project in Greater Copenhagen," Cities, 114, no. 7 (2021): 137-143, doi: 10.1016/j.cities.2021.103187.

[51] Saeid Pira, "The social issues of smart home: a review of four European cities' experiences," Pira European Journal of Futures Research 9, no. 3 (2021): 1-15, https://doi.org/10.1186/s40309-021-00173-4.

[52] Duncan Maclaren and Julian Agyeman, Case Study: Copenhagen. Sharing Cities, A Case for Truly Smart and Substantiable cities (Cambridge, MA: MIT Press, 2015), 138.

[53] Southwark Council, "Southwark Unitary Development Plan (1995): Policy R.2.1" (report presented at the London Borough of Southwark Council, London 1995).

[54] Roberta Comunian."Rethinking the Creative City: The Role of Complexity, Networks and Interactions in the Urban Creative Economy," Urban Studies Journal Limited 48, no. 6 (2011): 1157-1179, doi: 10.1177/0042098010370626

[55] Maurizio Carta, "The Fluid City Paradigm: A Deeper Innovation." in *The Fluid City Paradigm: Waterfront Regeneration as an Urban Renewal Strategy*, ed. Maurizio Carta et al. (Cham: Springer, 2016), 4.

[56] Marichela Sepe. "Urban history and cultural resources in urban regeneration: a case of creative waterfront renewal," Planning Perspectives 28, no. 4 (2013): 595-613, http://dx.doi.org/10.1080/02665433.2013.774539.

[57] Wellington City Council, "Wellington Urban Growth Plan: Urban Development and Transport Strategy: 2014-2043," Wellington: Wellington City Council. (Report presented at the Wellington City Council, Wellington June 2015).

[58] Michael Buxton, Robin Goodman and Susie Moloney, *Planning Melbourne: Lessons for a Sustainable City* (Clayton: CSIRO Publishing, 2016,), 1.

[59] Colin Fournier, "Cities on the Edge of Chaos," Architectural design 85, no 6, (2015):128-133, DOI: 10.1002/ad.1990

[60] Geddes, *Cities in Evolution*, 1.

[61] President Zelenskyy. "Breaking!" 0:24-0:33 https://twitter.com/i/status/1500472014452273157

[62] Jacobs, Downtown is for people, 140.

Chapter 1

[1] Hans Mommaas, "Spaces of Culture and Economy: Mapping the Cultural-Creative Cluster Landscape," Creative Economies, Creative Cities 98 (2009): 45, doi:10.1007/978-1-4020-9949-6_4

[2] Andre Raymond, *Artisans et commerçants Au Caire XVIIIe* Siècle (Damas: Institute Français de Damas, 1973).

[3] Hans Mommaas, "Cultural Clusters and the Post-industrial City: Towards the Remapping of Urban Cultural Policy", Urban Studies 41 (2004): 508, doi: 10.1080/0042098042000178663.

[4] Lewis Mumford, *The Culture of Cities*. (New York: Harcourt Brace Jovanovich, 1938), 20

[5] Jacobs, *The Death and Rise of Great American Cities*,

[6] Mark Stern and Susan Seifert, "Cultural Clusters: The Implications of Cultural Assets Agglomeration for Neighborhood Revitalization", Journal of Planning Education and Research 29 (2010), doi: 10.1177/0739456X09358555.

[7] Stern and Seifert, 265.

[8] "Cairo-Creative Cities Network", UNECO, accessed June 12, 2020, https://en.unesco.org/creative-cities/cairo.

[9] "Creative Cities Network", UNESCO, accessed April 24, 2021, https://en.unesco.org/creative-cities/cairo

[10] Salah Haridi, *Al-Hiraf wal-sina'at fi 'ahd Muhammad 'Ali (Crafts and Industries in the Age of Muhammad 'Ali)*, (Cairo: Dar al-ma'arif, 1985), 31.

[11] Natalia Ramirez and Alaa El-Habashi, "ReGREENeration of Historic Cairo: Hara al-Nabawiya and Bayt Madkour in al-Darb Al-Ahmar", The Journal of Public Space 5 (2020), doi: 0.32891/jps.v5i1.1251

[12] John T. Chalcraft, *The Striking Cabbies of Cairo and other Stories: Crafts and Guilds in Egypt 1863-1914*, (State university of New York press, 2005), 5.

[13] Chalcraft, 5.

14 Pascale Ghazaleh, *Masters of the Trade: Crafts and Craftspeople in Cairo 1750-1850*, (The American university in Cairo press, 1999), 55.

15 Ghazaleh, 55.

16 Ayman Fu'ad Sayyid, *The Topography and Urban Evolution of CAIRO*, (Cairo: General Egyptian book organization, 2015), 371.

17 Ali Pasha Mubarak, *Al-Khitat al-tawfiqiyya al-jadida li Misr al-qahira wa muduniha wa biladiha al-qadima wal-shahira*, Vol. I. (Cairo: General Egyptian Book Organization, 2014), 247.

18 Edward William Lane, *An Account of the Manners and Customs of Modern Egyptians*, Written in Egypt during the Years 1833-1835, (London: W.Clowes and sons, 1860), 183.

19 E. F Jomard, Wasf MAdinat Al-Qahira (Description of the city of Cairo), Translated by Ayman Fu'ad al-Sayyid, (Cairo: Maktabat al- khanji, 1988), 102.

20 Alaa El-Habashi and Aliaa Zidan, "The Creative Sustainable City: Application on the Regeneration of Crafts in Historic Cairo" (Tenth Conference of Sustainable Environmental Development, Sharm El Sheikh, Egypt, March 16-20, 2019), 2.

21 El-Habashi and Zidan, 3.

22 Andre Raymond, *Grandes Villes Arabes à l'époque Ottoman*, (Cairo: Dar Al-Fikr for Studies, Publishing and Distribution, 1991), 209.

23 Gaston Wiet, *Al-qahira madinat al-fan w-al-tegara (Cairo, city of art and commerce)*. Translated by Mustafa Al-'Abadi. (Cairo: General Egyptian book organization, 2015), 113

24 Alaa El-Habashi, "Athar to Monuments: The Intervention of the Comité De Conservation Des Monuments De L'Art Arabe," (University of Pennsylvania, 2001), 14.

25 Napoleon Le Grand, Plan Général de Boulaq, du Kaire, de l'Ile de Roudah, du Vieux-Kaire et de Gyzeh. In: Description de l'Egypte ou Recueil des Observations et des Recherches qui ont été faites en Egypte pendant l'Expedition de l'Armée Francaise. Paris: L'Imprimerie Impériale, p. Plate 15 (Environs du Kaire, 1809)

26 Andre Raymond, *Artisans et commerçants Au Caire XVIIIe Siècle*. (Damas: Institute Français de Damas, 1973)

27 Abd al-Rahman al-Jabarti, *The Marvelous Compositions of Biographies and Events*. (Beirut: Dar al-Faris, 1970)

28 Sayyid, *The Topography and Urban Evolution of CAIRO*, 408.

29 Mohamed Riad, Cairo: The people fabric in space and time and their problems in the present and future, (Cairo: General Egyptian book organization, 2007), 49.

30 Marion Séjourné, "The History of Informal Settlements" in *Cairo's Informal Areas Between Urban Challenges and Hidden Potentials*, ed. Regina Kipper et al. (Cairo: The Egyptian-German Participatory Development Programme in Urban Areas, 2009), 17.

31 Elena Piffero, "Beyond Rules and Regulations: The Growth of Informal Cairo" in *Cairo's Informal Areas Between Urban Challenges and Hidden Potentials*, ed. Regina Kipper et al. (Cairo: The Egyptian-German Participatory Development Programme in Urban Areas, 2009), 27.

32 Riad, Cairo:The people fabric, 86.

33 Riad, Cairo:The people fabric, 75.

[34] Steven Viney, "The state of urban planning and informal areas after the Egyptian Revolution", *Egypt Independent,* March 17, 2013, https://egyptindependent.com/state-urban-planning-and-informal-areas-after-egyptian-revolution/

[35] Ahmed Abd El Rahman et al., "Mapping Informal Areas in Egypt Between the Past Interventions and Next Urban Revolution," Journal of Urban Research 21, (2016): 116-129, doi: 10.21608/jur.2016.89852

[36] Evliya Celebi, *SEYAHATNAMESI: Misr,Sudan,Habes 1672-1680,* Translated by El-Safsafe Ahmed Al-Qattory, (Cairo: The National Center for Translation, 2010), 57.

[37] "Wood Working Craft", ARCHiNOS Architecture, accessed June 2, 2020, https://www.undeadcrafts.com/carpentry.

[38] Ali Fahim, *Al nigara al 'amalia (the practical carpentering),* (Cairo: al-tawfiq press, 1914), 170.

[39] As'ad Nadeem, *Traditional Arts and Crafts from Cairo,* (Cairo: Egyptian Archives for Folk life and Folk Traditions, 2014), 7.

[40] Raymond, *Artisans et commerçants,* 543.

[41] El-Habashi and Zidan, 8.

[42] Agnieszka Dobrowolska, *The Building Crafts of Cairo: A Living Tradition,* (Cairo: The American University in Cairo Press, 2005); and Ali Fahim, *al nigara al 'amalia* (Cairo: al-tawfiq press, 1914).

[43] El-Habashi and Zidan, 6.

[44] Ramirez and El-Habashi, 59.

[45] UNESCO, Urban Regeneration Project for Historic Cairo (URHC) Team, *The Outstanding Universal Value of Historic Cairo-draft URHC proposal,* (Cairo: URHC, February 2013), 5-6.

Chapter 2

[1] Jacob Burkhardt, *The Greeks and Greek Civilization,* trans. Sheila Stern and ed. Oswyn Murray (London: Harper Collins Press, 1998), 162.

[2] Johann P. Arnason and Peter Murphy, "Introduction," in *Agōn, Logos, Polis: The Greek Achievement and its Aftermath.* (Stuttgart: F. Steiner Publishing, 2001), 10.

[3] Plato. *Republic, Book 2.* ed. Edith Hamilton and Huntington Cairns and trans. Lane Cooper (Princeton: Princeton University Press, 1962)

[4] Dubbini, Rachele. "Agōnes on the Greek Agora between Ritual and Spectacle: Some Examples from the Peloponnese," In *Body, Performance, Agency, and Experience,* vol. II, edited by Angelos Chaniotis et al., 157-81. Wiesbaden: Harrassowitz, 2010.

[5] Alan Finlayson, *Democracy and Pluralism: The Political Thought of William E. Connolly* (London: Routledge, 2011

[6] Johann P. Arnason and Peter Murphy, "Introduction," in *Agōn, Logos, Polis: The Greek Achievement and its Aftermath.* (Stuttgart: F. Steiner Publishing, 2001), 10.

[7] Oswyn Murray, "Gnosis and Tradition" in *Agōn, Logos, Polis: The Greek Achievement and its Aftermath, ed.* Johann P. Arnason and Peter Murphy (Stuttgart: F. Steiner Publishing, 2001), 18.

[8] Jane Jacobs, *The Death and Life of Great American Cities* (New York: Vintage Books, 1992) 332, 433-439.

[9] Plato. *Republic, Book 2*. Section 368c The Collected Dialogues of Plato Including the Letters, ed. Edith Hamilton and Huntington Cairns and trans. Lane Cooper (Princeton: Princeton University Press, 1962), 615

[10] Ibid.

[11] Ibid, 614.

[12] Hagi Kenaan, "Human Cities and the Space of Conflict," in *Human Cities: Civil Society Reclaims Public Space*, eds. Rafaella Houlstan-Hasaerts et al. (European Project Human Cities, 2012), 39.

[13] Martin Heidegger, *Being and Time*. trans. J. Macquarrie and E. Robinson (New York: Harper & Row, 1962) 79.

[14] Ibid.

[15] Ibid, 80.

[16] Each of these expressions is supported by place. See, Martin Heidegger, *Being and Time*, trans. John Macquarrie and Edward Robinson (New York: Harper & Row, 1962), 80.

[17] "Democracy" accessed March 11, 2021. https://www.etymonline.com/word/democracy

[18] Nicole Loraux, The Divided City: On Memory and Forgetting in Ancient Athens, trans. Corinne Pache and Jeff Fort (New York: Zone, 2006).

[19] Aristotle, "Athenian Constitution" in *The Athenian Constitution; The Eudemian Ethics; On Virtues and Vices*, trans. H. Rackham (Cambridge, Mass.: Harvard University Press, 1935), 85.

[20] P. E. Van 'T Wout, "Solon's Law on Stasis: Promoting Active Neutrality," Classical Quarterly *60*, no. 2 (2010): 289-301.

[21] Plato, *Republic, Book 2*. Sections 422e-423a.

[22] Rachele Dubbini, "Agōnes on the Greek, Agora between Ritual and Spectacle: Some Examples from the Peloponnese," in *Body, Performance, Agency, and Experience*, Volume II, eds. Angelos Chaniotis et al (Leuven: Wiesbaden Harrassowitz, 2010), 157-81.

[23] Johann P. Arnason and Peter Murphy, "Introduction," 10.

[24] Ibid.

[25] Johan Huizinga, *Homo Ludens: A Study of the Play Element in Culture* (London: Maurice Temple, 1970), 68

[26] See for example: Frank Kolb, *Agora und Theater. Volks- und Festversammlung* (Berlin: Gebr. Mann Verlag, 1981).

On the architectural aspect in the agonistic agora see: Rachele Dubbini, "Agōnes on the Greek Agora between Ritual and Spectacle: Some Examples from the Peloponnes," pp. 157-181.

[27] Homer, *Odyssey*, Book VIII. 109-125

[28] Rachele Dubbini, "Agōnes on the Greek Agora between Ritual and Spectacle: Some Examples from the Peloponnese" pp. 158-160

[29] Ibid. p. 160

[30] Ibid. pp. 157-81

31 On the location of the Old Agora, see: John K. Papadopoulos, "The Original Kerameikos of Athens and the Siting of the Athenian Agora," *Greek, Roman, and Byzantine Studies 37*, no. 2 (1996): 109-12. Noel Robertson, "The City Center of Archaic Athens," *Hesperia 67* (1998): 283-302.

32 Prior to that an indirect route had been required in order to get to the Acropolis from the ancient agora.

33 Tasos Tanoulas, "The Pre-Mnesiclean Cistern," *AM 107 (1992):* 160.

34 Jessica Paga, "Contested Space at the Entrance of the Athenian Acropolis," *Journal of the Society of Architectural Historians 76*, no. 2 (2017): 166.

35 For more information, see the article by Paga Jessica, Contested Space at the Entrance of the Athenian Acropolis, Journal of the Society of Architectural Historians 76, no. 2 (June 2017), 154-174,

36 For example see: Jens A. Bundgaard, *Mnesicles: A Greek Architect at Work* (Copenhagen: Gyldendal, 1957); Hans Eiteljorg, "New Finds Concerning the Entrance to the Acropolis," *Athens Annals of Archaeology 8* (1976): 94–5; R. A. Tomlinson, "Review of The Sanctuary of Athena Nike in Athens: Architectural Stages and Chronology, by Ira Mark," *Journal of Hellenic Studies 115* (1995)" 238; Ira S. Mark, *The Sanctuary of Athena Nike in Athens: Architectural Stages and Chronology* (Princeton, N.J.: American School of Classical Studies at Athens, 1993); Ione Mylonas Shear, "The Western Approach to the Athenian Akroplis" *The Journal of Hellenic Studies 119* (1999): 86-127; Harold B. Mattingly, "The Athena Nike Dossier: IG I3 35/36 and 64 A–B," Classical Quarterly 50 (2000): 604-6; David W.J. Gill, "The Decision to Build the Temple of Athena Nike ('IG' I3 35)," Historia 51 (2001): 257-78.

37 Jessica Paga, "Contested Space at the Entrance of the Athenian Acropolis," p.166.

21 Aristophanes, *Lysistrata*, trans. Jack Lindsay (New York: Hartsdale House, 1920).

39 Jessica Paga, "Contested Space at the Entrance of the Athenian Acropolis," p.168.

40 For example: Alan Finlayson, *Democracy and Pluralism: The Political Thought of William E. Connolly* (London: Routledge, 2011); Chantal Mouffe and Markus Miessem, *The Space of Agōnism* (Berlin: Sternberg Press, 2012); Mark Wenman, "Agōnistic Pluralism and Three Archetypal Forms of Politics," *Contemporary Political Theory*, 2 (2003): 165-86; Mark Wenman, *Agōnistic Democracy: Constituent Power in the Era of Globalization* (Cambridge: Cambridge University Press, 2013).

41 For example, Hanna Arendt's idea of the commonality through diversity or Foucault's understanding of the power contest.

42 Chantal Mouffe, *The Democracy Paradox* (London and New York: Verso, 2000), 101-3. Aristotle indicates that the polis was more than a system of sharing, it was an expression of the ability to maintain various identities within the whole. These aspects were a part of a common base intended to incorporate within it the different, from a mutual recognition, however not from a need for one dimensional unity. Aristotle, *Politics*, 1261a.

43 This is reflected in Mouffe's statement on the grounds that cities do not have any special status: "I don't think that the city by itself is more conducive to an agōnistic form of conflict." Konstantin Kastrissianakis, "From Antagōnistic Politics to an Agōnistic Public Space. Interview with Chantal Mouffe," *Cities in Turmoil, Special Issue, Re-Public* (2010).

44 Hanna Arendt, *The Human Condition* (Chicago, IL: University of Chicago Press, 1958), 57.

45 Bernard Tschumi, *Architecture and Disjunction* (Cambridge, MA: MIT Press, 1994).

Chapter 3

[1] Gamble Jos, *Shanghai in Transition: Changing Perspectives and Social Contours of a Chinese Metropolis* (London: Routledge Curzon, 2003), 8.

[2] "Reply of the State Council on the General Urban Plan of Shanghai Municipality," The State of Council the People's Republic of China, modified December 25, 2017, http://www.gov.cn/zhengce/content/2017-12/25/content_5250134.htm.

[3] Non Arkaraprasertkul, "Power, Politics, and the Making of Shanghai," *Journal of Planning History* 9.4 (2010): 238.

[4] Arkaraprasertkul, 238-40.

[5] Arkaraprasertkul, 242.

[6] David Harvey, *A Brief History of Neoliberalism* (Oxford: University Press, 2007), 120.

[7] Yawei Chen, "Making Shanghai a Creative City: Exploring the Creative Cluster Strategy from a Chinese Perspective," in *Creative Knowledge Cities: Myth, Visions and Realities*, ed. Marina van Geenhuizen and Nijkamp Peter (Cheltenham, Northampton: Edward Elgar, 2012): 447.

[8] Harvey, *A Brief History of Neoliberalism*, 122.

[9] Nicholas R. Lardy, *China's Unfinished Economic Revolution* (Washington, DC: Brookings Institution, 1998), 21.

[10] Yawei Chen, Qiyu TU, and Ning Su, "Shanghai's Huangpu Riverbank Redevelopment Beyond World Expo 2010" (paper presented at the annual conference AESOP 2014: From Control to Co-Evolution, Utrecht/Delft, The Netherlands, July 9-12, 2014).

[11] "West Bund History," West Bund, accessed May 2, 2020, http://www.westbund.com/en/index/ABOUT-WEST-BUND/History/West-Bund-History.html.

[12] "District Overview," West Bund, accessed May 5, 2020, http://www.westbund.com/en/index/ABOUT-WEST-BUND/Area-Overview/District-Overview.html.

[13] "Suggestions for Accelerating Development of Culture and Creative Industries in Shanghai," Information Office of Shanghai Municipality, modified December 15, 2017, http://www.shio.gov.cn/sh/xwb/n790/n792/n989/n1027/u1ai14603_K318.html.

[14] "Industry Landscape," West Bund, accessed May 5, 2020, http://www.westbund.com/en/index/ABOUT-WEST-BUND/Industry-Outline/Industry-Landscape.html.

[15] "District Overview," West Bund, accessed May 5, 2020, http://www.westbund.com/en/index/ABOUT-WEST-BUND/Area-Overview/District-Overview.html.

[16] Yichun Qiu, "Stakeholders and Partnership in Urban Regeneration: The Case of Shanghai West Bund," (Master Thesis, Columbia University, 2019), 22.

[17] Henri Lefebvre, "The Right to the City," in *Writings on Cities*, ed. and trans. Eleonore Kofman and Elizabeth Lebas (Oxford: Blackwell, 1996), 173.

[18] Benjamin Fraser, *Toward an Urban Cultural Studies. Henri Lefebvre and the Humanities* (New York: Palgrave Macmillan, 2015), 70.

[19] Robert Layton, "Art and Agency: A Reassessment," *Journal of the Royal Anthropological Institute* 9.3 (2003): 449.

[20] Richard A. Lynch, "Foucault's Theory of Power," in *Michel Foucault: Key Concepts*, ed. Dianna Taylor (London. New York: Routledge, 2014), 13-26.

[21] Michel Foucault, "The Subject and Power," *Critical Inquiry* 8.4 (1982): 790.

[22] Francisco Klauser et al. "Michel Foucault and The Smart City: Power Dynamics Inherent in Contemporary Governing Through Code," *Environment and Planning D: Society and Space* 32 (2014): 872, doi:10.1068/d13041p.

[23] John Pløger, "Foucault's Dispositif and the City," *Planning Theory* 7.1 (2018): 53, doi: 10.1177/1473095207085665.

[24] Meiqin Wang, *Socially Engaged Participatory Art Practice in Contemporary China: Voices From Below* (New York: Routledge, 2019), 59.

[25] Carsten Herrmann-Pillath, "Fei Xiaotong's Comparative Theory of Chinese Culture: Its Relevance for Contemporary Cross-disciplinary Research on Chinese 'Collectivism'," *The Copenhagen Journal of Asian Studies* 34.1 (2016): 28.

[26] Xiaotong Fei, *From the Soil: The Foundations of Chinese Society*, trans. Gary G. Hamilton and Wang Zheng (Berkeley and Los Angeles, California, London: University of California Press, 1992), 125.

[27] Harvey, *A Brief History of Neoliberalism*, 46.

[28] "Global Public Space Toolkit: From Global Principles to Local Policies and Practice," United Nations Human Settlements Programme (UN Habitat), accessed June 3, 2020, https://unhabitat.org/global-public-space-toolkit-from-global-principles-to-local-policies-and-practice.

[29] Colin McFarlane, "Assemblage and critical urbanism," *City* 15.2 (2011): 206, doi: 10.1080/13604813.2011.568715.

Chapter 4

[1] Harvey Molotch, "The City as a Growth Machine: Toward a Political Economy of Place," *American Journal of Sociology* 82, no. 2 (1976): 309-332.

[2] Tracy Neumann, *Remaking the Rust Belt: the Postindustrial Transformation of North America* (Philadelphia: University of Pennsylvania Press, 2016), 1-13.

[3] Julia Sattler, "Narratives of Urban Transformation Reading the Rust Belt in the Ruhr Valley," in *Urban Transformations in the U.S.A: Spaces, Communities, Representations*, ed. Julia Sattler (Bielefeld: Transcript Verlag, 2016), 12.

[4] Barbara Buchenau and Jens Martin Gurr, "City Scripts Urban American Studies and the Conjunction of Textual Strategies and Spatial Processes," in *Urban Transformations in the U.S.A: Spaces, Communities, Representations*, ed. Julia Sattler (Bielefeld: Transcript Verlag, 2016), 399.

[5] Buchenau and Gurr, 399.

[6] I am doing this as a member of the research group *Scripts for Postindustrial Urban Futures* of the University Alliance Ruhr, which explores the imaginative strategies and narrative scenarios of post-industrial urban centers in the US and Germany, and which is funded by the Volkswagen Stiftung.

[7] Steph Lawler, "Stories and the Social World," in *Research Methods for Cultural Studies*, ed. Michael Pickering and Gabriele Griffin (Edinburgh: Edinburgh University Press, 2008), 36.

[8] Frederick J. Turner, *The Frontier in American History* (New York: H. Holt and Company, 1920), 2.

[9] Turner, 263.

[10] Turner, 300.

[11] Turner, 263.

[12] Neil Smith, *The New Urban Frontier: Gentrification and the Revanchist City* (London: Routledge, 2005), xiv.

[13] Senatsverwaltung für Stadtentwicklung, *Urban Pioneers* (Berlin: Jovis, 2007), 36.

[14] Rebecca J. Kinney, *Beautiful Wasteland: The Rise of Detroit as America's Postindustrial Frontier* (Minneapolis: University of Minnesota Press, 2016), 125.

[15] Kinney, 39.

[16] "Freiraumluxus für Kreative: Eine Potentialsammelmaschine für Wanne," Stadt Wanne, accessed May 07, 2021, https://www.freiraumluxus.de.

[17] Jörg Heiser, "Speaking through Masks," in *Waitin' Around to Die*, ed. Oliver Zybok (Hatje Cantz, 2010), 29.

[18] Ralf Schlüter, "Der Wilde Westen," *Art Magazine* (February 2010): 19.

[19] Stefanie Bremer and Boris Sieverts et al.,"Claiming Land," *Shrinking Cities*, accessed May 07, 2021, http://www.shrinkingcities.com/projekte2.0.html.

[20] Stefanie Krebs, "Landschaften der Piraterie - Eine Ästhetik des Habhaftwerdens," 2007. https://boku.ac.at/rali/ila/veranstaltungen-des-ila/archiv-veranstaltungen/lx-landschaft-denken/l2-24052007/stefanie-krebs.

[21] Florida, Richard. *The Rise Of The Creative Class, Revisited* (New York: Basic Books, 2011), 388.

[22] "Summer of Pioneers", Stadt Altena, accessed May 07, 2021, https://altena-pioneers.de.

[23] Steven Hankin, "The War for Talent," *McKinsey Quarterly* 3, no. 3 (January 1998), 46.

[24] Walter Grünzweig, "Parasitic Simulacrum. Ralph Waldo Emerson, Richard Florida, and the Urban 'Creative Class,'" in *Spaces – Communities - Representations: Urban Transformations in the USA*, ed. Julia Sattler (Bielefeld: Transcript Verlag, 2016), 87.

[25] Ruhrgestalten, *Konter - Free City Guide For Ruhr Area Travel*, ed. Florian Kolominski (Oberhausen: Ruhr Tourismus, 2018), 34.

[26] Ruhrgestalten, 34.

[27] Ruhrgestalten, 34.

[28] Ruhrgestalten, 34.

[29] Neil Smith, *The New Urban Frontier: Gentrification and the Revanchist City.* (London: Routledge, 2005), 17.

[30] Smith, 15.

[31] Smith, 16.

[32] Benjamin Davy, "Plan It Without a Condom!," *Planning Theory* 7, no. 3, (2008): 303.

[33] Davy, 304.

[34] On 21st und 22nd April 2016, workshops under the title "Urban Spaces of Possibility" ("Urbane Möglichkeitsräume") were organized by the Institute of European Ethnology by the Humboldt University Berlin, by the Zukunftsakademie NRW und by the Urbanisten. This project was funded by the EU initiative SEiSMiC.

35 My translation, German original: "Damit wagen wir den Blick über den Tellerrand und weg von klassischen Beteiligungs-prozessen und verfolgen die Ziele einer innovativen Planungskultur. Diese ist inklusiv, wächst langsam, integriert das lokale Wissen im Quartier, nimmt sich Zeit zur Selbstreflexion, denkt immer wieder neu über Alternativen nach und ist offen für unerwartete Möglichkeiten." "Neue Werk Union," Urbanisten, accessed February 28, 2021, https://dieurbanisten.de/urbanisten-projekt/kreative-stadtentwicklung-auf-dem-ehem-hsp-areal/.

36 "Smart Rino," Thelen Group, accessed February 28, 2021, https://www.thelen-gruppe.com/portfolio/projekt/smart-rhino/.

37 cf. "MitWirkung bei der Quartiersentwicklung von Smart Rhino," Stadt Dortmund, accessed February 28, 2021, https://www.dortmund.de/de/leben_in_dortmund/planen _bauen_wohnen/stadtplanungs_und_bauordnungsamt/nachrichten_spboamt/detailse iten_spboamt.jsp?nid=630144.

Chapter 5

1 "China Statistical Yearbook 2019," National Bureau of Statistics of China, accessed May 17, 2021, http:// www.stats.gov.cn/tjsj/ndsj/.

2 Jie Chen and Bruce Judd, "Relationality and Territoriality: Rethinking Policy Circulation of Industrial Heritage Reuse in Chongqing, China," *International Journal of Heritage Studies* 27 (2021): 16.

3 Yiming Wang, *Pseudo-Public Spaces in Chinese Shopping Malls: Rise, Publicness and Consequences* (London: Routledge, 2019), 123.

4 Jie Chen et al. "Adaptive Reuse of Industrial Heritage for Cultural Purposes in Beijing, Shanghai and Chongqing," *Structural Survey* 34 (2016): 341.

5 Sun Sheng Han and Yong Wang, "Chongqing," *Cities* 18 (2001): 116.

6 David S. G. Goodman, "The Campaign to "Open Up the West": National, Provincial-level and Local Perspectives," *The China Quarterly* 178 (2004): 317.

7 Sun Sheng Han and Yong Wang, "Chongqing," *Cities* 18 (2001): 117.

8 Sheng Zhong, "The Neo-liberal Turn: 'Culture'-led Urban Regeneration in Shanghai," in *The Routledge Companion to Urban Regeneration*, ed. Michael Leary and John McCarthy (London: Routledge, 2013), 495.

9 David Harvey, *The Condition of Postmodernity: An Enquiry into the Origins of Cultural Change* (Oxford: Blackwell, 1990), 222.

10 David Harvey, *The Condition of Postmodernity: An Enquiry into the Origins of Cultural Change* (Oxford: Blackwell, 1990), 101-102, 257.

11 David Harvey, *Seventeen Contradictions and the End of Capitalism* (New York: Oxford University Press, 2014), 146.

12 David Harvey, *The Condition of Postmodernity: An Enquiry into the Origins of Cultural Change* (Oxford: Blackwell, 1990), 102.

13 Sharon Zukin, *Naked City: The Death and Life of Authentic Urban Places* (New York: Oxford University Press, 2010), p.xiii.

14 Jiang Xu et al. "Land Commodification: New Land Development and Politics in China since the Late 1990s," *International Journal of Urban and Regional Research* 33 (2009): 9.

15 Xiaobo Su, "Urban Entrepreneurialism and the Commodification of Heritage in China," *Urban Studies* 52 (2015): 2874.

16 Tsu-Lung Chou, "Creative Space, Cultural Industry Clusters, and Participation of the State in Beijing," *Eurasian Geography and Economics* 53 (2012): 197.

17 Jie Shen and Fulong Wu, "Restless Urban Landscapes in China: A Case Study of Three Projects in Shanghai," *Journal of Urban Affairs* 34 (2012): 255.

18 Jing Wang, "The Global Reach of a New Discourse: How Far can 'Creative Industries' Travel?" *International Journal of Cultural Studies* 7 (2004): 17.

19 Jun Wang, "'Art in Capital': Shaping Distinctiveness in a Culture-led Urban Regeneration Project in Red Town, Shanghai," *Cities* 26 (2009): 318.

20 Jie Zheng and Roger Chan, "The Impact of 'Creative Industry Clusters' on Cultural and Creative Industry Development in Shanghai," *City, Culture and Society* 5 (2014): 9.

21 Jennifer Currier, "Art and Power in the New China: An Exploration of Beijing's 798 District and Its Implications for Contemporary Urbanism," *Town Planning Review* 79 (2008): 237.

22 Xuefei Ren and Meng Sun, "Artistic Urbanization: Creative Industries and Creative Control in Beijing," *International Journal of Urban and Regional Research* 36 (2012): 504.

23 Jie Chen and Bruce Judd, "Relationality and Territoriality: Rethinking Policy Circulation of Industrial Heritage Reuse in Chongqing, China," *International Journal of Heritage Studies* 27 (2021): 22.

24 Interview with the government official (G2), 2016.

25 Interview with the government official (G4), 2016.

26 Interview with the expert (E5), 2016.

27 Interview with the land banking agency (D1), 2016.

28 Interview with the land banking agency (D3), 2016.

29 Interview with the land banking agency (D4), 2016.

30 Interview with the urban designer (C5), 2016.

31 Interview with the urban designers (C4 and C5), 2016.

32 Interview with the government official (G4), 2016.

33 Interview with the architect (C9), 2016.

34 Interview with local artists (A6, A9, A10), 2016.

Chapter 6

1 "Constitution of the Commonwealth of Australia," Museum of Australian Democracy, accessed April 13, 2020, https://www.foundingdocs.gov.au/scan-sid-91.html.

2 Paul Reid, *Canberra Following Griffin* (Canberra: National Archives of Australia, 2002), 9-10.

3 "Information, conditions and particulars for guidance on the preparation of competitive designs for the Federal Capital City of the Commonwealth of Australia," Department of Home Affairs Australia, accessed April 13, 2020, https://nla.gov.au/nla.cat-vn921986.

4 David Headon, *The Symbolic Role of the National Capital: From Colonial Arguments to 21st Century Ideals* (Canberra: National Capital Authority, 2003), 33-36.

[5] "Suggested names for Australia's new capital," National Archives of Australia, accessed January 11, 2021, https://www.naa.gov.au/learn/learning-resources/learning-resource-themes/government-anddemocracy/federation/suggested-names-australias-new-capital.

[6] Robert Fishman, Urban Utopias in the Twentieth Century: Ebenezer Howard, Frank Lloyd Wright and Le Corbusier (Cambridge, Mass.: The MIT Press, 1982), 3-20.

[7] Tali Hatuka and Alexander D'Hooghe, "After Postmodernism: Readdressing the Role of Utopia in Urban Design and Planning," *Places* 19, no. 2 (2007): 20.

[8] Colin Rowe and Fred Koetter, *Collage City* (Cambridge, Mass.: The MIT Press, 1978).

[9] Steven Hurtt, "Conjectures on Urban Form: The Cornell Urban Design Studio 1963-1982," *The Cornell Journal of Architecture* 2 (Fall 1983): 71-78, https://issuu.com/cornellaap/docs/cja002-opt.; Joan Ockman, "Form without Utopia: Contextualising Colin Rowe," *Journal of the Society of Architectural Historians* 57, no. 4 (1998), http://www.jstor.org/stable/991461.; Rowe and Koetter, *Collage City*, 11-31.

[10] David Grahame Shane, *Recombinant Urbanism: Conceptual Modeling in Architecture, Urban Design, and City Theory* (Chichester: John Wiley & Sons, 2005), 128-138.

[11] Craig Johnson, "Utopia and the Dirty Secret of Architecture," *Colloquy: Text Theory Critique*, no. 14 (2007): 30-32.; Robert Klanten, Lukas Feireiss and Matthias Bottger, *Utopia Forever: Visions of Architecture and Urbanism* (Berlin: Gestalten, 2011), 5-9.; David Pinder, "In Defence of Utopian Urbanism: Imagining Cities After the 'End of Utopia'," *Geografiska Annaler* 84, no. 3-4 (2002): 231-233.

[12] Lyman Tower Sargent, "Utopia," in The New Dictionary of the History of Ideas, ed. M.C. Horowitz (New York: Charles Scribner & Sons, 2004), 2403-9.

[13] Verena Harz, "Building a Better Place: Utopianism and the Revision of Community in Toni Morrison's *Paradise*," *Current Objectives of Postgraduate American Studies* 12 (2011), accessed January 11, 2021, https://copas.uniregensburg.de/article/view/135/161; Thomas More, *Utopia*, ed. P. Turner (London: Penguin, 2003).

[14] Colin Rowe and Fred Koetter, "Collage City," *The Architectural Review* CLVIII, no. 942 (1975): 70.

[15] J. C. Davis, *Utopia and the Ideal society* (UK: Cambridge University Press, 1981), 38.; Rowe and Koetter, *Collage City*, 13-14.

[16] Frederick H. A. Aalen, "English Origins," *The Garden City: Past, Present, and Future*, ed. Stephen V. Ward (London: E&FN Spon, 1992), 28.

[17] Martin Meyerson, "Utopian Traditions and the Planning of Cities," *Daedalus* 90, no. 1 (1961), accessed January 22, 2021, http://www.jstor.org/stable/20026647.

[18] Rowe and Koetter, "Collage City," 68.

[19] Ernest Green, "The Social Functions of Utopian Architecture," *Utopias Studies* 4, no. 1 (1993): 1, accessed January 22, 2021, http://www.jstor.org/stable/20719143.

[20] Rowe and Koetter, *Collage City*.; Ebenezer Howard, *Garden Cities of To-Morrow*, ed. Frederick J. Osborn (Cambridge, Mass.: M.I.T. Press, 1965).

[21] Walter Burley Griffin, "American Designs Splendid New Capital for Australia," *The New York Times* (New York), 2 June 1912, accessed January 11, 2021, https://www.nytimes.com/1912/06/02/archives/city-twentyfive-miles-square-to-be-built-upon-what-is-now-a.html.

[22] Peter Harrison and Robert Freestone, *Walter Burley Griffin: Landscape Architect*, ed. Robert Freestone (Canberra: National Library of Australia, 1995); John Macarthur, "Appropriation," in *The Picturesque Architecture, Disgust and Other Irregularities* (Hoboken: Taylor and Francis, 2013).

[23] Rowe and Koetter, *Collage City.*

[24] Peter Hall and Colin Ward, *Sociable Cities: The Legacy of Ebenezer Howard* (Chichester, West Sussex, England: J. Wiley, 1998), 15.

[25] Headon, *The Symbolic Role of the National Capital*, 38-39, 44.; Reid, *Canberra Following Griffin*, 39-45.

[26] National Capital Authority, *The Griffin Legacy: Canberra, the Nation's Capital in the 21st Century* (Canberra: National Capital Authority, 2004), 33-34.

[27] Griffin, "American Designs Splendid New Capital for Australia."

[28] NCA, *The Griffin Legacy*, 48-58.; Headon, *The Symbolic Role of the National Capital*, 44.

[29] NCA, 54.

[30] Reid, *Canberra Following Griffin*, 47.

[31] Reid, 4.

[32] Walter Burley Griffin, *Walter Burley Griffin - Letter dated January 1913 - Re His plan*, letter, National Archives of Australia, NAA: A110, FC1916/186, Canberra, accessed April 13, 2020, https://recordsearch.naa.gov.au/SearchNRetrieve/Interface/ViewImage.aspx? B=55919.; Percy L. Sheaffe, S*heaffe Papers. Printed Material, 'Commonwealth of Australia, Department of Home Affairs. The Federal Capital. Report Explanatory of the Preliminary General Plan' by Walter Burley Griffin [3 Copies]*, National Archives of Australia, NAA: M4071, 49, Canberra, accessed April 13, 2020, https://recordsearch.naa.gov.au/SearchN Retrieve/Interface/ViewImage.aspx?B=1873728.; Reid, *Canberra Following Griffin*, 107-108.

[33] Reid, *Canberra Following Griffin*, 107

[34] Reid, 237-245, 251-253.

[35] Christine Ellem, "No little plans," *Thesis Eleven* 123, no. 1 (2014):113-114, doi: https://doi.org/10.1177/0725513614543412.; Reid, *Canberra Following Griffin*, 1-3.

[36] NCA, *The Griffin Legacy*, 109.; John W. Reps, Graham Foundation for Advanced Studies in the Fine Arts, and National Capital Planning Authority, *Canberra 1912: Plans and Planners of the Australian Capital Competition* (Carlton South, VIC: Melbourne University Press, 1997), 140-146.

[37] Marcello Balbo and Francoise Naves-Bouchanine, "Urban Fragmentation as a Research Hypothesis: RabatSalé Case Study," *Habitat International* 19, no. 4 (1995): 573.; Maria Cristina Bayón, Gonzalo A. Saravi and Mariana Ortego Brena, "The Cultural Dimensions of Urban Fragmentation: Segregation, Sociability, and Inequality in Mexico City," *Latin America Perspectives* 40, no. 2 (2013), accessed April 13, 2020, https://www.jstor.org/stable/ 23466021.; Elizabeth Delmelle, "The Increasing Sociospatial Fragmentation of Urban America," *Urban Science* 3, no. 1 (2019): doi: https://doi.org/10.3390/urbansci3010009.

[38] Shane, *Recombinant Urbanism*, 129-130.

[39] Alioscia Mozzato, "Colin Rowe and Aldo Rossi. Utopia as a Metaphor of a New City Analogous to the Existing One," *sITA* 6 (2018), accessed April 13, 2020, https://sita.uauim. ro/6/a/72/.

[40] Rowe and Koetter, *Collage City*,138-142; Arthur McIntyre, *Contemporary Australian Collage and Its Origins* (Australia: Craftsman House, 1990), 15.

[41] Rowe and Koetter, 149.

[42] Shane, *Recombinant Urbanism*, 129.

[43] Reid, *Canberra Following Griffin*, 1-4.

[44] "Discovering Mildenhall's Canberra: Capitol Theatre, Manuka," National Archives of Australia and Museum of Australian Democracy, accessed June 9, 2020, https://mildenhall. moadoph.gov.au/photo/5000.; Ken Roe, "Capitol Theatre," *Cinema Treasures, Cinema Treasures LLC,* accessed January 11, 2021, http://cinematreasures.org/theaters/35502.

[45] "Capitol Theatre, Manuka, ACT," National Film and Sound Archives, accessed January 11, 2021, https://www.nfsa.gov.au/collection/curated/capitol-theatre-manuka-act.

[46] "Register of Significant Twentieth Century Architecture - Sydney and Melbourne Buildings," Australian Institute of Architects, accessed June 9, 2020, https://www.architecture. com.au/ wp-content/uploads/sydney-amp-melbourne-buildings.pdf.

[47] "Sydney and Melbourne Buildings," ACT Government, accessed January 11, 2021, https://www.act.gov.au/cityrenewal/places/cityhill/sydney-and-melbourne-building-precinct.

[48] NCA, *The Griffin Legacy*, 54.

[49] ACT Government, "Sydney and Melbourne Buildings."

[50] "History," National Portrait Gallery, accessed January 11, 2021, https://www.portrait.gov. au/content/gallery-history/.

[51] "Architecture," National Portrait Gallery, accessed January 11, 2021, https://www. portrait.gov.au/content/the-building/.

[52] National Portrait Gallery, "Architecture."

[53] Headon, *The Symbolic Role of the National Capital*, 38-39, 44.

[54] Rowe and Koetter, *Collage City*, 119-149.; Shane, *Recombinant Urbanism*, 131.

Chapter 7

[1] City of Perth. *Modern Visions of the City of Perth,* Perth: City of Perth, 2009, accessed May 12, 2021. https://www.museumofperth.com.au/modern-visions.

[2] "Perth City Link - Overview" Development WA. Development WA, accessed October 17, 2020. https://developmentwa.com.au/projects/redevelopment/perth-city-link/overview.

[3] Reginald Appleyard, "Western Australia: Economic and Demographic Growth, 1850-1914." In *A New History of Western Australia,* Charles Thomas Stannage, ed., (Nedlands: University of Western Australia Press, 1981), 211-236.

[4] Alistair Sisson and Paul Maginn, "Reclaiming Northbridge: Urban (Dis) Order and Territorial Stigmatisation in Perth's Night Time Economy Precinct," *Urban Policy and Research* 36 (2): 123-137 (2018). http://doi.org/10.1080/08111146.2018.1460266.

[5] City of Perth, "City of Perth SafeCity Community Safety and Crime Prevention Plan 2010-2013," Perth: City of Perth, accessed August 15, 2018, https://catalogue.nla.gov.au/ Record/5785558.

6 Australian Bureau of Statistics [ABS], "2016 Census QuickStats: Northbridge (WA) Code SSC51149 (SSC)," Canberra: *Australian Bureau of Statistics* (2016), accessed January 20, 2017 http://quickstats.censusdata.abs.gov.au/census_services/getproduct/census/2016/quickstat/SSC51149.

7 SGS Economics and Planning, "Economic Performance of Australia's Cities and Regions," Canberra: *SGS Economics and Planning*, (2018): 11-34, https://www.sgsep.com.au/assets/main/SGS-Economics-and-Planning-Economic-performance-fo-asutralias-cities-and-regions-report.pdf.

8 Mark O'Connor and William Lines, *Overloading Australia: How Governments and Media Dither and Deny on Population.* (Canterbury, N.S.W.: Envirobook, 2010), 6.

9 Oxford Dictionaries, s.v. "Ideal," accessed April 8, 2021, https://www.oxforddictionaries.com/definition/english/ideal

10 Chris Dickman, "Whither Wildlife in an Overpopulated World?" in *Sustainable Futures: Linking Population, Resources and the Environment*, Jenny Goldie and Katharine Betts, ed., 13-23. (Victoria: CSIRO Publishing, 2014), https://doi.org/10.1002/psp.1965, 14.

11 Dickman, 14.

12 Perth Population, "Perth Population 2019," accessed January 5, 2021, http://www.population.net.au/perth-population/

13 Australian Bureau of Statistics [ABS], "2016 Census QuickStats: Perth (WA)," Canberra: *Australian Bureau of Statistics* (2016), accessed January 20, 2017, https://quickstats.censusdata.abs.gov.au/census_services/getproduct/census/2016/quickstat/SSC51218.

14 City of Perth, "City Planning Scheme No.2 (Part 2)," Perth: City of Perth, accessed August 17, 2018, https://www.perth.wa.gov.au/develop/planning-framework/planning-schemes.

15 Ed Melet and Eric Vreedenburgh, *Rooftop Architecture: Building on an Elevated Surface* (Rotterdam: Nai Publishers, 2005), 17-18.

16 Jennifer Shields, *Collage and Architecture* (New York: Routledge, 2014), 152.

17 Clive Forster, *Australian Cities: Continuity and Change* (New York: Oxford University Press, 2004), 110.

18 Jan Gehl, *Cities for People* (Washington, Dc: Island Press, 2010), 148.

19 City of Perth, "City Planning Scheme No. 2—Schedule 3: Use Group Tables." Perth: City of Perth, accessed May 13, 2021, https://www.perth.wa.gov.au/en/building-and-planning/planning-framework/planning-schemes.

20 Andrew O'Connor, "WA state budget deficit to surge to almost $4b," ABC News, May 12, 2016, accessed March 21, 2021, https://www.abc.net.au/news/2016-05-12/wa-state-budget-deficit-up-to-$4b/7409334.

21 Emily Piesse and Laura Gartry, "Apartment Glut Looms in Perth Market," *ABC News*, April 7, 2016, accessed March 21, 2021, https://www.abc.net.au/news/2016-04-07/perth-apartment-oversupply-fears-market-slows/7308280.

22 Patrick Cook, "The Cultural City: The Role of Culture in Perth City Planning Policy" (Bachelor's Dissertation, 2010), vii: 1-2.

23 Steven Miles, *Youth Lifestyles in a Changing World* (Philadelphia: Open University Press, 2000), 159-160.

[24] Steven Holl, Juhani Pallasmaa, and Alberto Gómez, *Questions of Perception: Phenomenology of Architecture* (San Francisco: William Stout, 2007), 48.

[25] Jennifer Shields, *Collage and Architecture* (New York: Routledge, 2014), 13.

[26] Lisa Given, *The SAGE Encyclopedia of Qualitative Research Methods*, vol. 2 (California: SAGE Publications Inc, 2008).

[27] Paula Gerstenblatt, "Collage Portraits as a Method of Analysis in Qualitative Research," *International Journal of Qualitative Methods* 12, no. 1 (2013): 294-309, https://doi.org/10.1177/160940691301200114.

[28] Lynn Butler-Kisber and Tiiu Poldma, "The Power of Visual Approaches in Qualitative Inquiry: The Use of Collage Making and Concept Mapping in Experiential Research," *Journal of Research Practice* 6, no. 2 (2011), 18.

[29] Solène Veysseyre, "Case Study: The Unspoken Rules of Favela Construction," ed. Vanessa Quirk, *ArchDaily*, accessed November 17, 2014, http://www.archdaily.com/531253/case-study-the-unspoken-rules-of-favela-construction.

[30] Remment Koolhaas and Brendan McGetrick, *Content: Triumph of Realization* (Köln: Taschen, 2004), 73-83: 510-12.

[31] James Gibson, *The Ecological Approach to Visual Perception* (New York: Psychology Press, 2015), 127.

[32] Frei Otto, *Occupying and Connecting Thoughts on Territories and Spheres of Influence with Particular Reference to Human Settlement*, ed. Berthold Burkhardt (London: Axel Menges, 2011), 116.

[33] Amale Andraos et al., "How to Build a City: The Roman Operating System," in *Mutations: Rem Koolhaas, Harvard Project on the City*, ed. Stefano Boeri et al. (Barcelona: ACTAR, 2000), 10-19.

[34] Amale Andraos et al., 14.

[35] O.M.A, Remment Koolhaas, and Bruce Mau, *S, M, L, XL* (New York: Monacelli Press, 1995).

[36] Planning Institute of Australia, "Planning Fact Sheet 01: What Is Planning," Perth, Planning Institute of Australia, 2018, https://www.planning.org.au/wa.

[37] Eric Weisstein, "Plateau's Laws" (Wolfram Research, Inc., 2016), http://mathworld.wolfram.com/PlateausLaws.html.

[38] Philip Ball, *Shapes. Nature's Patterns: A Tapestry in Three Parts* (Oxford: Oxford University Press, 2009), 66-71.

[39] Tom Ballow, *The New Science of Flight and Movement* (Victoria, British Columbia: Trafford Publishing, 2005), 33-34.

[40] University College London, "Humans Are Hard-Wired to Follow the Path of Least Resistance," accessed March 12, 2017, https://www.sciencedaily.com/releases/2017/02/170221101016.htm.

[41] Frei Otto, *Occupying and Connecting Thoughts on Territories and Spheres of Influence with Particular Reference to Human Settlement*, ed. Berthold Burkhardt (London: Axel Menges, 2011), 6.

Chapter 8

[1] Deane Simpson, Kathrin Susanna Gimmel, Anders Lonka, Marc Jay, and Joost Grootens, eds., *Atlas of the Copenhagens* (Berlin: Ruby Press, 2018).

[2] Hans T. Andersen and Lars Winther, "Crisis in the Resurgent City? The Rise of Copenhagen," *International Journal of Urban and Regional Research* 34.3 (2010): 693.

[3] Deane Simpson, "Copenhagen under the Metric Regimes of the Competitive and Attractive City," in *Atlas of the Copenhagens*, ed. Deane Simpson et al. (Berlin: Ruby Press, 2018), 17-53.

[4] Tom Nielsen, "The Making of Democratic Urban Public Space in Denmark," in *Public Space Design and Social Cohesion: An International Comparison*, ed. by Patricia Aelbrecht et al. (Routledge, 2019), 37-57.

[5] See, e.g., cross-disciplinary technological institutes like the Zigurat Global Institute of Technology, providing master's in "Global Smart City Management," accessed February 23, 2021, https://www.e-zigurat.com/en/smart-cities-masters-program/; and promoting smart city solutions through web articles like "Smart City Series: The Barcelona Experience," Zigurat Global Institute of Technology, accessed February 23, 2021, https://www.e-zigurat.com/blog/en/smart-city-barcelona-experience/.

[6] Several scholars made this argument. For instance, the Italian professor Pascual Berrone in the lecture "From Smart Cities to Smart Governance" (presentation at the conference "Business Improvement Districts—En ny samarbejdsmodel for vækst og udvikling i byområder," VIA University College, Aarhus, Denmark, November 29, 2017.

[7] Rem Koolhaas, "Rem Koolhaas Asks: Are Smart Cities Condemned to be Stupid?" ArchDaily, December 10, 2014, accessed February 23, 2021, https://www.archdaily.com/576480/rem-koolhaas-asks-are-smart-cities-condemned-to-be-stupid, ISSN 0719-8884.

[8] Shoshana Zuboff, *The Age of Surveillance Capitalism* (London: Profile Books Ltd., 2019).

[9] See, e.g., Boyd Cohen, "The 3 Generations of Smart Cities. Inside the development of the technology driven city," Fast Company, October 8, 2015, accessed February 24, 2021, https://www.fastcompany.com/3047795/the-3-generations-of-smart-cities.

[10] "Early stage planning. Re-imagined," Spacemaker, accessed February 24, 2021, https://www.spacemakerai.com/.

[11] See Alison and Peter Smithson, *Ordinariness and Light* (London: Faber & Faber Ltd, 1970) and Helena Webster, ed., *Modernism Without Rhetoric—Essays on the work of Alison and Peter Smithson* (Academy Editions, London, 1997).

[12] Robert Venturi, *Complexity and Contradiction in Architecture* (New York: The Museum of Modern Art, 1966).

[13] Thomas Sieverts, Michael Koch, Ursula Stein, and Michael Steinbusch, eds., *Zwischenstadt – Inzwischenstadt? Entdecken, Begreifen ,Verändern* (Wuppertal: Verlag Müller + Busmann, 2005). See also Thomas Sieverts, Zwischenstadt: zwischen Ort und Welt Raum und Zeit Stadt und Land (Wiesbaden: Vieweg+Teubner Verlag, 1997).

[14] Richard Sennett, The Uses of Disorder: Personal Identity and City Life (New York: Knopf, 1970).

[15] Richard Sennett and Pablo Sendra, *Designing Disorder: Experiments and Disruptions in the City* (London, New York: Verso, 2020).

[16] "Denmark is fourth most digital country in the world," Copenhagen Capacity, June 18, 2020, accessed February 24, 2021, https://www.copcap.com/news/denmark-is-fourth-most-digital-country-in-the-world. See also: "The Digital Economy and Society Index (DESI)," European Commission, accessed February 24, 2021, https://ec.europa.eu/digital-single-market/en/digital-economy-and-society-index-desi.

[17] Mette Frisk Jensen and Gert Tinggaard Svendsen, "Corruption and Bureaucratic Reforms 'Getting to Denmark'?" in *The Oxford Handbook of Danish Politics*, edited by Peter Munk Christiansen et al. (Oxford University Press, 2020), 177-192.

[18] "Bæredygtig byudvikling i Nordhavn," By & Havn, accessed February 25, 2021, https://byoghavn.dk/nordhavn/baeredygtig-byudvikling/.

[19] "A Smart City Energy Lab," Energylab Nordhavn, accessed February 25, 2021, http://www.energylabnordhavn.com/.

[20] See, e.g., the Danish office TREDJE NATUR (Third Nature) that has specialized in inventive sustainable solutions. See, e.g., the project 'Enghaveparken—Climate Park'. Here flooding becomes an attraction. See "Enghaveparken—Climate Park," TREDJE NATUR, accessed February 25, 2021, https://www.tredjenatur.dk/en/portfolio/enghaveparken-climate-park/.

[21] 'Østergro' is an example of a roof garden with local food production, see "Welcome to ØsterGro," ØsterGro, accessed February 25, 2021, https://www.oestergro.dk/in-english.

[22] See the Danish Building Regulations, § 250–§ 298 on Energy consumption "Energiforbrug (§ 250–§ 298)," Bygningsreglementet.dk/Indenrigs-og Boligministeriet, accessed February 25, 2021, https://bygningsreglementet.dk/Tekniske-bestemmelser/11/Krav.

[23] "Copenhagen International School—Nordhavn," CF Møller Architects, accessed February 25, 2021, https://www.cfmoller.com/p/Copenhagen-International-School-Nordhavn-i2956.html#.

[24] Georg Simmel, "Die Großstadt. Vorträge und Aufsätze zur Städteausstellung," in Jahrbuch der Gehe-Stiftung Dresden (Dresden: Th. Petermann, 1903), 185-206.

[25] Alex Paul Pentland, "*Society's Nervous System: Building Effective Government, Energy and Public Health Systems,*" MIT Open Access Articles, October 2011.

[26] Walter Benjamin, Berliner Kindheit um neuzehnhundert (Berlin: Suhrkamp, 2012).

[27] Tom Nielsen has addressed the role of "superfluous landscapes." See Tom Nielsen, "The Return of the Excessive: Superfluous Landscapes," *Space and Culture* 5, no. 1 (2002): 53-62.

[28] Tom Hodgkinson, "Adam Curtis: Social Media is a Scam" *Idler Magazine*, February 3, 2021, https://www.idler.co.uk/article/adam-curtis-social-media-is-a-scam/.

[29] Kristian Lindberg, "De elsker Københavns største betonklods: »Det ville være en katastrofe at fjerne Bispeengbuen. Jeg forstår slet ikke, at man kan få den tanke!«" Berlingske, October 21, 2018, https://www.berlingske.dk/kultur/de-elsker-koebenhavns-stoerste-betonklods-det-ville-vaere-en-katastrofe-at.

[30] Christian Bennike, "Den næste Amager Fælled-sag: Red Bispeengbuen!," Information, October 21, 2017, https://www.information.dk/moti/2017/10/naeste-amager-faelled-sag-red-bispeengbuen.

[31] "Transformation of The Boulevard," TREDJE NATUR, accessed February 25, 2021, https://www.tredjenatur.dk/en/portfolio/transformation-of-the-boulevard/.

[32] "Urban 13," Urban 13, accessed February 25, 2021, https://www.urban13.dk/.

[33] Kasper Bruun Vindum Brandt, "Politikere giver grønt lys til at rive halvdelen af Bispeengbuen ned," TV2/Lorry, January 13, 2021, https://www.tv2lorry.dk/koebenhavn/politikere-giver-groent-lys-til-at-rive-halvdelen-af-bispeengbuen-ned.

[34] Referring to the seminal publication: Manuel Castells, *The Rise of the Network Society* (Malden, Mass: Blackwell Publishers, 1996).

[35] Subsequent endnote: Koolhaas, "Are Smart Cities Condemned to Be Stupid?"

[36] "'Connecting Copenhagen' is the World's Best Smart City Project," State of Green, accessed February 25, 2021, https://stateofgreen.com/en/partners/city-of-copenhagen/news/connecting-copenhagen-is-the-worlds-best-smart-city-project/.

[37] "Projects," Copenhagen Solutions Lab, accessed February 25, 2021, https://cphsolutionslab.dk/en/projekter.

Chapter 9

[1] Richard Rogers, "Bankside Urban Study: The Bankside Triangle," *Tate Press Release*, May 11, 2001, https://www.tate.org.uk/file/bankside-urban-study-bankside-triangle

[2] Southwark Council, "Southwark Unitary Development Plan (1995): Policy R.2.1" (report presented at the London Borough of Southwark Council, London 1995).

[3] Mayor of London, The London Plan: Spatial Development Strategy for Greater London (Greater London Authority, London, February 2004). 235.

[4] Mayor of London (2004), 234-235.

[5] James Douet, "Introduction," in *Industrial Heritage Re-tooled: The TICCIH guide to Industrial Heritage Conservation*, ed. James Douet. (Lancaster: Carnegie Publishing Ltd., 2012), 1.

[6] Mayor of London, The London Plan: Spatial Development Strategy for Greater London: Consolidated with Alterations since 2004 (Greater London Authority, London February 2008). 45 & 168.

[7] Gert de Roo and Camilla Perone, "A multi-level rationality model for planning behaviour," in *Handbook on Planning and Complexity*, ed. Gert de Roo et al. (Cheltenham: Edward Elgar Publishing Ltd, 2020), 36.

[8] Terry Farrell, *Shaping London: The patterns and forms that make the metropolis*, (Chichester: John Wiley and Sons, Ltd., 2010), 36-60.

[9] Michael Jenner, *London Heritage: The Changing Style of a City*, (London: Michael Joseph, 1988), 13.

[10] Simon Bradley and Nikolaus Pevsner, *London 1: City of London*, (New Haven and London: Yale University Press, 1997), 32.

[11] Bradley and Pevsner, 35.

[12] Bradley and Pevsner, 38.

[13] Harvey Sheldon, "Roman Southwark," in *London Under Ground: the archaeology of a city*, ed. Ian Haynes et al. (Oxford: Oxbow Books, 2000), 130.

[14] Bridget Cherry and Nikolaus Pevsner, London 2: South, (New Haven and London: Yale University Press, 2002), 586.

[15] Paul L. Knox, *London: Architecture, Building and Social Change* (London: Merrell Publishers Limited, 2015), 236.

[16] Ben Campkin, *Remaking London: Decline and Regeneration in Urban Culture* (London and New York: I. B. Tauris, 2013), 39.

[17] Cherry and Pevsner, London 2: South, 582.

[18] Stephen Murray, "The Evolution and Transformation of Bankside, London, 1947-2019," Journal of Urban History 47, no. 1 (2021): 68-84, doi: 10.1177/0096144219864677.

[19] Stephanie Williams, *Docklands* (London: Architecture Design and Technology Press, 1990), 16.

[20] Tony Travers, *The Politics of London: Governing and Ungovernable City* (Hampshire: Palgrave Macmillan, 2004), 11.

[21] R. K. Home, "Deregulating UK planning control in the 1980s," Cities 8, no. 4, (1991): 292-300, https://doi.org/10.1016/0264-2751(91)90046-T.

[22] LPAC, *1994: Advice on Strategic Planning Guidance for London* (London: HMSO, 1994), 2.

[23] Caroline Donnellan, *Towards Tate Modern: Public Policy, Private Vision* (London and New York: Routledge, 2018). 15.

[24] Neil Lee. "The creative industries and urban economic growth in the UK," Environment and Planning A: Economy and Space 46, no. 1 (2014): 455-470. doi:10.1068/a4472.

[25] Richard Rogers, introduction to *Towards an Urban Renaissance (Final Report of the Urban Task Force,* by Urban Task Force (London: Taylor & Francis, 1999), 8.

[26] Peter Hall, "How much better than no bread?" Town and Country Planning 70, no. 1 (2001): 1-4, https://archive.tcpa.org.uk/archive/journals/2000-2009/2001/january-march-84/1617349?q=peter%20hall.

[27] San Wanamaker, "Shakespeare's Globe Reborn," RSA Journal 138, no. 5401, (1989): 25-34, https://www.jstor.org/stable/41375089

[28] Paul Teedon, "Designing a Place Called Bankside: On Defining an Unknown Space in London," European Planning Studies 9, no. 4 (2001): 459-481. doi: 10.1080/713666488

[29] Kenneth Powell, *City Reborn: Architecture and Regeneration in London, from Bankside to Dulwich* (London and New York: Merrell, 2004), 52.

[30] Donnellan, *Towards Tate Modern*, 97.

[31] Steven Miles and Ronan Paddison, "Introduction The Rise and Rise of Culture-Led Urban Regeneration," in *Culture-Led Urban Regeneration*, ed. Ronan Paddison et al. (London and New York: Routledge, 2007), ix.

[32] Ken Allinson, *London's Contemporary Architecture: A Visitor's Guide* (Oxford and Burlington MA: Architectural Press, 2003), 108.

[33] Mathew Gandy, "NEO Bankside," Architectural Design 82 no. 1 (2012): 50-53, https://doi.org/10.1002/ad.1348

[34] Oliver Wainwright, "New Bankside: how Richard Roger's new 'non-dom accom' cut out the poor," *The Guardian*, July 21, 2015, https://www.theguardian.com/artanddesign/architecture-design-blog/2015/jul/21/neo-bankside-how-richard-rogers-new-non-dom-accom-cut-out-the-poor.

[35] "London SE1 Community Website," London SE1, accessed May 8, 2022. https://www.london-se1.co.uk/news/view/8308.

[36] "Arbor reaches milestone with topping out ceremony," Bankside Yards London SE1, accessed May 8, 2022, https://banksideyards.com/press/bankside-yards-to-be-uks-first-fossil-fuel-free-major-mixed-use-development/.

[37] "Find an Architect: Bankside 123," RIBA, accessed May 8, 2022, https://www.architecture. com/find-an-architect/allies-and-morrison-llp/london/bankside-123

[38] Powell, *City Reborn*, 118.

[39] "The Blue Fin Building.," Skyscrapernews.com, accessed May 8, 2022, www.skyscrapernews. com/buildings.php?id=1447.

[40] "Climate Emergency: Our commitment to tackling the emergency," Southwark Council, accessed May 8, 2022, https://www.southwark.gov.uk/environment/climate-emergency? chapter=2.

[41] Stephen Witherford, *Bankside Urban Forest: To lose oneself in a city - as one loses oneself in a forest,* (Lausanne: LAPA studio publication, 2008). 15.

[42] "Bankside Urban Forest," Better Bankside, accessed May 8, 2022, https://betterbankside. co.uk/what-we-do/bankside-urban-forest/.

[43] "About," Low_Line, accessed May 6, 2022, https://www.lowline.london/#about

[44] Jacobs, *The Death and Life of Great American Cities*, 230.

[45] Francesca Froy et al. "Pragmatic urbanism: London's railway a rches and small-scale enterprise," European Planning Studies 25, no. 11 (2017): 2076-2096, https://doi.org/10.1080/ 09654313.2017.1367141.

[46] Murphy, *Landscape Architecture Theory*, 4.

[47] John D. Beasley, *Southwark Revisited* (London: Tempus, 2004), 60.

[48] Mayor of London, The London Plan, 235.

[49] Southwark Council, London Borough of Southwark Unitary Development Plan, section 1.22.

[50] Southwark Council, section 8.67.

[51] Powell, City Reborn, 66.

[52] Hana Morel, "Policy and Practice of London's Historic Environment," The Historic Environment: Policy & Practice 10, no. 2 (2019):152-177, doi: 10.1080/17567505.2019.157 4098.

[53] Andrew Jones, "Issues in Waterfront Regeneration: More Sobering Thoughts-A UK Perspective," Planning Practice & Research 13, no. 4 (2019): 433-442, doi: 10.1080/026974 59815987.

[54] Allinson, London's Contemporary Architecture, 122.

[55] Brodie Boland, Aaron De Smet, Rob Palter, and Aditya Sanghvi, "Reimagining the office and work life after COVID-19," *McKinsey and Company,* June 2020. https://www.mckinsey. com/business-functions/people-and-organizational-performance/our-insights/reimagining-the-office-and-work-life-after-covid-19.

[56] Steffen Lehmann, *Urban Regeneration: A Manifesto for transforming UK Cities in the Age of Climate Change* (Cham: Palgrave Macmillian, 2019), 3.

Chapter 10

[1] Wellingtonians have compared their city to Melbourne, Australia as they both have a similar cafe and arts culture. It is widely accepted that Wellingtonians look up to Melbourne as a bigger version of themselves.

[2] Dominika Byczkowska-Owczarek, "Researcher's personal experiences as a method of embodiment research," in *The Routledge Handbook of Planning Research Methods*, ed. Elisabete A. Silva et al. (Abingdon: Routledge, 2016), 202-212.

[3] Bent Flyvbjerg, *Making Social Science Matter: Why Social Inquiry Fails and How It Can Succeed Again Cambridge, UK.* (Cambridge University Press, 2001), 166-168.

[4] Murray Sherwin, "Towards better local regulation," Productivity Commission, New Zealand Government, May 2013. https://www.productivity.govt.nz/assets/Documents/f32eda4453/Final-report-Towards-better-local regulation.pdf.

[5] Michael Gunder. "Commentary: Is Urban Design Still Urban Planning? An Exploration and Response," Journal of Planning Education and Research 31, no. 2 (2011): 184-95, doi: 10.1177/0739456x10393358.

[6] Peter Nijkamp, "XXQ Factors for Sustainable Urban Development: A Systems Economics View," *Romanian journal of regional science* 2, no. 1 (2008): 325.

[7] Michael Porter, "Clusters and the New Economy," Harvard Business Review 76, no. 6 (1998), 77. (Reprinted in Managing in the New Economy, HBSP, 1999; and in Systems of Innovation: Growth, Competitiveness and Employment, Edward Elgar, 2000).

[8] Leanne Hodyl, "To Investigate Planning Policies That Deliver Positive Social Outcomes in Hyper-Dense, High-Rise Residential Environments," The Winston Churchill Memorial Trust of Australia, 2015, https://apo.org.au/node/52757, accessed 15th November 2020.

[9] "Building competitive cities: Reform of the urban and infrastructure planning system - A technical working paper," Ministry for the Environment, New Zealand, 31st October 2010, https://www.mfe.govt.nz/publications/rma/building-competitive-cities-discussion-document.

[10] Jamie Peck, "Austerity Urbanism," City 16, no. 6 (2012): 626-55, doi: 10.1080/13604813. 2012.734071.

[11] "Creating the Plan," City of Melbourne, Victoria, Australia, accessed March 21, 2021, https://www.melbourne.vic.gov.au/about-melbourne/future-melbourne/creating-the-plan/Pages/creating-the plan.aspx.

[12] "Development Activity," City of Melbourne, Victoria, Australia, accessed March 21, 2021, https://www.developmentactivity.melbourne.vic.gov.au/.

[13] Cristina Martinez-Fernandez et al. "Shrinking Cities: Urban Challenges of Globalization," International Journal of Urban and Regional Research 36, no. 2 (2012): 213, doi:10.1111/j. 1468-2427.2011.01092. x.

[14] In May 2013 John Key spoke at a conference in Takapuna, Auckland. He was documented as saying "Wellington is dying." There was much debate in the media at the time. Marine Hallahan et al. "Prime minister side-steps "dying" comment," *Stuff News.* May 07, 2013, https://www.stuff.co.nz/national/8639116/Prime-minister-side-steps-dying-comment.

[15] In the last 3 months Wellington has undergone a development resurgence. There is a "donut effect" where areas surrounding the CBD are seeing a flurry of new and repurposed residential structures. While construction and crane numbers have increased the projects are limited to maximizing internal site conditions with limited contribution to the wider external built environment.

[16] Rebecca Kiddle. "Where Do We Dance? Planning Social Spaces in the Suburbs." *NZ Local Government Magazine*, no. 56 (June 2019): 10-13.

17 "Urban design and city building are surely among the most auspicious endeavors of this or any age, giving rise to a vision of life." Donald Watson, Time-Saver Standards for Urban Design (McGraw-Hill Education, 2003), https://www.accessengineeringlibrary.com/content/book/9780070685079.

18 The Urban Design Protocol identifies: Context, Character, Choice, Connections, Creativity, Custodianship and Collaboration as key considerations for designers. "3 Key urban design qualities – The seven Cs," Ministry for the Environment, New Zealand, accessed March 13, 2021, https://www.mfe.govt.nz/publications/towns-and cities/new-zealand-urban-design-protocol/3-key-urban-design-qualities-seven.

19 "Vancouver Plan," City of Vancouver, accessed March 21, 2021, https://vancouver.ca/home-property development/vancouver-city-wide-plan.aspx.

20 Sune Blicher, "New Danish Architecture Policy Is Putting People First," Danish Agency for Culture, accessed April 5, 2021, https://news.cision.com/danish-agency-for-culture/quotes.

21 Malcolm Smit. "Towards a Complex and Integrated Urbanism," UrbanNext, accessed March 21, 2021, https://urbannext.net/towards-a-complex-and-integrated-urbanism/.

22 Joss cites Tom Saunders and Peter Baeck "Rethinking smart cities from the ground up," Nesta, accessed April 5, 2021, https://media.nesta.org.uk/documents/rethinking_smart _cities_from_the_ground_up_2015.pdf. Sander and Baeck state that "collaborative technologies offer the opportunity to engage and enable citizens and, thus, to help citizens themselves to shape the future of their cities." Simon Joss, "Future Cities: Asserting Public Governance," Palgrave Communications 4, no. 1 (2018), doi: 10.1057/s41599-018-0087-7.

23 Golam Mathbor, "Enhancement of community preparedness for natural disasters: The role of social work in building social capital for sustainable disaster relief and management," International Social Work 50, no.3 (2009):357-369, doi: 10.1177/0020872807076049.

24 CoCityApp enables decision makers to get a real-time image of their city through the eyes of its citizens and has the potential to replace outdated approaches to community engagement such as a questionnaire or online survey. Rasmus Frisk et al, "Building cities with people," (paper presented at the 8th International Urban Design Conference Empowering Change: Transformative Innovations and Projects Brisbane QLD, 16-18 November 2015). https://www.arkilab.dk/wp-content/uploads/2016/06/1.pdf.

25 Louise Fabian and Kristine Samson. "Claiming Participation – a Comparative Analysis of DIY Urbanism in Denmark," Journal of Urbanism: International Research on Placemaking and Urban Sustainability 9, no. 2 (2015): 166, doi: 10.1080/17549175.2015.1056207.

26 Ray Edgar, "Architecture students envision a new-look Melbourne." *The Sydney Morning Herald,* December 18, 2020, https://www.smh.com.au/culture/art-and-design/architecture-students-envision-a-new-look melbourne-20201214-p56n8d.html.

27 "Melbourne Now 2023," City of Melbourne, Victoria, Australia, accessed March 21, 2021, https://www.onlymelbourne.com.au/melbourne-now-ngv#.YFbwDq8zZyw.

28 "Sampling the City," City of Melbourne, Victoria, Australia, accessed March 21, 2021, https://www.ngv.vic.gov.au/melbournenow/projects/528.html.

29 "Have your say – Shelly Bay Development," Wellington City Council, New Zealand, August 14, 2017, https://wellington.govt.nz/~/media/have-your-say/public-input/files/consultations/2017/07/shelly-bay/shelly bay-proposal.pdf?la=en.

30 Guy Julier, "Political Economies of Design Activism and the Public Sector," (paper presented at Nordic Design Research Conference 2011, Making design matter, Helsinki, Finland, May 29-31, 2011, https://teputahi.org.nz/wp-content/uploads/2015/10/Julier_Design_Activism.pdf.

31 "The Value of Urban Design: The economic, environmental and social benefits of urban design," Ministry for the Environment, New Zealand, June 2005, http://www.mfe.govt.nz/publications/urban/value-urban-design-full-report-jun05/index.html.

32 Ajay Garde, "Citizen Participation, Design Competition and the Product in Urban Design: Insights from the Orange County Great Park," Journal of Urban Design 19, no. 1 (2013): 89, doi: 10.1080/13574809.2013.854697.

33 Cesar Hidalgo, "A bold idea to replace politicians," Ted Talk, April 2018, https://www.ted.com/talks/cesar_hidalgo_a_bold_idea_to_replace_politicians?language=en

34 "Social media fact sheet," Pew Research Centre, June 12, 2019, https://www.pewresearch.org/internet/pi_14-01-30_factsheet_2-copy/.

35 Devon Maloney and Lucas Puente. "The app era is here: Now to optimize for it," Slack, October 31, 2019, https://slack.com/intl/en-nz/blog/transformation/the-app-era-is-here.

36 Brian W. Head. "Community Engagement: Participation on Whose Terms?" Australian journal of political science 42, no. 3 (2007):441-454, doi: 10.1080/10361140701513570.

Ingram Content Group UK Ltd.
Milton Keynes UK
UKHW020821160423
420240UK00011B/129